I Have Kept the Faith

Other books by Emil G. Kraeling:

The Book of the Ways of God
The Brooklyn Museum Aramaic Papyri
The Old Testament Since the Reformation
Rand McNally Bible Atlas
Historical Atlas of the Holy Land
Our Living Bible (with Michael Avi-Yonah)
The Clarified New Testament Vol. I The Four Gospels
The Prophets

The Literature of the Old Testament, Bewer, Julius A.
3rd edition revised by E.G.K.

I Have Kept the Faith

THE LIFE OF THE APOSTLE PAUL

by Emil G. Kraeling

RAND McNALLY & COMPANY

Chicago • New York • San Francisco

Map from Atlas of World History
edited by R. R. Palmer, 1965

First paperback printing, 1979

Table of Contents

	Introduction	7
1	The Tarsus Boyhood	13
2	Going to Jerusalem	22
3	The Quest	29
4	The Persecutor	39
5	Arabia and Damascus	53
6	The Hidden Years	65
7	Antioch the Great	77
8	The First Missionary Journey Cyprus	89
9	The First Missionary Journey Asia Minor	94
10	The Crisis at Jerusalem	105
11	The Battle over Segregation at Antioch	117
12	The Second Missionary Journey From Antioch to Troas	125

13 The Second Missionary Journey
      Through Macedonia   133

14 The Second Missionary Journey
      Athens, Corinth, and Return   145

15 The Third Missionary Journey
      Through Asia Minor to Ephesus   162

16 The Third Missionary Journey
      The Crisis in Paul's Career   180

17 The Third Missionary Journey
      Corinth and the Letter to the Romans   196

18 The Third Missionary Journey
      The Return to Palestine   204

19 In the Holy City   215
20 The Captivity at Caesarea   229
21 From Caesarea to Malta   239
22 Arrival and Captivity at Rome   248
23 Before Caesar   257

    Chronological Table   268
    Sources   269
    Abbreviations   271
    The Chronology   272
    Notes and References   276
    Index   308

Introduction

NO ONE CAN pass by this extraordinary man. Paul helped build the house of the Christian civilization that we inhabit and his thought helped to give generations of our ancestors their outlook on life. But he is a controversial figure. Says Renan, "The Writings of Paul have been a danger and a hidden rock—the causes of the principal defects in Christian theology. Paul is the father of the subtle Augustine, of the unfruitful Thomas Aquinas, of the gloomy Calvinist, of the peevish Jansenist, of the fierce theology which damns and predestinates to damnation." Renan here is forced to omit Martin Luther, who found in Paul a joyous and victorious faith. But we do not need to concern ourselves with the more abstruse elements in Paul's thinking. In this book we are concerned primarily with Paul the man and his great struggle. To put that in proper perspective is our aim.

In trying to bring to life persons of the past about whom the knowledge is fragmentary, some exponents of modern popular biography exercise considerable freedom not only in dramatizing the happenings but in filling in gaps with the imagination. There is no reason why this should not be done in the case of Paul. For an incomplete "Life" is unsatisfactory. A biography must begin, according to M. Maurois, "with one object—of placing the reader in an atmosphere which will facilitate his understanding of the first feelings of the hero in his youth." The reader wants to see a life unroll in such a way that the young man discovers the problems that involve the mature man in his struggle. He wants to see development take place. He desires, too, to know whether the individual was true to himself to the end.

Obviously this can only be done for Paul with the aid of the imagination on the basis of carefully sifted surviving indications—not in the sense of certainty, of course, but by way of suggestion to satisfy the cravings of the reader for a total picture. It should, however, remain within the realm of probability and not take on too much of the nature of fiction. An admitted reconstruction, plausibly done, should be just as acceptable to a reader as the type of reflective filling of gaps, recommended by Paul Murray Kendall in his recent discussion of the art of biography.

Even in the reported history of Paul many things are controversial, such as the chronology and the order of some events. There is no one who can settle the argument about them with present means. Alternate views are admissible. But for the purpose of narrative an author must make his decision and not leave his reader dangling in uncertainty.

The works cited in the notes will show those familiar with the research in this field the main influences to which I yielded or reacted in developing my views. I have, however, refrained from heaping up titles of books and articles on special points.

E. G. KRAELING

New Canaan, Conn.

To my daughter
CECILIA

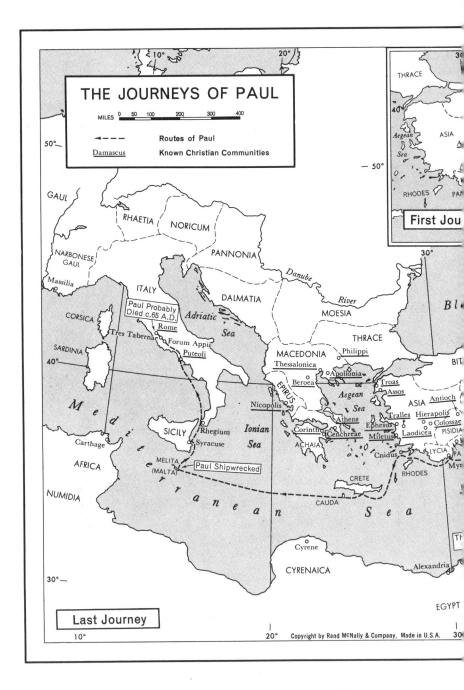

THE JOURNEYS OF PAUL

MILES 0 50 100 200 300 400

◄- - - Routes of Paul

Damascus Known Christian Communities

GAUL

RHAETIA NORICUM

PANNONIA

NARBONESE
GAUL

Massilia

ITALY

Danube

DALMATIA

River

MOESIA

CORSICA

Paul Probably
Died c.65 A.D.

Adriatic

Rome

Sea

THRACE

SARDINIA

Tres Tabernae

Forum Appii

Puteoli

MACEDONIA

Philippi

Thessalonica

EPIRUS

Beroea

Apollonia

Troas

Assos

Mediterranean

Nicopolis

Aegean
Sea

ASIA

Antioch

SICILY

Rhegium

Ionian

Syracuse

Sea

Athens

Corinth

Cenchreae

Tralles

Ephesus

Miletus

Hierapolis

Colossae

Laodicea

PISIDIA

Carthage

AFRICA

MELITA
(MALTA)

Paul Shipwrecked

Cnidus

LYCIA

CRETE

RHODES

NUMIDIA

CAUDA

Sea

Cyrene

CYRENAICA

Alexandria

Black

BIT

THRACE

Aegean
Sea

ASIA

RHODES

PA

First Jou

Cnidus

Myr

EGYPT

Last Journey

Copyright by Rand McNally & Company, Made in U.S.A.

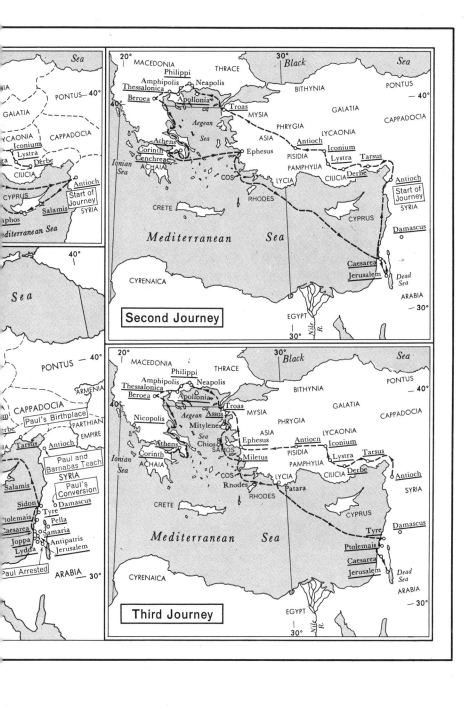

1 THE TARSUS BOYHOOD

Of the people of Israel, of the tribe of Benja-
min, a Hebrew born of Hebrews.

PHILIPPIANS 3:5

I am a Jew, from Tarsus in Cilicia; a citizen of
no mean city. ACTS 21:39

But I was born a [Roman] *citizen.*

ACTS 22:28

IN THE REIGN of Caesar Augustus, in an unknown year
and day, a son was born to a Jewish couple in a city of Cilicia
named Tarsus.[1] This is all we know specifically about the
child of destiny with whom we are concerned until the day
when he steps forth as a "young man" on the stage of history.
However, just as one could, without going far astray, reconstruct the early life of a Negro boy in a southern town, so
one can recapture much of this child's development from the
knowledge of his social and religious background in the frame-
work of time and place. With the philosopher Xenophanes,
a much earlier native of Asia Minor, we say, "Let these be
taken as fancies, something like the truth."

13

Every child is a miracle to its mother. When this young Jewish woman held her little son's body against her own and he went about sucking nourishment in a business-like way, she thought that there was never a child like this and that no name was too great for him. And when on the eighth day the friends and relatives assembled for the usual celebration and she was asked what the boy was to be called, she replied, "His name is Saul."

This response evoked a nod of dignified approval from her husband, who traced his descent from the tribe of Benjamin which of old had given the Hebrew people its first king, Saul, the son of Kish. The guests rejoiced and spoke their well-wishes, whereupon the babe was circumcised. Suddenly finding that this world was not just a bed of roses as he thought while being cuddled and fed, he complained bitterly for three days until healing set in, and thereafter became content with his lot.

The news of the birth of a son in the house of a patrician among the Jews leaked out of the Jewish district and into the city. When the boy's father went forth into the marketplace and was congratulated by some of the Gentiles and asked what the child's name was to be, he answered, "His name is Paul." This was because the child's real name was reserved for use among his own kind, while among Gentiles a Jewish boy bore another name, more familiar to the ears of Greek-speaking people. But this was a very special child and actually had a longer name than that, for his father was not only a citizen of Tarsus but also, and quite separately from that, a Roman citizen.

Every real Roman had three names:[2] a first name, which was commonly reduced to an initial when written; a second one, which was the clan name and remained constant like our family names, and a third name, which was the one by which the individual was commonly called—something like our first name in function. Thus G. (Gaius) Julius Caesar belonged to the Julian family but was called Caesar. Those who succeeded him and were of this family are known as the Julian emperors. So great was the fame of this man that his third name Caesar (or *Kaisar* in Greek spelling) became the imperial Roman title.

Now Paul's father was not of a Roman family, but when citizenship was conferred on foreigners they usually took the first two names of the dictator or general from whom they had received the grant. Paul's father had already inherited that citizenship privilege, for the great occasions when it might have been conferred on a Tarsian Jew lay in the past. It may have been granted to an ancestor by the immortal Julius himself, who had honored Tarsus and called it Juliopolis, a name which was to prove evanescent after his demise. Paul's first and second Roman name thus could have been Gaius Julius. The third name Paul was chosen for a twofold reason: because it was Roman and famed as the third name of a great Roman general, L. Aemilius Paulus, and because it sounded much like the boy's Hebrew name, Saul.

Paul, we will suppose, was born in the spring, when the rainy winter was at an end. From May to October the weather was humid, and a haze lay over the Cilician plain. Tarsus was about ten miles from the coast, and the region in which it lay was immensely fertile. A few miles to the north the land became hilly, and these ridges paralleled the great wall of the snow-capped Taurus Mountains which rose behind them to a height of nine thousand feet. There was a great pass in the mountain wall leading up to the high plateau of the interior. During the long winter there was no travel through this snow-choked defile; but when the road became open again in late spring the camel caravans began to come down from the interior through those so-called Cilician Gates, bringing their wealth to Tarsus for export.

When the summer came the infant Paul was taken to a summer home on the slopes of the Taurus, there to breathe the fresh air of mountain and forest and to escape from the dreadful heat and the fevers that racked the bodies of all those who did not flee. Only a century ago "the ague" was a similar and inescapable terror to people in our own country wherever there were swamps and marshes, and none realized that it was the mosquito that caused the havoc. At Tarsus it was, of course, the same enemy and not some dreadful fever-demon, as the people believed.

The founder of Paul's family was a man of some consequence, for unimportant people were not made Roman citizens. While Palestinian Jews were mainly agricultural, Jews in foreign lands sometimes found greater opportunities. We will assume that Paul's father was carrying on an inherited textile business. The caravans brought him numberless hides of black goats from the imperial properties in the Lycaonian plains. The cloth called *Cilicium* or "the Cilician product," made from this remarkably fine hair, was much in demand for warm mantles for soldiers and sailors. Such a man also had land holdings in the rich Tarsus plain and slaves to work his acres.

In that old world a man's home was his castle. He went forth from it on horseback to inspect field and factory, leaving behind him a housebound wife, who freed from his dominion could now do a little dominating of her own over the servants. When she went out she was veiled—a point the Tarsians insisted upon. Her main joy in life was to spoil her sons, and she bore their selfishness and tyranny with inner joy. Was not a boy, who would go out into the world and be somebody, the main excuse for a woman's existence, the future source of life's chief satisfaction? So Paul grew to be a willful, tempestuous lad, like a wild young colt of the pastures.

Paul's father could have held the rank of a citizen of Tarsus only as member of a tribal association for that was how the citizenry was organized.[3] It must have been a Jewish one, for a Jew could not have been a member of the other associations, since he would have had to participate in their pagan religious rites. An all-Jewish group, however, could substitute the service of its synagogue for the latter.

The remarkable institution of the synagogue had spread among the Jews ever since the so-called law of Moses, which prohibited their having temples and bringing sacrifices outside of Jerusalem, was adopted (Nehemiah 8-10). It provided a spiritual service composed of a confession of faith, scripture reading, homily, and prayer. It thus is ancestral to the Protestant type of service as the temple cult is to the Catholic service.

What the education of a Jewish boy of a well-to-do family in the Hellenistic cities of that day was is not completely known. It may have varied greatly in different places and in individual cases. Paul being of the class that did not restrict itself to a ghetto was given instruction that would enable him to move about with freedom and self-confidence among the Greeks. If he is reported as saying that from his youth he spent his life among his own nation (Acts 26:4) this is to be taken with a grain of salt, both in view of its formulation by the author of Acts and the audience there addressed. His family background was, however, conservative since he asserts that he was born "as to the law a Pharisee" (Philippians 3:5). At home the Aramaic language was spoken, for this is probably what he meant when in that same connection he calls himself "a Hebrew born of Hebrews."[4] With Jewish boys of his kind the main educational effort was directed to learning to read the Greek Bible-translation, just as the main education of Turkish boys until the modern revolution was sitting with a teacher in a mosque and learning to read the Koran.

In some way the young Paul learned a craft that was to stand him in good stead (Acts 18:3). It was beneath the dignity of a man of Paul's father's status to let his son work seriously at such an occupation. The boy may have picked it up visiting with his father's workmen, as boys like to do. Literally rendered the Greek term for the craft means "tent-maker." But such terms often took on broader meanings. One must not be misled by the example of the nomads of Asia Minor and of the other eastern lands, among whom the women on their primitive looms weave strips of a coarse, firm material from black goats' hair and then sew them together to make tents. There are no grounds for thinking that this was the sort of work in which Paul became skilled. One of the church fathers with a knowledge of the living language renders the term used of Paul's craft as "leather-worker,"[5] for in the Graeco-Roman world tents were made mainly of leather. Many other things could be made from leather, notably shoes and containers for water or wine (the "wine-skins" of Mark 2:22). A whole city like Colophon north of Ephesus could even specialize in the leatherworking trade.

Can we suppose that Paul as he grew up shared in any of the educational opportunities enjoyed by the Greeks of his city? Ever since the emperor Augustus had sent his teacher, the Stoic Athenodorus, a native of Tarsus, to oust the corrupt gang that was in control there, the city was fortunate to have been governed by philosophers.[6] After the sway of Athenodorus was over came that of Nestor of the "Academic" school, whom the boy Paul must often have seen. Tarsus thus had become a great center of learning, not one to which students from other countries were attracted, but rather one from which many teachers went forth to other places to carry the torch of knowledge.

But Paul nowhere shows acquaintance with the Greek classics. The few quotations from Greek literature that he is credited with were of the widely known type and prove no acquaintance with their actual sources. Homer was the bible of the Greeks, but Paul apparently was unfamiliar with *Iliad* or *Odyssey*. A Jewish father like Paul's would have been too horrified by the world of the Homeric gods with their immoralities and jealousies to let his son read these epics. Paul can hardly have attended the theater—though Jews sometimes did, as the Alexandrian Jew Philo reports of himself—or appreciated the plays of the Greek dramatists. However, we may imagine the youth as pausing to listen to the itinerant philosophers who addressed people in the marketplace. It was a speechmaking in which the speaker not only set forth his viewpoint, but took up and refuted the objections that someone might raise. From these public speakers, Stoics and Cynics, Paul evidently learned the manner of arguing that he later used so effectively.

One must certainly suppose that Paul often went to the "gymnasium" or athletic field where the Gentile youths cultivated physical fitness. It lay on the banks of the Cydnus, which in those days flowed through the city. The participants, in the customary Greek manner, laid aside their garments and were completely naked.

Did Paul ever join in this activity which was open to him as to all young men? If he did, the chances are that he would have been the butt of ridicule for being circumcised.[7] The experience would have led him to remain on the sidelines. One can imagine also that it might have raised in his mind the question whether circumcision was not an unnecessary handicap that the Jew carried into the world. That problem was to be a great concern in his life. However this may have been, Paul's interest in athletics was real.

Often, too, he must have visited the harbor—the *rhegma*, a lakelike basin five miles below the city. Light vessels could go up to the city itself, as did one that had brought Egypt's queen, Cleopatra, to Tarsus. People of Paul's time were always talking of that day. The ship had purple sails and a gilded stern, and silver oars beat time to the music of instruments. The people, unaware of who was coming, had run out of the city to see the spectacle, leaving Mark Antony seated alone on his tribunal at the marketplace. Cleopatra, lying under a canopy of gold, with cupid-like boys fanning her and maids dressed as sea-nymphs and graces steering the rudders and working at the ropes, was beauty incarnate. The superstitious sank down to pray, thinking that the goddess Aphrodite was arriving to feast with Dionysus for the common good of Asia.[8]

In the harbor Paul saw ships from all lands; from Greece and Italy, from Syria and Egypt, from Cyprus and Crete unloading foreign wares or taking on the products of Cilicia and Cappadocia. Travelers visited the city, while waiting for the ships to unload and load. The seamen were a tough lot, and many of them spoke dialects, Phoenician and Punic, that Paul recognized as similar to Hebrew.

We can imagine the boy dreaming of visiting some of the distant lands from which the ships came—especially those of the west: Macedonia, whence Alexander had gone forth, bringing Greek civilization in his train; Greece, with her famous cities, Athens and Corinth; Rome where the men who ruled the earth resided; Spain and the pillars of Hercules, the very limit of the west. Boyish longings arose in his bosom. If he were only a captain of one of those sea-going ships that carried hundreds of passengers and crew; if he were only commander of a thousand (chiliarch) in the Roman army and could go to the Danube or the Rhine, to the Euphrates or the Nile, wherever the emperor Tiberius would send him! But no, he was a Jewish boy, for whom the battle would have to stop on the Sabbath; who could not eat this and that which Gentiles ate. He was hemmed in by decrees of the Jewish "philosophers," who started their thinking with the premise of a sacred book from which all truth had to be deduced, instead of with what was reasonable, as did those fascinating teachers whom he heard in the colonnades of Tarsus.

Perhaps when he was about seventeen years old[9] Paul was imprudent enough to voice such thoughts. The paternal brow clouded; a storm was brewing. But when the lightning fell it did not seem so bad.

"Saul," said his father, "I am going to send you to the land of your fathers, to Jerusalem to study our philosophy. There you can learn that we must above all else keep the law of our God."

2 GOING TO JERUSALEM

*I was glad when they said to me, "Let us go
to the house of the LORD."*

PSALMS 122:1

IT IS A GREAT day when a youth can set forth to a far
country in a sea-going ship, free for the first time from fa-
therly commands and motherly solicitude, full of self-reliance
and ready to meet the world. The bravado may not last long,
but it is vastly satisfying while it does.

It was, we will suppose, the year A.D. 28.[1] We can visualize
in our imagination the scene at the harbor of Tarsus, where
family and friends were on hand in the hour of sailing. The
ship was a small merchantman with upturned prow, ascend-
ing stern, and a cabin on the afterdeck. Her sailors stood
ready to cast off from the mole, loosen the paddles with which
she was steered, and to unfurl the sail. Paul's father went
aboard to speak with the captain, ostensibly about the ship-
ment of goods which Paul was to deliver to a merchant at
Jerusalem,[2] but actually about looking out for his son. Seizing
the opportunity, Paul's mother took her boy aside for a few
private words. He felt annoyed and embarrassed to have the

22

onlookers observe this. Her eyes behind her veil were tearful. She expressed the hope that he would not stay away for more than a year, and then would return to help his father in business. A suitable marriage would be arranged for him. Paul knew the girl she had in mind. But he must let his father know within the year for it would soon be necessary to reach a definite accord with the girl's father and arrange the engagement. Then after another year was up he could marry her.[3]

There was a faraway look in Paul's eyes as his mother poured out her parting song.

"We will see, Mother. Right now I feel something drawing me, and I do not know where it will lead me."

At this reply his mother's fears for him were intensified. Swiftly her words gushed forth. Let him not disappoint her hopes! She had carried him under her heart for nine months; she had born him in pain; she had suckled him with the milk of her breasts till the long weaning was ended; she had nursed him through fevers, amid fervent prayers for his life. Let him not disappoint her by striking off on some wayward path. He was stiff-necked, she knew it; he was just like his father in that respect. Let him recognize it as a dangerous failing.

Paul turned away with relief as his father approached. How tiresome were those maternal warnings, and yet how disquieting too! They cast a pall over the enthusiasm with which he had come down to the harbor. He received the well-wishes of his friends and relatives, kissed his younger sister[4] and his parents, took his dunnage bag into which his mother had stowed clothing and some of those edibles for which Tarsus no doubt was famous as it still is, and got aboard the vessel.

Sailing hours were adjusted to catch the breeze coming from the land. When the sail was unfurled—a single square one, not too large—it bosomed out like a billowy cloud, and the ship began to move away. Paul stood near the two paddle-like rudders, each of which was managed by a sailor to steer the ship towards the outlet, as they went through the lakelike basin.

He felt remorse for having brushed aside his mother and her counsel. Was she right after all? Should he come back and marry? The girl she had mentioned was very nice, and suited him better than any other he knew of. She was very much like his mother who had a subtle way of making his father think that everything he did flowed from his own ideas. Dear mother—there she was waving to him, though little he knew how much it cost her. His forceful father had a big smile as he waved his hand; Paul did not know how heavily the responsibility he had taken of sending the boy to Jerusalem weighed on him, and with what anxiety he anticipated a repetition of his wife's accusations once they were at home.

The group on shore receded into the distance, and as the ship passed out of the lake and into the stream it disappeared from view.

Down the Cydnus they went, past fields bearing rich crops, and in sight of herds of cattle. The city government of Tarsus had a constant task of keeping the river open. Boats were at work, and men—prisoners at hard labor—were dredging up silt with copper buckets fastened to ropes. Soon Paul could hear the roar of the sea—a sound that he came to love. It was exciting to go through the breakers and into the open water where the waves cradled the ship. Looking back he could see the Cilician plain and in the background the mighty Taurus Mountains. He did not dream how long it would be before he would see them again.

The ship had a full cargo for Caesarea of Palestine. Catching the favorable prevailing westerly winds it sped ahead. They passed other merchantmen bound in the opposite direction and making only slow progress by tacking. Soon they were off the blessed isle of Cyprus that pointed its sharp finger at the gulf of Issus.

Nearer came the Syrian coastline. Paul's eager eyes took in the new scenes with delight. The captain pointed out the forested Amanus range ending in Mt. Rhosus at Seleucia, the harbor of the great Syrian capital, Antioch; the mouth of the Orontes River; the Casius Mountain, in passing which all the mariners lifted up their hands in prayer to the god Zeus or Baal, while Paul prayed to the God of heaven and earth; then came the long Lebanon range and the narrow Phoenician coastal strip before it. Berytus was passed, below the mouth of the Lycus river, where there were said to be strange rock carvings; then the famed island city of Tyre, which Alexander had overcome by building a mole out to it. The high, many-storied houses crowded together, were visible far out at sea.

Next came white ledges above the sea. Paul was told that this was the Tyrian ladder; it was traversed by a narrow road with steps hewn into the rock. Over it many an army had passed in olden times. Soon the bold headland of Mt. Carmel hove into view. Here, too, the sailors offered prayers to the god of the mount. Paul, mindful of the story of the prophet Elijah which had impressed him so when he heard it read in the synagogue, thought of how the fierce old fellow had outdone the Baal prophets up there. In the bay on its northern side lay Sycaminos (now Haifa), the best natural harbor of Palestine. Passing Dora (the biblical Dor), they at length neared their destination, Caesarea.

This powerful fortress city was a great sight to behold from the sea. It was built by King Herod in approved Hellenistic style, with stone brought from afar.[5] On an unfavorable coast he had created a harbor that was a marvel of Greek engineering. A great breakwater had been established and a bay dug out in which a whole fleet could ride safely at anchor. There was a mole with towers on it, the largest of which was named the Drusium in honor of Drusus, a son-in-law of

Caesar. There was a great hippodrome, from which the spectators could view the chariot races, while at the same time facing the sea. There was the royal palace where the Roman governor of Judea, Pontius Pilate (a.d. 26–36), now lived and a heathen temple dedicated to Roma (a goddess symbolizing the city of Rome) and to Caesar (imagined as deified after death like the Egyptian Pharaohs). These edifices showed that Herod did not build for the Jews but rather for the Hellenistic population which was predominant in the area. Paul would have liked to linger there but that was impossible.

The ship captains had agents with whom they were accustomed to do business. These men took care of the delivery of shipments to the places for which they were intended. We may imagine that the right agent was soon on hand and that to him the captain entrusted Paul who was to go along to Jerusalem with the goods shipped by his father. The unloading of the vessel and the careful checking of all the boxes, bags, and parcels and their destinations took time, during which Paul was able to walk about in the city. He was, indeed, permitted to sleep another night on the vessel.

The following morning, however, the goods were loaded on the backs of camels, and caravans heading for Samaria and for Jerusalem were gradually organized and got under way. The owner of such a caravan became responsible for the delivery of the goods. Paul went with the one going to Jerusalem, and was provided with a donkey to ride. It was a nimble animal and gave him a lot of amusement.

The distance from Caesarea to Jerusalem was sixty-five miles. The slow travel of a heavily burdened caravan made this a three-day journey. Two stops thus had to be made at caravanserais. In the ascent from the lower to the upper Beth-horon, Paul must have noted with some dismay how bare these rocky ridges of Palestine were—how different from the beautifully forested slopes of the mountains adjoining the Cilician plain. When he was thirsty he had to drink cistern water out of goatskin containers. The first time he spat it out. Natives of Asia Minor, such as Paul, weie connoisseurs of water, tasted it much as one tastes the flavor of wines, and praised the waters of one place as superior to those of another.[6] He thought of the noble rivers and streams of Cilicia, and wondered that any land could be so destitute of moisture as was the one through which he was riding. But when he mentioned this to an elderly camel driver, the man's eyes glowed with a prophetic light. "Think," he said, "what it will be like when from the Temple the River of Life will break forth, lined with trees bearing fruit and with leaves for healing."[7]

On the afternoon of the third day they reached a rise called in Greek, Mount Scopus, or "Prospect Hill" where Jerusalem first came into view. Coming from the north it was disappointing to see it standing, not on a height as Paul had expected, but on land sloping off to the south in two ridges with a gradually deepening depression between them. On the left, in front of the city, there was a grim-looking fortress with numerous Roman soldiers moving about. Behind it one could look into a part of the great Temple area. A ravine slanted down from the northeastern corner of the city, beneath the wall, and west of it rose a hill planted with olive orchards. The city walls were broken down in various places on the north side so that it was not immediately defensible. Three high towers were visible on the western side of the city, belonging, so Paul was told, to the palace of the late King Herod. It was now at the disposal of Pontius Pilate, when he came up from Caesarea to show the Jews that Rome kept a vigilant eye on the city.

The road led straight to the northern gate of the city. The

caravan with its burdens went to the bazaar district, where shopkeepers soon thronged about to receive goods for which they were waiting.

Here Paul found the merchant to whom his father's goods were addressed—an elderly man, a Cilician Jew by birth. He received the youth with great kindness and brought him to his wife. She was a motherly woman, very happy to have a guest and to hear news of Tarsus, her childhood home.

So Paul at last was in the city, whose name had a sacred ring in the ear of every Jew. He did not know it, but he now stood at that crucial point in life where every step is fraught with fate. He could not have told anyone what he was going to be, and certainly did not wish to be what he became. One step leads to another and a higher power holds the reins. The impulse of his father to send him to Jerusalem, opened the door to Paul's destiny. He would pass through it and help to shape a new world.

3 THE QUEST

I advanced in Judaism beyond many of my
own age among my people, so extremely zealous
was I for the traditions of my fathers.

GALATIANS 1:14

Brought up in this city at the feet of Gamaliel,
educated according to the strict manner of the
law of our fathers, being zealous for God as
you all are this day.   ACTS 22:3

THERE WAS MUCH for Paul to see and do in the holy
city. The first thing of course was to visit the Temple.[1] He
was astonished at its great size and the mighty stones of
which it was constructed. Especially impressive were the
great colonnades adjoining the walls of the outer court, and
providing a shaded walk. He could not go beyond this court
because he was considered unclean since he came from a
foreign land. A seven day period of purification was required
before he could enter the Court of the Women and go up
the steps and through a gate to the innermost court where
the holy altar and the "House" stood. At the terrace be-

29

fore the Court of the Women, he saw a posted warning tablet
in the Greek language which stated:

> NO HEATHEN SHALL ENTER WITHIN THE HEDGE
> AND WALL ABOUT THE SANCTUARY. WHOEVER IS
> CAUGHT CAN ONLY BLAME HIMSELF, BECAUSE
> DEATH WILL FOLLOW.

As he read the inscription[2] Paul had a vague and strangely
disturbing premonition that somewhere in the corridors of
the future, evil was brewing for him from those solemn words.

Though he had to delay going into the inner courts he
was able to attend a synagogue with his host on the next
Sabbath. There was one especially built for Greek-speaking
Jews—the Synagogue of the "Libertines" (i.e., Roman freedmen), Alexandrians, Cyrenians, and Cilicians, and this was
naturally the one to which they went.[3] Here the lessons were
read and an exhortation was given in the Greek language.
As a stranger Paul might have been asked to speak, but he
was still too young to be considered for that role. The "ruler"
or president of the synagogue had appointed a visitor from
Alexandria for the office, and Paul was very much interested
to hear the fine Greek spoken by the man, as well as his
unusual type of scripture interpretation. He often quoted the
great Alexandrian teacher Philo, who was proving to the
Greeks that all their wisdom was already contained in the
books of Moses (the Pentateuch).

Paul, eager to hear more about Philo, sought the acquaintance of this speaker after the service. He learned that Philo
believed in the contemplative life. He often left friends and
relatives to retire into the desert where, without distraction by
earthly matters, he could look upon the world as from above
and where his spirit could soar aloft in an inspired state.
This thinker had a great admiration for a Jewish monastic
group in Egypt called the "servers of God" (Therapeutae),

and for the Essenes. Paul had never heard of either of these.

Paul's father had sent him to Jerusalem both to labor and to learn.[4] He worked for some hours of the day for the merchant, but then had time also to pursue other interests. His father hoped that he might become a Pharisee by conviction. This, Paul found, was going to take a great deal of study, which he felt like postponing. With his newly gained independence he decided to become acquainted first of all with the Sadducees, who were the party of the more sophisticated Jews.[5] They were said to be named after the priestly family of Zadok (1 Kings 2:35), and included all those who favored restoration of Zadokite high-priestly rule such as had existed in the period from the coming of the Greeks (333 B.C.) to the usurpation of the office by Simon the Maccabee in 141 B.C. and its transformation to a kingship in 104 B.C.

By associating with the Sadducees, Paul came into the house of the high priest Caiaphas (A.D. 18–36),[6] and was introduced as a young man from Tarsus and a Roman citizen. The keen eyes of the high priest seemed to pierce through him. Paul felt himself sized up, classified, and tucked away in memory's file for further reference.

"Sometimes young men like you can be very useful to our people's cause," the high priest said graciously. "I hope we can depend on you, Paul, if the need arises."

"I have not made up my mind yet to which party I am going to belong," said Paul. "My father wants me to be a Pharisee."

"The difference amounts to very little out in the Greek and Roman world. We even have priests here tonight who are Pharisees by conviction. The nation is more than the party. Keep in touch with us in the future."

Paul thanked him and promised to do so.

As he mingled with the Sadducees he found that there were a number of families that were eligible for the high

priestly office, and that the rivalries between them were keen
on this account. It was puzzling, too, that a great many persons were called "high priests" beside the one who actually
was the incumbent of the office. The title was given to former
high priests and even to their sons.

The Sadducees did not have the piety Paul expected to
find; they were worldly and given to associating with foreigners. Many of them had been in Rome on political missions. They were inclined to look patronizingly on the Pharisees as narrow-minded. They loved banquets and good living,
and did not practice self-denial and frugality like their rivals.

Paul soon had found out all he needed to know about this
"philosophy," and so he now turned to the study of Pharisaism. His father had told him that Pharisees were something
like the Greek Stoics. There were various Pharisaic teachers,
but the most famous was a man named Gamaliel (Acts 6:35;
22:3). Paul decided to visit his class. He found the teacher
seated on the hard floor before his students, lecturing in Hebrew, the language of the Scriptures, not in the Aramaic dia-
lect spoken by the people. These teachers accepted no money
for their teaching, but held that as God had given the law
without charge to Moses and through him to Israel, so the
instruction in it was to be free. Thus, they had to eke out
their livelihood as best they could—often by manual labor.
This made a lasting impression on Paul. There must be no
profit-motive in the heart of the true teacher of men.

But Paul was not at home sufficiently in the ancient
tongue or in the Hebrew Scriptures to benefit much from
Gamaliel.[7] His scriptures were the Greek Bible translation.
He sought out a teacher who was of the school of Gamaliel,
but who taught Greek-speaking persons like himself, for the
Pharisees saw to it that their teachings were made available
to Hellenistic Jewry too. Paul had no aspiration to become a
rabbi, but only to discover the right philosophy of life. The

teacher did not confine himself to legal casuistry (*Halakah*) but gave a great deal of practical religious instruction (*Haggadah*). In this way Paul learned some of the peculiar methods of proof from Scripture used in the schools and certain legends and speculations not found in Scripture itself, though suggested by it.[8]

Paul found the students among whom he entered excited about questions which seemed far removed from the things that animated the priestly and the political leaders he had met among the Sadducees. His new friends were concerned with avoidance of defilement, based on the Mosaic laws about clean and unclean. Several dangers in particular threatened. One was that the tithe might not have been paid on produce bought in the market. Under Pharisaic rules the buyer was liable before God for using only that which had been properly tithed and a conscientious Pharisee would pay the tithe himself if uncertain whether the seller had done it. This was what Jesus was soon to satirize as straining out a gnat (Matthew 23:24). Another danger was that one might have had contact with someone or something that was unclean, ritually speaking (Mark 7:3-4).[9]

But avoiding these perils only belonged to the sphere of obligation under the law. Fulfillment of the law did not yet guarantee salvation. "What must I do to inherit eternal life?" (Mark 10:17). That was the anxious question which the best young men among the Pharisaic Jews were asking.

This quest, quite remote from older Jewish ways, was parallel to the philosopher's quest of the Greek students, whom Paul had heard debating the way to higher wisdom at Tarsus. The intelligentsia among the Greeks sought wisdom; the Pharisaic intellectual sought righteousness and justification, *i.e.*, being acknowledged as righteous by God. Behind this desire to please God and even to obtain a store of merits lay the expectation of a world to come, in which some would be saved and the majority lost. There were books in circulation, called "apocalypses" in which the last judgment, hell and paradise were vividly described. This vast panorama, the stimulus of which was to carry on through the ages to Dante, Milton, and Bunyan, was tremendously impressive. Any reader of such a book would be driven to ask that selfsame question: "What can I do to be saved?"

It is the experience of many who go to the fountains of learning that they become absorbed in ultimate questions. Before long the young man may be lured into paths that will use up his strength for years to come, and will find himself doing what he had not planned to do. So this son of a Roman citizen of Tarsus found himself striving to outdo his fellows by scrupulously living up to the law and in laying up a treasure in heaven by good works. He fasted twice a week (Luke 18:12) instead of only the legally required once a year, gave alms to the poor, and made and executed vows. What the teachers before Gamaliel such as Hillel and Shammai had taught, and what Gamaliel had added of new insight, he tried to obey in an intensive quest of righteousness.

There were indeed some who "trusted in themselves that they were righteous" (Luke 18:9). But Paul had received a concept from the Stoics of Tarsus that did not permit him to indulge in such an illusion: conscience.[10] His conscience revealed to him how sin permeated his motives and actions. Knowledge of the law in its full range of 365 prohibitions and 248 commandments, as elaborated by Pharisaic tradition, only made the reaction of conscience the more overwhelming. O blessed ignorance of childhood! In retrospect he would say many years later: "I was once alive apart from the law, but when the commandment came sin revived (better, sprang into life) and I died" (Romans 7:9).

Those who pursue a great goal and cannot attain it may suffer despair, which those who set their sights lower, escape.

Paul, the most zealous of pupils, now became despondent. He begged the merchant to excuse him from any activity in the marketplace. He did not want to defile himself. At the same time he wondered whether there was not some way to a holier life than Pharisaism afforded.

One day Paul asked his host about men in the streets wearing white garments that seemed worn out.

"Those are Essenes," his host said. "They are our third major party. Do not be surprised that their garments are worn out. They have only the one and get no other until the old one falls to pieces. They represent the most peculiar 'philosophy' in our midst today. Their main community is near the head of the Dead Sea."

This information intrigued Paul so much that he decided to go to their community, observe their life, and perhaps apply for membership.[11]

He went down to the Essene Gate of the city, which was used largely by men of this sect in coming to Jerusalem from their Dead Sea habitat, and intercepted one who was leaving, asking whether he might go with him. Consent was gladly given, and so Paul soon found himself descending through the great gorge southeast of the city toward the head of the Dead Sea. The way led through the dreadful "Wilderness of Judah"—a kind of "Death Valley" country. The Essene settlement, with a walled-in compound serving as its center, lay on a shelf above the plain bordering the Dead Sea near its head.[12] Here they had their refectory, workshops, and meeting room as well as a refuge in time of danger. For there were always bands of nomads who might seek to attack an outpost like this, and put themselves in possession of it. There were many caves in the area, in which people lived or at least sought relief from the heat of the day. There was a good spring in the plain near the Dead Sea, and here there was another settlement. Agriculture was practiced diligently, for the community had to sustain itself by this means, since the Dead Sea was devoid of fish.

Paul was taken to the "inspector" who conferred with those seeking admission to the order. He was asked immediately whether he was prepared to become a life member, for they wished to receive only serious seekers. It would take several years before he could become a full-fledged member, and in the final stage he had to turn over to the order all he had of earthly possessions. Paul did not wish to commit himself as yet and simply asked for the privilege of staying a few days and observing their way of life. His request was granted and he was able to move about freely in the settlement.

He was much interested in the scriptorium, where men sat with pen in hand copying books for their own use and for sale. They wrote mainly on leather that had been properly prepared for the purpose. Successive pieces of hide would be inscribed and sewn together, so that they formed a long strip, which could be rolled up. The writing consisted of columns of text written from right to left, with the successive columns following in that direction.

The members of the sect ate together. A third of all the nights in the year each man kept vigil, and spent the time in reading aloud from the sacred books, and singing praises taken from biblical psalms as well as from newer hymns.

Particularly noteworthy was the affection they had for one another. This impressed Paul so much that he never forgot it.

It was difficult to find out anything about Essene tenets, however, since they took an oath not to divulge these to outsiders. Priests were a prominent element among them, and so one could infer that they were in some respects like the Sadducees in their teachings but more devout.

When Paul went down to the Dead Sea he was surprised to see that the shore was pebbly instead of sandy. The water was so shallow that he could walk several hundred feet before it came to his knees. As he looked at the grand scene—the sea, with the mountain wall of Moab in the background— some shepherds came down with a flock of sheep and gave the reluctant animals a bath in the brine.

Under a tree not far from the lake, Paul saw a man seated and went to converse with him.[13] He was evidently very old. The frugal existence people led here was so healthy that many of the sect lived a hundred or more years. The man pointed out Mt. Nebo on which Moses had died, aged 120, of whom it was said "his eye was not dim and his natural force not abated" and hoped he would reach the same age.

He also told Paul that a few miles above the head of the lake there was a ford of the Jordan, near which John the Baptist had immersed his converts. The young man had heard of him, had he? He was like one of the ancient prophets, the old man reported. Thousands of people had come to hear him, for he had proclaimed the coming judgment and called for repentance. John had denounced Herod Antipas the tetrarch— popularly called "king"—of Galilee and Peraea, and had been put to death. And now, the old man went on, there was another prophet in Galilee, Jesus of Nazareth, who was making a great name for himself as friend of the common people, healer of diseases, and preacher of a coming new order. The Pharisees were said to be very much opposed to him, because he denied the authority of the tradition of their teachers, and held that some laws given by Moses were of less importance than others or even in need of revision.

Paul was shocked at this report. The law of Moses was revered by the Pharisees with whom he had studied. It was in their view the basis of all Jewish life. He was sure he would have no use for the man from Nazareth.

"Did John the Baptist have any disciples?" he asked.

Yes, but these had been scattered after his death. However,

there now was another man living where John had lived; this
man was Bannus. He clothed himself with what could be
made from vegetation, and had no other food than what grew
wild—herbs, roots, and the like—and was also attracting some
disciples. He prescribed bathing frequently in cold water by
day and also in the night to preserve one's purity.[14]

Paul decided that he would seek out this holy man and
try his way of salvation. He obtained a guide and with his aid
found the ascetic in a grove of willows east of the Jordan,[15]
not far from the ford where one went up to Moab. He was a
kindly man, with unusual eyes. Paul felt drawn to him as to
no one he had ever met.

"I have been a disciple of the Pharisees," Paul said, "but I
cannot find the righteousness I seek, in order that I may receive life eternal."

"Dwell here for a season among us at Israel's holy river,"
Bannus replied, as he sized up the ardent youth before him.
"I do not know whether you will find what you are looking
for, but you will be free from the temptations of the world."

4 THE PERSECUTOR

*For you have heard of my former life in Juda-
ism, how I persecuted the church of God violently and tried to destroy it.*

GALATIANS 1:13

THE TWO YEARS that Paul may have spent at the Jordan
(which we take to have been A.D. 28–30)[1] were perhaps the
most significant years in the history of the ages. At that time
Jesus of Nazareth carried on his great ministry in Galilee.
When in the spring of A.D. 30 Jesus went up to Jerusalem
he passed through Jericho, only a few miles from the Jordan
ford, but the little group we have described in the willow
grove on the other side of the river had known nothing about
it. He had been arrested, tried, crucified, and buried, but no
echo of the events had reached them—so great was their
monastic isolation.[2] But then one day a former disciple of
John the Baptist came to the place with the message that
Jesus the crucified had appeared to his disciples. Many of
them who had fled at the time of his arrest had returned to
Jerusalem. Now they were establishing a synagogue. People
called them the Nazarenes.

For some time Paul had been feeling restless in his monastic existence. He had come to realize that there was no escape from sin in the monk's cave. He came to doubt that he was building up any store of merits in heaven by living in contemplation and with frequent ablutions in water. He discussed the matter with Bannus, who told him, "Paul, you are by nature a man of action. Go back into the world of men where you belong."

So Paul quietly left the group at the river and went back by way of Jericho to Jerusalem. It seemed to him as though he had come out of a long illness.

Paul now decided to be a Pharisee, but without going to such an extreme as he had previously done. The quest for personal righteousness was not enough to satisfy him. He longed to play a role, however modest, that would serve to advance his people in foreign lands. The influence of the Jews was constantly increasing in the outside world. It made him proud to hear how numerous and important they were in Egypt, Syria, and Cyprus. But at all costs they would have to remain loyal subjects of the empire which had held its protecting hand over them in the past.

But there were clouds on the Jewish horizon. There was, for example, the new sect of the Nazarenes. They claimed that the promised prophet-Messiah of whom Isaiah had spoken had come in the person of Jesus of Nazareth. Only through faith in him, they taught, could one be saved.

To any Pharisee it was unthinkable that God would reveal himself among the common people (the 'Am-ha'ar ets, as the rabbis called them), who were regarded as not scrupulously law-abiding. The inhabitants of Galilee, in particular, were all of that sort. They lived too far from the Temple and were too much involved with Gentiles, or hindered by their occupations to live the holy life.

The Nazarene movement was threatening to pass over

into Hellenistic Jewry. A number of the people in the synagogue which Paul attended were adherents of it. They believed that though Jesus had been crucified, this was in accordance with scriptural predictions and that he would return as the Son of man of whom Daniel had prophesied (7:13).

This seemed to Paul a teaching prejudicial to Jewish interests. There was much distrust and dislike of the Jews in the world. It was insulting to a Gentile to be treated as unclean by a Jew, or to have his viands rejected. Jews were very forward, too, in political matters. Wherever they were strong and numerous the Gentiles were seeking to curb them. Street battles between the rival groups were common in cities like Alexandria and Antioch. A teaching about a Jewish Messiah, if it were carried into the Gentile world, could only endanger the safety of the Jews there. The Romans had given the Jews many privileges in addition to those obtained from the Seleucid and Ptolemaic kings and from free cities. All this could be lost if the Romans saw a menace to their state in this message of a Messiah.

Paul often went to the house of one of the high priests, who was fond of associating with Jews from the Roman world. Here he found much concern about the new movement. The priestly party wanted no talk about a Messiah. The high priest, they held, was the Anointed of the Lord. After the king of the Greeks, Alexander, had come, the high priests had actually governed Judah for nearly two hundred years. It was that kind of government that the Sadducees wanted to have restored.

The high priest Caiaphas had seen this dream of a Temple-state threatened by the movement led by Jesus. For that reason he had spoken the fateful words, "It is expedient for you that one man should die for the people, and that the whole nation should not perish" (John 11:50). But instead of being destroyed the movement was becoming all the more deeply rooted through the witness and activity of the followers of Jesus.

One of the younger men of the high priestly group suggested that what was needed now was a band of counteragents to curb this movement. But, he complained, a leader was lacking who could take charge of such an action. They themselves could not be involved directly in it.

The eyes of a senior high priest fell upon Paul, and several others cried out his name.[3] Heaven had put the right man in their midst! He was a "Hellenist" or Greek-speaking Jew and a Roman citizen. His actions would be less subject to scrutiny than those of a native of Judea.

Paul was startled, but at the same time felt honored. He declared that he was willing to head what we might call a "vigilante" group, composed of young men from abroad. He would, however, confine himself to dealing with Hellenistic Jews who had become followers of Jesus, for his real concern was to see this sect stopped from spreading from Judea into the Roman world.

The high priest agreed that this was an urgent problem and to solve it would be a great service to world Judaism. The native Galilean followers of Jesus, it was admitted, were faithful temple-goers and the great teacher of the Pharisees, Gamaliel, had recommended dealing leniently with them (Acts 5:39),[4] but some of the Hellenists were reported to have radical ideas. There was, for instance, a man named Stephen, who was a leader among them. It was said that he considered God's holy temple superfluous. Paul's eyes flashed fire. Yes, he would organize a band to take care of such destroyers of the very basis of Judaism.

Paul went forth from the meeting with determination to accomplish something.

It is so satisfying to find oneself dedicated to a cause one thinks is noble. True, the inner voice whispered, "Paul, what are you doing?" but he failed to heed it, so proud was he of being on the side of the high priest and of God. He soon found four young men from Alexandria and from Cyrene. They were athletic and intrepid, and with these he formed a little society of adventurers that bound itself to secrecy and to his command and had for its aim the suppression of the Nazarene movement among Hellenistic Jews.

They would make a beginning with a leader of this group named Stephen, who was always debating with others in the synagogue about Jesus. We may tentatively reconstruct what happened from certain elements of the highly dramatized Acts account.

A favorable opportunity presented itself when Stephen visited the temple.[5] Near the entrance the five surrounded him and involved him in debate. They spoke loudly so that people ran to the scene to see what the argument was about.

Did he say, they asked, that Jesus of Nazareth would destroy this holy place and change the customs given by Moses?

Stephen defended himself in a discourse[6] in which he declared that God did not, like the deities of the heathen, dwell in houses made by hands. Quoting a prophet he declared that heaven was his throne and earth his foot-stool. Who could make a house worthy of him or able to contain him?

"Blasphemy!" cried Paul. Bystanders echoed his words.

But Stephen's face was like that of an angel—awesome to behold. He recognized the evil intent of those who had cornered him. "You stiff-necked people," he charged, "uncircumcised in heart and ears, you always resist the Holy Spirit. As your fathers did, so do you. Which of the prophets did not your fathers persecute? And they killed those who announced beforehand the coming of the Righteous One, whom you have now betrayed and murdered—you who received the law as delivered by angels and did not keep it."

The hearers were enraged. They gnashed their teeth at his words. So blinded were they that they did not see the transformation that was taking place in Stephen. It was as though the man's countenance became glorified before them. His eyes shone and a beatific smile lighted his face. He was overcome by a vision. Forgetting those around him, Stephen described in soliloquy what he was seeing.

"I see the heavens opened and the Son of man standing at the right hand of God."

Paul was fascinated. It was the first time he had seen a man in the visionary state.

It was clear that by this "Son of man" Stephen meant Jesus who had himself quoted the seventh chapter of Daniel before his judges (Matthew 26:64; Luke 22:69).[7]

Blinded by their prejudice his hearers disregarded the evidence of the Holy Spirit's presence, shut their ears in horror at the supposed blasphemy and rushed upon Stephen.

They pushed and pulled and dragged him away from the Temple and through the nearby city gate. Hundreds more joined the mob. Paul's helpers took off their robes and laid them at his feet,[8] and then proceeded to pelt Stephen with stones. Paul saw the stones strike him, knock him down, saw the blood streaming from his head. What was the man saying? He was praying, "Lord Jesus receive my spirit."

A heavy stone brought him to his knees. Once more he cried out with a loud voice, "Lord, do not hold this sin against them!"

When he had said this his broken body gave a quiver, and he died.

The crowd left him where he lay in his blood, and departed with jeers and laughter.

Paul was troubled that night about what he had done in bringing this man to death. What did it matter if Stephen was mistaken in believing that Jesus was Israel's Messiah, who would come again as Son of man? Was he not harmless, and a saintly man at that?

The death of Stephen was investigated by a Roman centurion. The high priest was asked if religious authority had been given to stone the man. This was denied and it was pointed out that there had been no regular procedure, even in the manner of the stoning. The high priest implied it was a case of mob violence pure and simple. The investigators found it impossible to learn who had instigated the stoning or participated in it. So the report sent to the Roman authorities at Caesarea was simply that a man was found slain near the city gate; cause of slaying and slayer, unknown; disposition of the body: friends who could not now be found had come and buried it.

Whatever qualms Paul had, he was able to put them aside. None of the leaders referred directly to what had happened, but Paul found himself treated with great respect. One of the younger high priests said to him, "In Rome they like to see young men hunt down guilty persons of all kinds as a noble dog does game. You are worthy of being a Roman."[9]

With his sworn followers Paul now instituted a reign of terror among the Hellenistic Nazarenes of Jerusalem. If one was caught on the street he was railroaded into the synagogue and beaten. Several times it happened that a frail man or a man advanced in years died from the beating. The occurrences led to an exodus of Christian Hellenists from the city. Sometimes the noble conduct of these people made such an impression on Paul that he felt guilty about persecuting them. More than once he was even conscious of a strange inner urge to join the Nazarene sect himself. But he brushed such a thought aside.

Part of the day Paul now spent regularly in the marketplace with the merchant selling his father's exports of Cilician cloth. His newly gained reputation attracted many people, including veiled women who found that his material was superior to any other.

Before long news reached the high priestly circles that the Nazarenes who had fled from persecution in Jerusalem were having great success winning converts in other cities and villages of the land. There was one named Philip who was carrying on a mighty missionary activity in the coastal region from Azotus in the south all the way to Caesarea in the north (Acts 8:40). In Peraea (the other side of the Jordan), in Galilee, and in the Decapolis—cities in northern Transjordan extending as far as Damascus—little groups of Nazarenes were forming, filled with devotion and zeal for their cause.

Paul was urged to extend his inquisition activity into some of these areas. He thought it best to avoid the coastal plain, owing to the fact that it was under close supervision of the Roman governor. In the inland areas, however, Roman forces were weak and there could be more persecution without attracting the attention of the legal authorities. All Paul needed was letters of recommendation from someone in the high priestly group to the presidents of synagogues in the various places.[10] In this way he would be received with respect and confidence, and would get all necessary information and help. Since the young men who had aided him in Jerusalem had returned to their homelands, it was necessary for Paul to enlist and train local help wherever he went.[11]

His abettors in the high priestly group were only too glad to have him continue these activities. He thus was able to sally forth to various towns north of Jerusalem and in the Jordan valley, ranging as far as Scythopolis, to deal with the troublesome Nazarene groups. Scenes with the Nazarenes were provoked in synagogues; inquisitions, with torture and beatings of suspects, were held. He would return to Jerusalem from such missions, make his reports to the priests and resume his business role for a while, until pressed to go on another expedition.

One day a letter came from Paul's father notifying him that his brother-in-law was coming to Jerusalem to take part in the Jerusalem business, and buy out the merchant who was anxious to return to Cilicia.[12] This was good news to Paul. He would no longer be so alone. His brother-in-law had been a young boy when Paul left Tarsus. When the family arrived, it was strange to find his little sister a grown up, sweet woman, and a joy to hear from her lips of all the happenings at home and among friends and acquaintances. When she told him of how his mother and father were longing for his return he said quietly that he could not yet leave Jerusalem. He had work to do for the high priests. But it was of a secret nature and he could not speak about it.

His brother-in-law was a born trader and was quickly at home in the street of the merchants. After Paul had introduced him to various customers and taken him to the synagogue, he himself became quite dispensable. This was a relief to him and made possible his ranging farther in the search for the Nazarenes.

It was not long before his sister received some intimation of what he was doing during his absences. His reputation for cruelty shocked her. She asked him if it was true that he was trying to destroy the new sect of the Nazarenes. How had these people offended him personally? Everybody said that they were very pious, and in the Temple she had even had several of their leaders pointed out to her. They looked like good men. Paul told her not to worry. He would not harm the Galileans. He was only trying to dissuade Greek-speaking Jews from adopting this cause. If unchecked they would make trouble for the Jews living abroad. What he did had the approval of the priests of God, and surely she had confidence in them and their authority.

But she laid her arms on his shoulders and looked into his eyes anxiously.

"Please Paul, give this up. It would grieve our mother to hear what you are doing. Go home to her, I beg you."

"Soon, soon," he replied indulgently. "I still have an important trip to make to Damascus, and then I may consider my work done."

It was true that Paul had become a hard young man. To direct and witness so many acts of brutality had made him callous, and it was this change in him that his sister sensed.

Still her words troubled him, and some of the scenes he had witnessed actually haunted him. The cries and pleas of the tortured rang in his ears. The night before his departure for Damascus he dreamed that his mother was bending over him and weeping. But when he awoke he brushed the dream aside. He was serving the cause of his God and of his people. Thus the holy heresy hunters have always comforted themselves.

It was a week's journey to Damascus. Paul had rented a horse and several mules with their handlers to carry a tent, bedding, and all equipment needed for the journey.[13] These men knew the road, but not much else and contracted to take him to the city whither he was bound.

At the time agreed on they were on hand with their animals and the party left the city. Day was just breaking in the east. From Mt. Scopus Paul looked back at Jerusalem aglow in the early light. It lay at peace; life was not yet astir.

The road was familiar to him as far as Ginnaea (Jenin) in the plain of Esdrelon.[14] From here his guides chose to take the track that would lead them to the western shore of the lake of Galilee. This was the region in which Jesus had carried on his ministry. But the Nazarenes had been driven out.

We may imagine Paul spending a night by the lakeside, very near the spot where Peter and the others had seen the risen Lord. Some fishermen whom he saw there and sought to engage in conversation were at first very reluctant to speak when asked about Jesus. Yes, he had performed some marvelous healings. He was a merciful man. One loved to hear him discourse about the coming kingdom of God and those who would enter it. He spoke with compassion—not like the Pharisees. It was sad to think that they had crucified him. He had not deserved death, certainly not such a cruel death. Paul listened and wondered how deep the influence of Jesus had penetrated.

His party crossed the river Jordan halfway between the lake of Galilee and the lake of the marshes farther to the north, and headed eastward for the upland region. In about five hours they came to a small town at the junction with the road coming up from the Galaditis (or Gilead). From the villagers here they learned that tribesmen from the east were committing robberies on the Damascus road, and were advised to await a caravan that was now due. But Paul was unafraid and insisted on pushing on the next morning.

Rather strangely his guides with their pack mules seem to have fallen behind.[15] This did not matter since Paul was now on the straight road to Damascus. The city was some twelve and one-half hours ahead and another night's stop would have to be made en route. The road ran through a bare and rocky region. On the east was the Trachonitis, its volcanic hills a deep purple in the distance. On the northwest was the huge massif of Mt. Hermon, still covered with snow, though it was the month of May. Paul would have to pass by the entire base of the mountain before reaching Damascus.

As he traveled on, the weather seemed to be changing. A brooding hush came over the land.[16] The solitude suddenly became awesome. He looked back to see if his muleteers were coming, but there was no one in sight. They must have tarried in the hope of being overtaken by the caravan.

His horse grew nervous and forged ahead more rapidly. Black clouds suddenly came scudding over Mt. Hermon. Paul now had traveled about five hours since his morning's start, and was directly opposite the main bulk of the mountain. A hawk came hurtling past, like an arrow shot from a bow. Paul thought of the superstitious belief of some Roman acquaintances that a bird coming from the left meant misfortune. This was nonsense, of course; the bird was evidently seeking to escape from something.

A moment later came a terrible windstorm, descending from the snowfields of Mt. Hermon with a chill that struck the thinly clad traveler with murderous force. Where was his warm coat of Cilicium? It was being carried by one of the pack mules, somewhere behind him. He was defenseless against the blast. His limbs became numb, as though frostbitten.[17]

Suddenly a great rift was torn into the clouds over Mt. Hermon and an eerie light fell upon the landscape. The chill gripped his heart, his bones quaked. He gave a cry of terror and his horse shot forward. There was a walled enclosure ahead—a khan for travelers—and his horse made for it at top speed. Almost at the door it stumbled, threw the rider, and then darted into the corral.

Paul was powerless to rise. He became conscious of a form standing silhouetted in that weird light.[18] Strangely, there was a lull in the sound and fury of the wind and in the mere sigh that was left of it he heard a voice speaking to him in his native tongue.[19]

"Saul, Saul, why persecutest thou me?"

As in a dream Paul asked, "Who are you, Lord?"

Again the reply came in the sigh of the breeze.

"I am Jesus of Nazareth, whom you are persecuting. It is vain for you to kick against the goads."

Paul found strength enough to answer.

"What shall I do, Lord?"

"Rise and go into Damascus, and you will be told what you are to do."[20]

The vision was gone. But as he struggled to his feet Paul realized that he could not see. Struck blind! That was what happened to men who saw what human eyes should not see. He groped to find his way to the door of the enclosure, managed to gain the interior of the shelter, and fell down unconscious.

When he came to again he sensed the presence of men and animals in the enclosure. His limbs were being rubbed by his muleteers. It took a long time before the circulation came back. He felt the warmth of a fire that had been kindled against the stone wall and was grateful for it, but he would not eat. Wrapped in his warm Cilician coat he slept in complete physical and nervous exhaustion.

In the morning they went on to Damascus. Paul's mount was led by the bridle by one of his companions. Crossing a river before they came to the city provided an obstacle that had to be negotiated with care, as it was high from the melting snows of Hermon, but it was effected without incident. Because of his impaired vision Paul missed experiencing one of the greatest thrills to be had in the Near Eastern world— the sight of Damascus in its glorious setting.

At the gate of the city Paul dismounted, for here his muleteers considered their contract fulfilled. But one of them agreed to lead him by the hand[21] to his destination. As they passed through the portal, a guard grumbled:

"Haven't we enough blind beggars in Damascus that you bring us another?"

"He is no beggar, and only became blind yesterday on the way," said the muleteer. "I am taking him to the street called Straight."

"Turn right at the next cross-street," said the guard.

Paul intended to go to the house of a man named Judas.

It turned out that the latter had gone to Emesa, but a servant received him on hearing his name and after the muleteer had been paid off took him to the room that was made ready.

Paul would eat nothing and desired only to be left alone with his thoughts, and try to understand what had happened to him. His whole existence was shattered and a new one had to be built out of the wreckage.

5 ARABIA AND DAMASCUS

*I did not confer with flesh and blood, nor did
I go up to Jerusalem to those who were apostles before me, but I went away into Arabia;
and again I returned to Damascus. Then after
three years I went up to Jerusalem to visit Cephas [Peter].*

GALATIANS 1:16-18

WHEN GOD'S CHOICE falls upon a man whom He wants
for His service the call is irresistible. Moses and Jeremiah
sought to evade it but could not. And now Paul had tried to escape it. All along, while he was persecuting the Nazarenes, an
inner voice had been summoning him to become one of them
and in their midst to find his life's service. Blinded by his
passion for the advancement of his nationality in the empire,
he had ignored this voice and had run away from its gentle
invitation. But now the stark reality was revealed to him. He
was like the ox that is being taught to draw the plow and is
kept moving by a prod—in the ancient East a long, pointed
stick held behind the animal's haunches by the plowman. If
the ox kicked he hurt himself, and the harder he kicked

the greater the hurt. "It is useless for you to kick against the goads."

Paul's hurt was indeed grievous.

The full realization that he had been fighting not for God but against Him prostrated him. How could there be forgiveness for what he had done in torturing and even bringing to death some of the followers of Jesus? What Jesus had said, "Inasmuch as ye have done it unto the least of these brethren, ye have done it unto me," Paul understood without knowing those words. Had the Lord's utterance to him not been, "I am Jesus whom thou persecutest?" The scar of the conscience was to remain with him throughout the years. Long afterward he was to call himself "the foremost of sinners" (1 Timothy 1: 15), was to concede that he was unworthy of the title "apostle," because he had persecuted the church of God (1 Corinthians 15:9).

From a persecutor of the new movement he was to become one of its proponents. He was to draw a furrow, but though willing to do so he had to learn how. In the vision Jesus had said that in Damascus he would be told what he was to do. So in the house of Judas, on the street called Straight, he awaited the fulfillment of this promise.

We see him as sitting in the courtyard of the house in the shade of trees fragrant with blossoms. Here he could hear the splashing of waters in a fountain piped in from the river Amana that watered the city as no other city of all Syria and Palestine was watered. But Paul was not listening for that. He was awaiting a knock on the door.[1] He had refused all food in the meantime.

The knock came. The servant admitted a visitor who wished to see the man who had come from Jerusalem.

Paul arose expectantly. His eyes sought to penetrate the dimness that lay upon them, but saw only a vague form approaching.

"Brother Saul!" said the visitor, "I am Ananias. The Lord has sent me to you that you may regain your sight and be filled with the Holy Spirit."

And lo, as Ananias placed his fingers upon Paul's eyelids, he felt a power proceeding from them, and it seemed as though the film that clouded his vision fell away. Thank God he could see again!

"And now, brother Saul, you must come with me to my house, for we have much to say to each other."

The transfer to the quarters of Ananias was soon made but when he arrived there Paul felt dizzy from weakness. He had eaten no food since the hour of his vision, and that day had itself been most exhausting even on the purely physical side. Yet he was not ready to eat.

Near the house of Ananias was a branch of a river hastening eastward to lose itself in the plain. Paul could hear the murmuring of the waters.

"What is to prevent my being baptized?" he asked, for he knew that baptism into the name of Jesus was the Nazarene initiation rite.

Ananias led him to the stream and casting off his outer garment, Paul lay down in the water so as to become fully immersed for a moment, and then rose up again, Ananias helping him. Suddenly, he felt as though all the evil were washed out of his heart, and as if he were beginning life anew.

Ananias watching, saw illumination appear on his face.

"The Holy Spirit has come upon you," he said simply.

Paul put on his robe again, and now food was set before him that he might eat after his long fast.

Ananias ate with him and at the end of the meal inducted Paul into the chief rite of the Nazarenes. He recited the words of the institution.

"The Lord Jesus, in the night when he was betrayed, took bread and when he had given thanks he broke it, and said,

'This is my body which is for you. Do this in remembrance of me.'

"In the same way also the cup after the supper, saying 'This cup is the new covenant in my blood. Do this as often as you drink it in remembrance of me' " (1 Corinthians 11: 23-25).

Along with the recitation Ananias broke a piece of unleavened bread and shared it with Paul, then poured wine into a cup and shared that. And they were conscious that the Lord was with them, blessing them as his beloved brethren.

From Ananias Paul now heard how the latter had known of his coming, and of the blindness that had befallen him. It had been revealed to him by the Lord (Acts 9:10-16).[2]

"Brother Saul," Ananias concluded, "you have added to the sufferings of Jesus by persecuting his followers. You will yourself suffer for his sake. As Stephen was stoned, so you will be stoned, yet escape death. As others died under beatings, so you shall be beaten five times but you will survive. When these things happen remember what you did. And much else must you suffer in Christ's name before he comes. But be of good cheer. His strength will be upon you, for you are to carry his name before the Gentiles."

Out of Paul's experience was born new religious insight. He now had his answer to the question that had led him to despair: "What must I do to inherit eternal life?" The answer was the one that Jesus had given to the man who asked him this same question, "Give up everything else and follow me."

The whole Pharisaic system of ritualistic cleanness and measured good works suddenly became for Paul a false and misleading way to salvation. He had been utterly mistaken in his Pharisaic assumption that God could not reveal himself to common men. The revelation of Jesus as the Messiah to Paul now convinced him that God had made himself known among people who did not share the Pharisaic doctrine. Those like himself, who were "according to righteousness in the law blameless" (Philippians 3:6) had erred. Their ideal had proven illusory. Man was not saved by his own efforts, by observing the law, and accumulating merit. Man was saved by God's mercy. That was the meaning of the mission of Jesus. Allegiance to him was the way to life eternal.

Years later Paul was to write: "For his sake I have suffered loss of all things, and count them as refuse, in order that I may gain Christ and be found in him, not having a righteousness of my own based on the law, but that which is through faith in Christ—the righteousness from God that depends on faith" (Philippians 3:8 f.). He thus counted as nothing all the high advantages which in his former opinion gave him reason "for confidence in the flesh" (Philippians 3:4-6).

There was no doubt in Paul's mind of the new insight thus given to him. It was nothing he needed to think out. It had come to him by revelation. What need was there of consulting others about it? He knew that the Nazarenes at Jerusalem were still under the influence of the old Jewish piety. They were trying to live according to the law while waiting for Jesus to return. There was nothing to be gained by going back there. The Lord who had instructed him could reveal his truth to them also at the right time. It would be embarrassing, too, to face the high priestly group and his former associates.

He had been given his own special task: to carry the good tidings of the grace of God to the Gentiles, and it was essential that he be about his business without delay. He left Damascus without consulting anyone. "I did not confer with flesh and blood," he declares (Galatians 1:16). Ananias found him gone one morning, without a farewell. Paul went in the full consciousness of being sent by Christ. He was an apostle, just as were Peter and the rest.

Whither should he go? Damascus was the great frontier city of Syria on the border of Arabia. It was there that Paul

went (Galatians 1:17).[3] Arabia was a term which included, as
it still does, all the areas east of Syria and Palestine and south
of the Euphrates to the Red Sea and Indian Ocean. The geog-
rapher Strabo, who died A.D. 20, so uses it. But Paul, we may be
sure, did not try to cross areas of desert or badlands where a
man might perish if he did not know where the wells were to
be found, but rather kept on the beaten track to cities such
as Bostra and Adra'a.[4]

The Nabataeans, an Arab people whose royal city, Petra,
was farther south in the land once belonging to the Edomites,
ruled this borderland[5] which later was to become the Roman
"Province of Arabia." The god Dusares, who was identified
with the Greek god Dionysius, was the most prominent Nabataean deity. At Petra he was worshiped in the form of an
unhewn quadrangular black stone. One is reminded of the
stone so greatly revered at Mecca.

Since both Greek and Aramaic were spoken in the regions
south and southeast of Damascus, Paul entered a mission field
for which he was eminently fitted. There were many Jewish
groups in these cities, and their basic tenets, such as their observance of ritual laws, abhorrence of idols, belief in only one
God, and practice of meeting on Sabbaths to hear reading of
their sacred books, were known to their Gentile neighbors,
some of whom had become worshipers of God. It was thus as
a Jew and through making contacts with synagogues that Paul
was best able to become acquainted with those Gentiles who
were most ready to hear him. He could build on what they
knew to apprise them of the new revelation that God had
given his people in and through Jesus Christ.

The Arabian ministry provided Paul with his first proving
ground. He had to learn by trial and error how to bring forward the message he was to deliver. What he accomplished
is wholly unknown, for the author of Acts does not even mention the Arabian sojourn, and Paul makes only that single

passing reference to it. Yet several centuries later we find numerous Christian churches in these regions. It is reasonable to believe that some of these came out of congregations originally founded by Paul. The God who had called him to his task must have given him enough success to sustain his faith in the reality of his commission.

At least one echo of Paul's sojourn of two years or more in those regions survives. We encounter it in his words, "Now Hagar is Mount Sinai in Arabia" (Galatians 4:25). Hagar, found in Nabataean inscriptions as Hagra (today el Hejr) was a town that lay twelve miles north of ancient Dedan (el Ela), a ten days march south of the head of the Gulf of Akabah.[6] It was the royal city of an Arab people called the Lihyanites. Paul thought the sacred mountain lay in its territory. He probably received this information from Arabian Jews. Had he traveled in the Negev, he would have been told that Sinai was in the peninsula west of Akabah where others sought it.

Some bold act, we suspect, terminated Paul's ministry in Arabia. We may imagine him as appearing at a heathen festival of the god Dusares and calling for repentance and conversion to the one true God and his Son, Jesus the Messiah. He may have been ordered to leave, as Amos the ancient prophet had been when he created a commotion at Bethel (Amos 7:12-13). A report about Paul may have been sent to King Aretas (IV) at Petra. Aretas had reason for anger against the Jews, since King Herod Antipas had dealt evilly with Aretas' daughter, Herod's wife, when he wanted to rid himself of her so that he could marry Herodias (Mark 6:17). Fortunately the Nabataean princess had divined what was being planned and had escaped to her father.[7]

On hearing of Paul's doings, Aretas issued an order that he be arrested.[8] But Paul, foreseeing this, fled to Damascus.

When he reached that city Paul first went to Ananias. The latter had a keen understanding of how a man could be driven

to strange actions by the Spirit, and had not been surprised
by Paul's sudden departure. He took him to the Christian
group at Damascus for the first time. They had all heard of
Paul's remarkable conversion and had given thanks to the
Lord that he had been stopped from undertaking his cruel
work in their midst. It seemed a miracle to find him a man so
full of humility and peace. How was it possible that he could
have been such a terrible persecutor?

Continuing to live under the roof of Ananias, Paul now
undertook to bring the gospel forward more vigorously in Damascus itself.[9] He went to a Jewish synagogue, which in this
city was also a Greek speaking one, and bore witness that Jesus
was the Messiah.

Paul's appearance in the synagogue caused great amazement. It was known that he had been the persecutor of the
Nazarenes, and that he had been sent to Damascus to carry
on inquisition there. Judas of the street called Straight may
have reported his arrival in a sorry condition and his going
away with the Nazarene, Ananias. That was the last anyone
had seen or heard of him. People had wondered what had become of him. Judas had received inquiries on behalf of Paul's
relatives through one of the high priestly group in Jerusalem,
but had been unable to say what had become of him.

The amazement of the people of the synagogue turned to
anger. This fellow had been zealous for the faith of their
fathers. Now he himself had joined the Nazarenes! He was an
apostate! It became intolerable to have him cast confusion
into one synagogue after another, for there were always some,
and especially proselytes from paganism to the Jewish faith,
who were infected by his reasoning. He was a skillful arguer
and there was no one at Damascus who could put him down.

Under these circumstances some Jews took the same stand
the high priest Caiaphas had taken in the case of Jesus: "the
man must die." Persons willing to kill him could readily be

found. Did not Brutus plunge his knife into Caesar, his intimate friend, because of disapproval of his becoming dictator?
A radical difference of opinion or philosophy has often been
considered warrant enough to assassinate someone.

Somehow the Nazarene group close to Ananias received
secret information about what was planned. They hid Paul
so that the assassins stalked him through the city in vain.

The Jews now enlisted the support of the head of the
Nabataean colony at Damascus, "their ethnarch," as he was
called.[10] For they had learned that Paul was wanted by their
King Aretas for a disturbance he had caused in his kingdom.
The ethnarch willingly aided by posting certain Nabataeans
outside of the gates of Damascus to seize Paul if he should try
to leave the city. They would whisk him away to Petra for
trial, and nobody would be the wiser.

In this perilous situation, Paul's friends decided that he
must be helped to escape. In the darkness of the night they
took him to one of their number who lived in a house at the
wall of the city. The building was several stories high and evidently overhung the ancient wall, now no longer needed for
defense. Out of a window of this house Paul was let down
over the wall in a basket and thus was able to elude the watch-
ers at the gates. He gives his own account of this incident in a
letter (2 Corinthians 11:30-33), in describing circumstances of
weakness that were not to his liking.

With his usefulness in Arabia and Damascus ended, Paul
now was in haste to go to his native Cilicia. He determined,
however, to make a quick visit to Jerusalem first. He felt that
he should become personally acquainted with Peter, the acknowledged leader of the Jerusalem church, before he went
far away.

It was perilous for Paul to enter the city in which there
now were so many against him, both those who knew of his
previous illegal activities and might have him arrested by the

Romans, and those who were shocked by his joining the Naza-renes. He determined, therefore, to employ the utmost secrecy. We can imagine him entering the city from the poorer and less-guarded section in the southwest, near nightfall, and mak-ing his way to the home of his sister.[11] That she rejoiced to see him still alive, we may be sure. But she had heard with alarm of his conversion to the Nazarene sect and of his missionary activity on its behalf. He was being denounced as an apostate. She begged him to go home to their parents at Tarsus.

That, Paul said, was just what he was planning to do. But first he wanted to confer with the men in Jerusalem who had known Jesus in his earthly ministry, especially Peter.

Paul's brother-in-law told him how the business was faring and of having met a man of Cyprus who was a Nazarene and who had returned to Jerusalem after his previous flight. People called him Barnabas. He was a good man, impressive in ap-pearance. Though a Hellenist, he had been active in the Naza-rene group from the first. Paul decided to send for him.

When Barnabas came Paul welcomed him as a brother of whose faithfulness in the service of Christ he had long heard. Was Barnabas astounded that Paul, the persecutor of the church of Christ, was now bent on its upbuilding? Christ had appeared to Paul and called him to his service—that was the explanation of this complete about-face. Now Paul was going back to his native Cilicia to carry on work there, but before he went he desired to speak with Peter. The latter had been the first to see the risen Lord, and he, Paul, now was the most recent one to do so. It was fitting that they should meet. Paul would not like to leave Judea without having made an attempt to see him. But he had to move in secret and did not wish to attend any group gatherings.

So the meeting was arranged.[12] According to Paul himself he stayed with Peter for fifteen days (Galatians 1:18). In that time his knowledge of the ministry of Jesus in Galilee and

Judea and of all he had said and done, was vastly increased. And he learned a great deal about the organization of the primitive church. He met "none other of the apostles except James the brother of the Lord" (Galatians 1:19). Paul thus seemingly, as also in 1 Corinthians 15:7, includes this man among the "apostles," and if that is correct we must infer that the title was not at that time restricted to the twelve disciples, as it was when Luke wrote. It seems likely that it was originally shared by all who had seen the risen Christ and received a commission of service from him. For it is on that basis Paul claims the title for himself, when he writes, "Am I not an apostle? Have I not seen Jesus our Lord" (2 Corinthians 9:1)? James, too, had seen the Lord (1 Corinthians 15:7).

On his part Paul must have told during the visit of how he was called by Jesus for work among the Gentiles. Since prophecy predicted the conversion of the Gentiles and since even the Pharisees, in the words of Jesus, "traversed sea and land to make a single proselyte" (Matthew 23:15) neither Peter nor James raised any objections. Paul was able to leave Jerusalem with the feeling that his ministry to the Gentiles was endorsed by the leaders.

Did he perhaps temporarily vacillate in his own mind whether or not he should preach to the Hellenistic Jews in Jerusalem?[13] The author of Acts has him relate how he fell into a trance at a last visit to the temple and was instructed:

"Make haste and get quickly out of Jerusalem, because they will not accept your testimony about me." Paul in his trance, had argued with the Lord. He held that since the Jews knew how he had persecuted the Nazarenes his testimony ought to impress them. But the Lord commanded, "Depart; for I will send you far away to the Gentiles" (Acts 22:17-21).[14]

Luke, who describes Paul as having disputed openly with the Hellenists so that they wanted to kill him, has the brethren bring him to Caesarea and send him off by ship to Tarsus.

Perhaps it is only unconscious humor when he continues, "so the church throughout all Judea had peace" (Acts 9:29 ff.). In reality Paul went forth without preaching at Jerusalem, and no doubt as secretly as he had come. For he says, "I was still not known by sight to the churches of Christ in Judea, they only heard it said 'He who persecuted us is now preaching the faith he once tried to destroy,' and they glorified God because of me" (Galatians 1:23-24).

6 THE HIDDEN YEARS

Then I went into the regions of Syria and Cilicia.

GALATIANS 1:21

THUS AFTER AN absence of about eight years, perhaps in A.D. 36 or 37, Paul again found himself sailing up the Cydnus River on a merchantman and seeing before him the great Taurus Mountains, upon which his eyes had opened at birth. "Home" sang the birds; "home" lowed the kine. He stepped forth upon the mole in the harbor with springy step, and took the road to the city.[1] He passed through the familiar streets unrecognized and came to the Jewish district. Some women eyed him curiously as he passed by and whispered to each other. He came to the door of his father's house which was opened by a slave whom he did not know. But his mother heard his voice and knew it, ran out and embraced him crying, "My son, my son." Then she saw through her tears how lean and emaciated he was.

"What have they done to you, my poor boy! How my heart has longed for you all these years! Why did you not come home when the year was up?"

"God wanted me to stay, Mother! He has called me to his service—a service I did not want nor desire, and woe to me if I do not serve."

She had been so worried since she had heard of his not returning from Damascus. Had he had no thought of his sister and his parents to let them know whether he was alive and what he was doing? They feared he had been slain by Arabs, or held for ransom by robbers.

"Never fear for me, Mother! The Lord has said to me, as he did to Jeremy the prophet, 'Be not afraid of them, for I am with you to deliver you.' I have hardly begun the work for which he chose me."

She looked at him with wide-open eyes. This was strange talk for a young man. Was his mind deranged?

It was even more difficult to face his father upon his homecoming. While he was kind, it was rather evident that he had written Paul off. The man's disappointment was grievous. He had hoped for a son who would follow in his footsteps, and be a help to him. What a mistake it had been to send him to Jerusalem! He had meant to do the right thing, and it turned out like this! The immature, he now realized, were a prey to all kinds of influences when left to themselves. His wife's anxiety at the time had been vindicated.

But hope springs eternal in the human heart, and especially in that of a mother. She pleaded with her husband to deal gently with Paul. Perhaps if he stayed at home with them he would gradually settle back into their life and would participate in it. Let him share in the work or business—perhaps in the shipping end of it, since he was so fond of ships and of the sea. If he found satisfaction in the work, he might yet decide to marry. The right kind of wife and children might be a great help in bringing him back to the normal interest in a livelihood.

When it became known that Paul had returned after years of roaming, friends and relatives of the family were curious to see him. Was it true that he had joined a new sect in Judea? The question came up again and again. He promised to speak about it in the synagogue on the Sabbath, but would not say anything until then. Yes, he had studied much at Jerusalem, had even sat at the feet of Gamaliel, though he had not wanted to become a rabbi. But he now was a teacher in the sect of the Nazarenes.

He revisited the scenes of his youth in and around Tarsus. In the marketplace he even encountered former fellow students. To their questions he replied that he had been in Judea and had studied a philosophy lately arisen there.

The Sabbath came and a large crowd assembled in the synagogue. Gentiles came too, drawn by curiosity. The ruler of the synagogue asked Paul to give the message. He outlined how the Hebrew people had hoped for a Messiah, and declared that this hope had been fulfilled in the only possible way, in the way predicted by the prophet Isaiah: that of the redeeming teacher-martyr, and in the person of Jesus of Nazareth.

The Gentiles present were inclined to scoff at the idea of a barbarian teacher being mankind's savior. Now, if it were another Greek, a second Heracles, they might find the idea attractive. Their savior would have to be a great athlete, a superman.

The proselytes on the other hand, those of pagan background who had become worshipers of God, were much interested and desirous of hearing more about the new Jewish sect and its Messiah. But the Jews were hostile.

"Who is this fellow that the LORD should have waited all these years for him to enlighten us and to lead us aside from the ways of our fathers? Let us not give him room to speak further in our synagogue."

Paul's father was instructed to tell his son not to step forward again in their midst.

But this caused dissatisfaction among the proselytes, and Paul was invited to address a meeting of them in a private house on the next Sabbath. It was held in a spacious court-yard under the shade trees. Many came, impelled by curiosity, to hear a message that promised so much to those of Gentile origin.

In his discourse Paul told them that the ritual laws were intended for Jews only, and that Gentiles need not be burdened with them. A man could be justified by God through faith alone.

Faith! This was a new accent in religion. Hitherto it was fear that had been uppermost in the consciousness. Those raised under paganism had not only the fear of one god to consider but fear of many gods, since the deities were often in rivalry and one god would cause misfortune to another god's devotees. The pages of Homer were full of instances of this. Judaism had reduced this anxiety by teaching that there was only one God to fear, and this was a great relief, especially since this God was believed to act according to moral principle rather than whim or favoritism. It was because of this teaching that many persons had become "God-fearers" and worshiped with the Jews. The Nazarenes kept this basic position and purified it further. God no longer had to be propitiated by rites and sacrifices. His helping hand was outstretched to all men. One need only take it. He had shown his love by sending his Son Jesus Christ, who proclaimed the new order and established the new covenant by becoming the single sacrifice that made all other sacrifices unnecessary. By confession of faith and a simple act of baptism one became initiated into the sect of the New Covenant. One could remain in the Jewish synagogue, but hold other meetings with those of like mind in houses until this group could establish a synagogue of its own.

The message was refreshing. It had the hope which Judaism promised, without the aggravating emphasis on promoting the Jewish nationality. It had the morality of the Hebrew prophets, without the ritualism that the noblest of the prophets condemned. Men and women could join in this fellowship, in so far as custom permitted their association, and the slave was as much beloved of God as his master.

A group of those accepting baptism was thus established by Paul at Tarsus and held their own meetings.

The absence of most of the proselytes from the synagogue service was quickly felt and greatly resented by the Jews. Their anger turned against Paul's father. It was his son who was throwing discord into the hitherto peaceful life of the Jewish community. The man was upset and distraught. Paul's mother was deeply worried. She had so longed for her son's return, yet now when she saw the consequences she wished he had stayed in Judea.

Paul was happy holding meetings with the Nazarene group. He wrote down for them many sayings of Jesus and testimonies from biblical prophecy. He taught them to pray and to repeat the sacred story of the Passion. They held common meals and celebrated the remembrance of the last meal of Jesus and his disciples, as often as they met. He laid down rules for their self-government and for their association with Jews and Gentiles, thus putting them into a position where they could function as a group without him if necessary.

That necessity soon came. Paul's father became alarmed by the reprisals visited on him by the Jewish community.[2]

A painful scene took place between father and son.

"You are destroying my position among our people," said his father. "There is only one way in which I can save myself and that is by disowning you. You must either give up being an apostle of the Nazarenes or leave my house forever."

"Before I was born God called me to be his servant. Woe unto me if I do not follow his call."

"These are vain delusions, my son. Cast them aside and take your place in the world of real life. See what an advantage you have: the son of a man of substance, a citizen of Tarsus, a Roman citizen."

"This world age is ending, father. A new one is coming from heaven in power. Only faith in the Messiah Jesus can save men on that day."

"This age will end, so we Pharisees, too, believe. But it may not be as soon as you think. Meanwhile let us look to a useful life in the world while it lasts."

"The day of the Lord will come like a thief in the night. When people say there is peace and security, destruction will come upon them and there will be no escape."

"Hear, hear the prophet!" mocked his father grimly. "There is only one thing more to say. Moses has commanded us 'Honor thy father and thy mother' (Exodus 20:12). You do this by obedience. As your father I call upon you to obey me and desist from your course."

"God is a greater father, and one must obey him first of all. He bids me do what I am doing."

"This means that you are disinherited."

"Our Messiah said to a rich young ruler, 'Go sell what you have, and give to the poor, and you will have a treasure in heaven; and come and follow me.' "

"Go then, son of my sorrow."

The following morning, when the household awoke Paul was gone. He had written on a wax tablet, "I must do the work of him that sent me."

Paul now became a wanderer in the land. He made himself independent by carrying on the leather-working trade, especially in the winter, which with its pouring rains was unfavorable for travel. While this was no occupation for the son of a man of rank, the loss of status now meant little to him. He worked only to support himself and to finance his travels.

The field he had before him was a large one.[3] To the east of Tarsus on the river Sarus was Adana; beyond that, on the next great river, the Pyramus, was Mopsuestia, with Anazarbus and Hieropolis-Castabala on its northern confluents. South of the Aleian field in the shore area there were places like Mallus, famed for reports about seers of the Homeric age, and Aegae, which Apollonius of Tyana aged eighteen chose in preference to Tarsus, when he studied philosophy and lingered at the temple of Aesculapius. West of Tarsus was the former Soli, now named Pompeiopolis, since Pompey had settled there the remnant of the pirates subjected by him. The city, so beautiful with its double colonnade of two hundred columns leading down to the harbor, had produced famous men, notably the poet Aratus. Between Soli and the next city on the west was the great river Lamus. This was a dividing line, for on the other side of it lay the "rough Cilicia" (*Cilicia aspera*) which is geologically a very different region.

We must assume that Paul made many journeys in this period of his life. In a rehearsal of what he had endured in his ministry (2 Corinthians 11:23 ff.), he makes allusion to events for which there seems to be no room in his history as related in the book of Acts. It is likely that some of these belong to this period, which may well have covered eight or nine years. A few of these items deserve mention here.

Five times I have received at the hands of the Jews the forty lashes less one.

These lashes, which were decreed by three judges from the membership of a synagogue, were applied with a whip wielded with the administrator's full strength. The victim lay prostrate, hands bound to a pillar or post, and if he died, there was no guilt resting on the executioner unless he had perchance exceeded the count prescribed in Deuteronomy 25:2. It was to lessen the hazard of this that "the less one" principle

was introduced by the Pharisaic lawyers. What a constitution
Paul must have had to endure so many cruel punishments!
The book of Acts does not report a single one of these happenings. When he refers to "countless beatings often near
death," he is thinking of buffetings received in irregular fashion,
as well as these legal synagogal lashings.

*Three times I have been shipwrecked; a night and a day
I have been adrift at sea.*

This is a particularly intriguing reminiscence. The author
of Acts does not mention any shipwrecks in Paul's Aegean
journeys, and there appears no time for any—unless the whole
account is woefully incomplete. Barring that, these shipwrecks
must have taken place along this southern Asia Minor coast
during his Cilician ministry. Did he venture by ship beyond
Cilicia to the Lycian and Carian shores and get thwarted by
repeated shipwrecks? Places like Rhodes and Halicarnassus,
where there were Jewish colonies and hence also Gentile
proselytes, were certainly important and alluring objectives.
It is strange that Acts makes no reference to them. Failure
to reach them would have indicated to Paul that the Spirit
did not want him to go there. On one occasion he had to float
about on a plank or spar for twenty-four hours, until picked
up or carried to shore by the tide. Perhaps, in the other cases
of which he makes mention, the ship was close enough to
the coast for him to swim ashore.

In danger from rivers.

In Cilicia there was always one more river to cross, for
many came down out of the gorges of the Taurus for a quick
run to the sea. Some were large and powerful rivers. Ferrymen
made a living at certain crossings, but in the freshet stages
such torrents were dangerous. Especially was this so with the
streams where there was no ferryman, and which one had to
ford. Should one starve while waiting for a freshet to subside,
or take a chance to cross over? A fall on a slippery rock could

result in injury, so that one would be swept helplessly away.
In danger from robbers.

Nowhere was that danger greater than in Cilicia and the
mountain regions adjacent to it where piracy and banditry
had been powerfully entrenched until Pompey undertook his
great campaign to exterminate it from the Mediterranean
world. But one can never catch the last robber and Paul's
remark suggests that he was held up more than once.

What the results of his single-handed mission work were
is unknown. But there can be no doubt that during those
years Paul was learning all the time, deepening his understanding of God's revelation in Jesus Christ, and developing
the strength of character and of mind, the skill in dealing
with people, the strategy and technique of the missionary
operation, that was in due course to make him the greatest of
all those who have borne the missionary title. But we can
imagine, too, his discouragements. He stood alone, wholly
dedicated to his work and to the menial labor needed to
sustain himself. The pressure of that isolation, when coupled
with so many hardships, rebuffs, and persecutions must have
been tremendous. As a counterweight he had the deep satisfaction of what he later called "an abundance of revelations"
(2 Corinthians 12:7). These were inward spiritual experiences
of an inspiring nature, wholly unlike the occasion on the road
to Damascus, for in that he had been conscious of the real
presence of a person and had heard himself addressed.

One of these new, strange incidents in particular impressed itself indelibly on his memory. He writes of it in
mysterious words:

"I know a man in Christ who fourteen years ago was caught
up to the third heaven—whether in the body or out of the
body I do not know, God knows. And I know that this man
was caught up into Paradise—whether in the body or out of
the body I know not, God knows—and he heard things that

cannot be told, which man may not utter (2 Corinthians 12:2-4)." This may have taken place late in 43—according to our chronology near the end of his lone missionary existence in Cilicia. He does not say where or under what circumstances it happened. His sensation was one of being borne aloft. He assumes that it was to the third stage of heaven in which the deity was held to dwell and where paradise was believed to be situated. It is vague whether it was the deity or an angel that spoke, but mysteries were imparted that were arcana—things one must not communicate to other persons. Hence he speaks as though of another individual. The incident had great importance for Paul. He felt as though a high privilege was given him. It is mystical in a way, but differs in that it was not sought, but granted without seeking.[4]

During this period, through his contacts with both Jews and Gentiles, Paul kept informed about what was going on in the world—above all in Palestine, Syria, and Asia Minor. He had heard of the earthquake that had visited Antioch in April, A.D. 37, after his return to Tarsus, and only a month after the emperor, Tiberius, died. The new emperor Gaius, better known by the cognomen Caligula (A.D. 37–41), who had lived at Antioch in childhood, took a great interest in the restoration of the damaged city. He sent money from the treasury and three prominent Romans to deliver it and to lend aid in the work of restoration.

Like all other Nazarenes, Paul had shared in the Jewish excitement caused by Caligula's edict of the winter of 39-40 that a statue of the emperor be set up in the Temple at Jerusalem.[5] Was this the "desolating sacrilege set up where it ought not to be" (Mark 13:14)? Would the terrible tribulation of which Jesus had spoken be ushered in when this edict was carried out? Fortunately, Caligula had died and his successor Claudius (41–54) had rescinded the edict. But Paul believed that "a man of lawlessness," who would take his seat in the Temple and proclaim himself as God, would yet come (2 Thessalonians 2:3 ff.).

More recently, grim times had befallen the followers of Jesus in Palestine. Herod Agrippa (I), thanks to the intimacy he had enjoyed with both Caligula and Claudius, had come to Palestine in A.D. 41 to reign over almost the entire realm once ruled by Herod the Great. He sought the favor of the Pharisaic element among the Jews by conducting himself as a Pharisee. While he resided at Caesarea he often came to Jerusalem, and it was not very long before he found out that he could ingratiate himself with the leaders of the people by proceeding against the Nazarenes.

He began, late in 43 or early in 44, by "laying violent hands on some who belonged to the church." He had James, the son of Zebedee, put to death by beheading. Soon afterward,[6] he had Peter arrested, but the latter had escaped and apparently had not been apprehended (Acts 12:1-19). This news had reached the Christians of Tarsus very quickly through reports from Caesarea. The little congregation was deeply stirred and prayed for Peter's deliverance. It took pride, too, in the fact that James had been able to drink the cup of martyrdom from which his Lord had drunk (Mark 10:38).

It was soon after the news of this came, in the early spring of A.D. 44, we believe, that a visitor of distinguished appearance came to Tarsus looking for Paul.

No one seemed to know where he was. The slave at the door of his father's house refused to answer any questions. Finally, the stranger located the small Christian group, and a messenger was dispatched to summon Paul from another city.

When Paul arrived he found that the man seeking him was none other than Barnabas. The latter told Paul that some men from Cyprus and Cyrene had come to Antioch and had preached Christ successfully to the Greeks. The Jerusalem church, on hearing of this, had dispatched Barnabas to that city to supervise the work there (Acts 11:19-24). This was prior to the recent persecution, news of which had reached him, too. He had a proposition to make: that he come with him to Antioch and aid in the work of winning Gentiles, for he knew that Paul considered that to be his special mission.

He likewise told Paul of the great preparations that were being made to hold Olympic-style games at Antioch in the month of October.[7] The occasion would bring great numbers of visitors from all over. It would provide an opportunity to make many contacts with persons from distant cities.

Paul was excited and enthusiastic about this news. There was no doubt in his mind that this invitation of Barnabas was a signal from the Lord. Painful as it was to leave his Cilician congregations, he made the necessary arrangements to appoint leaders in each and promised to keep in touch with them and to pray for them at all times.

Did he pay a parting visit to his father and mother? It would be the last time that he would set foot in Tarsus. It seems likely that he refrained for their sake. He knew he was hated by the whole Jewish community, not only of Tarsus, but of the other cities of Cilicia, for the damage he was doing to the synagogues.

It was no doubt a relief to his parents to hear indirectly that Paul was transferring his activities to Antioch. How proud they ought to have been to have given to the world a son whose influence on human history was to be so vast! But that high destiny of his was hidden from their sight in the bosom of time. What availed his mother's tears? Paul would never mention her but would later refer to the mother of a distinguished Christian named Rufus as his mother, too (Romans 16:13). The very names of his parents would be forgotten.

Thus Paul went forth from the city of his childhood with Barnabas and down to the harbor to set sail for Syria.

7 ANTIOCH THE GREAT

*For a whole year they met with the church,
and taught a large company of people; and in
Antioch the disciples were for the first time
called Christians.*

ACTS 11:26

IT WAS A significant day in Paul's life when he first came
to Antioch, once the capital of the Seleucid empire, but now
the seat of government of the Roman province of Syria-
Cilicia.[1] The city, with a population of 500,000 inhabitants,
was third in rank in the Mediterranean world, being preceded
in importance only by Rome and Alexandria.

Paul and his companion had come on foot from the sea-
port of Seleucia. As they crossed the bridge over the Orontes
River and reached the city, they saw a wall-lined island about
a mile upstream. There, Barnabas told him, the Roman governor of Syria, Petronius, had his residence in the palace of
the former Seleucid dynasty which had ruled over a mighty
realm originally extending from the Aegean Sea to India and
from the Caspian to the Mediterranean, but sadly reduced
when Rome gave it the coup de grace in 64 B.C.

Before them now loomed the Bridge Gate. Stuck on a rod on top of the city's wall was a skull. When Paul glanced up at it, Barnabas said, "The head of the priest Phineas of Tiberias."

There had been a great riot in Antioch in which many Jews were killed and their synagogues burned. To avenge this a Jewish force from Galilee, under the leadership of this Phineas, had surprised and terrorized the city. The emperor Gaius had penalized some of the leading men of Antioch for not stopping the original riot and for laxity in guarding the city. He had sent troops down to Galilee, who put to death many of the Jews. Phineas was beheaded and his head hung on the wall of Antioch as a gruesome warning.[2]

Passing through the gate, Paul found that he was near the southern limit of the city. A little below this point the wall ran eastward to the top of Mt. Silpius, where it turned northward to embrace the citadel and after dropping to the ravine of the winter-torrent Parmenius, partly ascended another ridge and then looped down to the river. Near that point was a bridge over the Orontes to the north end of the island and the hippodrome.

The city was laid out according to the city planning system of Hippodamus of Miletus, in regular streets, with a long avenue lined with colonnades passing through its center. The pavement of the southern portion of this avenue, which Paul and Barnabas soon had to cross, was a gift of King Herod of Judea to the city. At the nearby end of this thoroughfare the road went out through a gate to Daphne, a suburb five miles to the south. A few decades later the Roman general Titus returning from the successful siege of Jerusalem would set up some figures of cherubim from spoils of the Jewish temple, outside of the Daphne Gate, which would then become known as the Cherubim Gate.

The streets of Antioch were so laid out that they had

shade and westerly breezes in the summer and sun in the winter—a degree of sophistication in city planning that one must certainly admire. Of its public buildings little is said in the records, but of its works of art, above all of its many statues, a great deal is recorded. The Tyche of Antioch, goddess of Fortune, was particularly renowned. Seleucus I had had the original statue made in bronze by a famous sculptor in Sicyon, near Corinth. Tyche in her long robe was seated on a rock symbolical of Mount Silpius, holding a sheaf of wheat in her right hand and wearing a turreted crown symbolizing the walls of the city. At her feet was a swimmer representing the Orontes River. While in Syria Paul handled many a coin bearing Tyche's image.

On the mountainside above the city Paul saw a bust hewn into the rock. Strangely the face was featureless—a mere mask. Barnabas told him that the people called it the Charonion. Charon, as Paul was aware, was the ferryman of Hades in Greek mythology. Barnabas only knew that long ago a seer had advised making the image to drive off a plague that was afflicting the city.

According to later tradition the church at Antioch lay in the southeastern part of the city, in the district of Epiphania (named for its builder, Antiochus IV Epiphanes, 175–164 b.c.), in a street called Singon Street, not far from the Pantheon (the site of which unfortunately is unknown).[3] Hereabouts was the main Jewish community in Paul's time, though there were several others in this region—one in the plain of Antioch, near the lake, and one at Daphne.[4]

Paul's coming to Antioch was, of course, the occasion of celebration among the Nazarenes. Everyone knew of his history and his work in Arabia, Damascus, and Cilicia. He had the knowledge and training possessed by no other missionary to carry on debate with the Greeks as well as with the Jews.

The joy of the occasion was sobered by the recent hap-

penings in Judea, of which we have already heard: the martyrdom of James and the arrest and escape of Peter (Acts 12:1-18).
The first apostolic martyr was an important and powerful
figure, and his death was regarded as heroic. God was praised
who had made him strong to bear witness without flinching.
Prayer was made for the preservation of Peter.

Perhaps, it was at this time that the prophet Agabus, accompanied by others, came up from Jerusalem and disturbed
the congregation with prophecy of terrible things to come
(Acts 11:27 ff.). While his predictions may have been of a
world's end, they were later regarded as fulfilled in some
calamities of nature that befell eastern lands. That very year
news would be received of crop failure in Egypt, owing to
floods of the Nile, a condition that was to be repeated the
following year (45).[5] This would mean very high grain prices.
It would seriously affect Rome, whose huge population had
to be fed with Egyptian grain. It could affect Palestine and
other areas if the harvests were poor.

But other news was to come too: that of the sudden death
of the persecutor, Herod Agrippa (spring of A.D. 44). Luke
has included a popular account of it (Acts 12:20-22). An
angel of the Lord smote the king because he did not reject
a popular cry that arose when he seated himself on his throne
in royal regalia and began to speak. The cry was "Behold the
voice of a god, and not of a man!" For such overweening
pride he reportedly was "eaten by worms" and died.[6] One can
appreciate the relief with which the news of the death of this
evildoer was received everywhere by the Nazarenes. His death,
too, was to have the advantage for them of a return of Judea
to direct Roman rule. Henceforth, there could be no officially
sanctioned persecution.

The congregation at Antioch was well supplied with prophets and teachers (Acts 13:1). The report about this is so
unusual that one must conclude that each man had played an

important role in the origin and history of this congregation. Besides Barnabas there was a Symeon who was called "Niger" (black), Lucius of Cyrene in Lybia, and Manaen (Menahem), an intimate of Herod Antipas, the former tetrarch of Galilee, who had lost his kingdom to his brother-in-law, Herod Agrippa I in A.D. 39 by decision of the emperor Caligula. Paul is added to the list as a junior member. But this is scarcely doing justice to Paul's importance at this time. When he later speaks about the various functions in the church, he says, "God has appointed in the church first apostles, second prophets, third teachers" (1 Corinthians 12:28). The author of Acts, with all his admiration for Paul, was forced by developments in the church since Paul's time to reserve the title of "apostle" for the twelve disciples of Jesus. But Paul himself is so emphatic in claiming the apostolic title in his letters that one can hardly believe that he only assumed it later on.

Seleucus in founding Antioch had required that everyone who dwelt there become a citizen, and so Paul, too, may soon have been enrolled as one. This comprehensive citizenship brought about a great mixture of peoples—Greeks, Syrians, and foreigners from many lands who had come in the time when the Seleucid kings ruled a far-flung empire. The Jews, too, were thus citizens and this resulted in a great deal of anti-Semitism. Their special privileges, which were even inscribed on bronze tablets, greatly aggravated the Greeks. Why should people who were exempt from military draft because no army could operate with men who refused to move on the Sabbath and to eat the food of the Gentiles, enjoy so much consideration?

The followers of Jesus, though considering themselves a Jewish sect, did not strive for an active political role, or insist on civil rights. That fact modified hostility toward them and put them in a different class. At some point in the development at Antioch the name "Christians" was applied to them

(Acts 11:26), though the mention of it in connection with
the stay of Paul in that city should not be pressed. He nowhere in his letters uses this term so it probably came up
later. The author of Acts uses it here and in 26:28 only. It is
of Latin rather than of Greek formation and so may first have
been coined by Roman authorities to differentiate the followers of Jesus from the Jews. The word "Christ" was the Greek
translation for the word "Messiah" (Aramaic *Meshiha*), but
many thought it to be one of Jesus' names.

Paul made himself entirely independent of the congregation and accepted no support. This meant that he had to
labor part of the time in the leather-working trade as he had
done in Cilicia. But it also made it evident to all men that
he did not preach for a livelihood, but rather because of dedi-
cation to his cause. He once mentions the fact that Barnabas
followed the same principle (Corinthians 9:6).

The trade Paul practiced brought him many contacts and
these probably were very useful for his missionary work. The
persons most likely to come to a leather worker were slaves
sent on errands by their masters. Such people were particularly
good prospects for Christian discipleship. Often, no doubt,
Paul had to deliver work he had finished and go to the houses
of the wealthy. This got him out of the Jewish district, and
enabled him to see how and where the Gentiles lived.

In the hours when all laid off working, Paul sought to
further his mission by teaching and counseling Gentiles who
were favorably inclined toward the Jewish religion. The contacts usually came through Gentile women, who had attended
the synagogue. Some of these now saw in Christianity a modified type of Judaism, to which their men could be more readily
persuaded to turn.

Paul had become acquainted with a young man named
Titus, the son of Greek parents.[7] In a society that existed by
slave labor, there was little for young men to do except to

indulge in the life of pleasure. Titus' boon-companions were of the sporting set who were fond of hunting, playing games, feasting, and drinking. Happily these activities were now interrupted by a strenuous course of training for the forthcoming sports events in which these young men all wanted to compete. Titus came to the Christian gathering with his mother one evening, and seemed impressed by the experience. Paul loved him the moment he saw him, and made himself his friend.

In the early fall (A.D. 44) visitors from everywhere streamed to Antioch for the newly instituted Olympics. Such an event was somewhat like a World's Fair of today. Accommodations were at a premium and amusements of all kinds flourished. But the significance of the occasion was even greater, for it represented the whole Greek culture in contrast to Oriental life. It brought together the delegations of the far-flung cities, with the consequence that much politicking was done, trade relations were formed, and cultural institutions were compared and improved. The people were reminded of the great heritage that Alexander had brought to the East. He was the true sun king, of whom Plutarch wrote, "But if the deity that sent down Alexander into this world had not recalled him quickly one law would be given to all mankind and they all might look toward one rule of justice, as though toward a common source of light. But as it is, that part of the world which has not looked upon Alexander has remained without sunlight."[8]

The festivities were carefully planned and organized.[9] The officials bore·the same titles as those at Olympia in Greece, but their functions were upgraded from the secular to the religious, so that they were virtually priestly. The head man in charge of the games had the title *Alytarch* (chief police officer) and was one of the foremost and wealthiest citizens of Antioch. He was expected to contribute generously to the cost of the games. As he represented Zeus for whom the games were held, the Alytarch received divine honors as the god's representative. He was clad in a white robe embroidered with gold, had white sandals and wore a crown studded with rubies, pearls and other precious stones, and carried a scepter of ebony. The *Grammateus* or secretary of the games represented Apollo and received the honors due that deity. He too wore a white garment and had a gold crown in the form of laurel leaves. A third official, the *Amphithales* ("one whose parents are both alive") was always a boy. He wore a white silk robe and a crown of laurel leaves containing a small gold bust of Zeus. But he represented Hermes and received the honors due him. Perhaps, as at Olympia, he cut with a golden knife the seventeen branches from the sacred olive tree, from which was made the crown that was the highest honor for the victor in the games.

The opening day was marked by a grand parade. However, the demilitarization prevailing under Roman rule left the occasion bereft of that splendor which ever attends the display of armed might. Well may some scions of the old families have mourned for those days, when Antiochus IV Epiphanes held his great games and some fifty thousand men both infantry and cavalry led the parade, with war chariots and war-elephants bringing up the rear.[10] Most of the horsemen wore golden breastplates, and nearly all had on coats of "purple" (scarlet). But even with the accent on the side of peace and cultural activities, the parade was able to inspire the spectators.

There were a hundred or more delegations in attendance, each eager to win honors for its city. Images of all the gods revered in that world of western Asia had been brought to pay homage to Zeus, the king of the gods. Some were gold-covered, while others were clad in gold-embroidered garments. Representations of mythological scenes were borne along with them. There were horsemen mounted on the finest Arabian racers and two- and four-horse chariots driven by drivers who would compete in the hippodrome. Two hundred women sprinkled perfume out of precious vessels, while hundreds of others were borne on divans by slaves. The different classes of athletes—runners, fencers, boxers, long-jumpers, pole vaulters, discus throwers—went past. Since the games included hunts, theatrical and musical events, competitions in poetry and in the arts, such contestants too were in the parade. There were also numerous beautiful girls who competed in events arranged for them and each had taken a vow of chastity before going on the journey,[11] for the sacred nature of the festival demanded high moral standards.

What were the thoughts and feelings of a man like Paul as he stood among the throng watching this parade through the great avenue of the city? His Jewish soul would have been repelled at the sight of the idols. We can hear him mumbling into his beard the words of the prophet. "Behold, you are nothing, and your work is nought; an abomination is he who chooses you" (Isaiah 41:24).

But must not something like admiration have stirred in his heart at such a congress of Hellenism? And must he not have felt the division of loyalties in his own nature? He was brought up in the Hellenistic world, and deeply influenced by it. Yet a large part of its life—all that was connected with mythology and religious custom—was a strange world to him, which he had had to shun because he was a Jew. He was stirred by those marching thousands. But alas, he could not be one with them. He was forced to discriminate between what was acceptable and what was not acceptable. As an ascetic he may have viewed with pain and distaste the exhibition of beauty, the appeal of perfumes to the senses, the display of so much wealth. But the athletes and other contestants, the horses and the chariots, must have given him great delight, and made him wonder at the poverty of his own people in such enrichment of man's existence on earth. His association with Greeks had taught him that there were many wonderful people among them. Some of their thinkers spoke of God in terms more universal than the Jews. It raised the question in his mind whether they would all be lost when God's judgment came? Surely the rabbis were wrong when they delivered all the Gentiles over to destruction. Paul's mind here already forged the belief which he was to express later that the law was written in the hearts of all mankind, and that those who observe it, though not members of the chosen people, will be able to condemn those who have the advantage of possessing the written code but break the law (Romans, ch. 2). God will judge all on how they lived up to the moral standards of which they were aware.

In the Antioch delegation Paul saw Titus, who was a track athlete, and gave him a friendly wave of the hand. He would have liked to attend some of the races in which the youth was going to compete. But the demand for his services was such that he had no time. Indeed, Titus himself sent him many customers. Harnesses required repair. A lot of shoe leather had been worn out in the travel of the multitude to Antioch. These dealings with persons from far places interested Paul intensely; they gave him the opportunity to hear of other regions and cities and to learn what kind of people lived there and how they spoke and thought.

But the thirty days of the month went by and therewith the games ended. The visiting thousands departed, each to his own city and country. Life at Antioch settled back into its accustomed routine. Titus, who was very proud of having won a race for Antioch, felt the letdown from the excitement very much. He often sat at Paul's workbench to talk over the happenings he had witnessed or heard of.

"It is wonderful to be an athlete," said Paul one day, as Titus was leaving. "We Nazarenes, too, are that in our own way," he added. "Every athlete exercises self-control in all things. You do it to receive a perishable wreath, but we an imperishable one."[12]

Through his association with Paul, Titus found less pleasure in the company of his boon companions. He became very thoughtful.

At one merry gathering he announced to his friends that he was quitting their society and joining the Nazarenes. He wished all an affectionate farewell, including the flute girls who made music at their festivities. The friends protested, the flute girls laughed—though one wept—and Titus, shaking himself free went forth to tell Paul what he had done. Paul praised him as his "true child in the common faith," and began to train him to be his helper.

But the Olympics also had an effect on the Nazarene group. They had given everyone a broadened horizon. It was impossible to have seen and met people from many regions of the East, all speaking Greek, though with dialectic differences, without gaining a new idea of the unity of the Greek world. Paul more than anyone else was moved by this insight and conceived a great idea. If delegations could come a thousand miles to Antioch for athletic games, could not representatives of the church of Antioch go equally far carrying the gospel?

Such thoughts put forward by Paul produced among the prophets and teachers the wish to seek divine counsel (Acts 13:1). They resorted to fasting, meditation, and prayer. At length a revelation came to one of them, perhaps to Symeon Niger. "Thus says the Spirit: set apart for me Barnabas and Saul for the work to which I have called them" (Acts 13:1 f.).

They were electrified by the message. In part it was cryptic as oracles often were. What the work was to be was left unstated, but that it implied travel outside of Syria was clear in view of what they had inquired about. The Spirit, one could be sure, in due course would give the two men illumination as to where they were to go.[13]

A special consecration of the two missionaries was allegedly held (Acts 13:3). Mention of this is significant. The author of Acts knew that this was the beginning of a great development, and sought by this dramatization to bring home to his readers that missionary enterprise should be initiated with suitable ecclesiastical ceremonies. We are more inclined to think of the importance of this decision for foreign missions as such. It made Antioch the new center of Christianity. "Jerusalem," says Renan, "remained the city of the poor of God, the ebionim, of those simple Galilean dreamers, intoxicated as it were with the expectation of the kingdom of Heaven. Antioch, almost a stranger to the words of Jesus which it had never heard, was the church of action and progress—Antioch was the city of Paul."[14]

8 THE FIRST MISSIONARY JOURNEY

Cyprus

> *For the kingdom of God does not consist in talk but in power.*
>
> 1 CORINTHIANS 4:20

IT WAS IN THE spring of 45, according to our reckoning, that Barnabas and Paul set out from Antioch for Seleucia, with the brethren giving them escort. It was a five hour walk to that harbor city and one-time powerful fortress. The road ran parallel to the Orontes, passing villages perched on the inclines of the mountains of Pieria to the north. Across the valley to the south loomed the noble summit of Mt. Casius, which Seleucus I Nicator is said to have ascended in 300 B.C. to inquire of the god of the mountain, Zeus, as to where he should build his new Seleucia. The way was familiar to Paul, for he and Barnabas had traveled it together in coming to Antioch.

Seleucia had an inner harbor within its walls, with a channel leading into it from the sea. From one of its two moles, the two men set forth in a ship to cross over to Cyprus, a distance of about 125 miles. As Barnabas was the leader, he had proposed the objective and Paul had concurred. Being a native of Cyprus, Barnabas had knowledge of conditions there and saw great prospects in that field. He had decided, too, to take along his cousin John, later known by the Roman name Marcus (Mark), who, we will assume was a young man of eighteen to twenty.[1] Barnabas probably felt it was more dignified for him to have an adjutant, who would do the errands, arrange for lodgings, and keep accounts. Paul was certainly glad to have John go along.

Sailing to Cyprus was not as simple as coming from Tarsus had been, for the prevailing winds were adverse. The ancient navigator had to take advantage of the current and do a great deal of tacking. With good luck they made the island in several days. The city at which they landed was Salamis, the most important city of the island in those times, and famed in history for the naval battles fought off this harbor in 498 and 449 B.C. The island was now a Roman province, and since 22 B.C. was governed by a proconsul appointed by the Roman Senate for a year's term.

There were very many Jews in Cyprus.[2] Half a century later they were so numerous that they could even seek to exterminate the non-Jews. As the Phoenicians must have formed an important part of the older population it seems likely that here as elsewhere the Jews had succeeded in converting and absorbing many of them. In Paul's time, however, the Greek element was dominant.

Paul and Barnabas preached the word in the "synagogues" of Salamis (Acts 13:5). Nothing is said of their having any success, but the mention of the place suggests that there was a congregation there in Luke's time. Since the next place mentioned is Paphos on the western end of the island, they must have chosen the southern route which led them through Famagusta and Larnaka. Strangely, Paul did not want to

linger on the way but pressed forward to the Paphos objective.
The Holy Spirit seized him in a manner that made it necessary for the others to follow Paul's wishes. He was a man who
drove himself and drove others without mercy, and this quality
was now asserting itself. On the human side we can perhaps
infer that Paul did not like islands. He wanted to be where
the currents of history were flowing freely, on the great high-
ways of the world. To have become involved in missions in
the towns along the line would have been time consuming.
He felt that he had a rendezvous with destiny at the western tip of Cyprus. We can well imagine that this haste was
not too pleasing to Barnabas, since Cyprus was his home
country.

Before coming to the Paphos of that day, they passed Old
Paphos which lay about a mile from the sea and had a very
ancient temple of the goddess Aphrodite. Her connection
with the island was of long standing and Homer speaks of
it in a vivid passage.[3] Seven miles beyond they came to New
Paphos. It had a fine harbor and was adorned with heathen
temples. Annually a celebration was held here which drew
pilgrims from all over the island, and a procession was made
from Paphos to Old Paphos and the parent shrine.

At Paphos the proconsul resided, who at this time was
Sergius Paulus[4]—perhaps the same man who, according to a
Latin inscription, held office under the emperor Claudius, as
"curator" of the shores and channels of the Tiber River, L.
Sergius Paulus. Was Paul's hastening toward Paphos due to
the desire to go to the very seat of government and, as it were,
beard the lion in his lair? Or did the man's cognomen, identical with his own, exercise an attraction as a kind of good
omen?

Their preaching here at Paphos brought them in touch
with one whom the author of Acts calls a *Magus*.[5] This term,
once used for the priests and wise men of Persia, now meant

an enchanter or wizard. This particular individual is described as a Jewish false prophet, named Bariesus ("son of Jesus"— the same name as the Lord's) but subsequently referred to as "Elymas." Luke asserts that the meaning of the latter name is "a magician."[6] He was one of those men who went about spreading some form of theosophical speculation and enjoyed a reputation for having unusual powers. Paul and Barnabas may have seemed to him like fellow craftsmen whose wisdom he would wish to explore.

The report of a new teaching by the two strangers evidently interested the proconsul, and led to a desire on his part to give these men an audience. For a cultured Roman, life was very boring at a provincial city and any novelty was highly welcomed. Providence thus aided Paul's innermost wish to present his gospel to Romans. If this man listened, it would be a great gain and establish a precedent to which he could appeal later.

The Magus, too, was present at the audience. As a Jew by origin, even though, perhaps, not in good standing in the synagogue, he knew the Jewish viewpoint, and so was probably consulted by the governor. Paul was the orator, while Barnabas stood by. This would have indicated to others that the latter was the more important personage for whom Paul was acting as spokesman. When the Magus interrupted, Paul became angry. The narrator makes the scene vivid: Paul fixed his eye on the man and allegedly addressed him with a ferocity that takes one's breath away:

"You son of the devil, you enemy of all righteousness, will you not stop making crooked the straight paths of the Lord?"

Paul here plays a role parallel to that of Peter, who launched forth in a similar violent attack on the Magus Simon at Samaria (Acts 8:9 f., 18 ff.). These wizards were causing Christianity a great deal of trouble in the time when Luke wrote his book of Acts, and even long after that.[7] Luke is warning his Christian readers of such people, and showing what Paul thought of them.

Allegedly, Elymas was smitten with blindness when Paul denounced him. The miraculous happening leads the governor, Sergius Paulus, to "believe." Luke means that he became a Christian, but the account he was using may only have meant to say that Sergius Paulus was convinced of the miraculous power of the speaker. There is no mention of a baptism. That the gospel was presented to a prominent Roman is made the outstanding event of the mission on Cyprus. From here on, furthermore, the author of Acts stops using the name Saul and instead speaks of "Paul." It seems almost as though Luke had the idea that Paul now adopted the name of the proconsul in place of the name "Saul." But this is not reconcilable with Paul's Roman citizenship, which required men to have Roman names, and as these were a matter of record, they could not readily be changed. Perhaps Paul had avoided using his Roman name when he became involved in the persecution of the Nazarenes, but now found it useful to resume it.

The thing we hear next about Paul is also surprising: "Now Paul and his company set sail from Paphos." Suddenly it is no longer Barnabas who is considered the leader, but Paul. Luke is bringing him to the fore since from now on he will be the central character in his story. It is like the falconer's removal of the hood from the head of the falcon.

9 THE FIRST MISSIONARY JOURNEY
Asia Minor

> *We are not, like so many, peddlers of God's*
> *word; but as men of sincerity, as commissioned*
> *by God, in the sight of God we speak in Christ.*
>
> 2 CORINTHIANS 2:17

THE VESSEL THEY were able to get from Paphos took
them across to Perga in Pamphylia—the region west of Cilicia
on the coast of Asia Minor. We can imagine how reluctant
Barnabas was to give up the mission on his native Cyprus.
But Paul was as one possessed. He felt the Spirit calling him
to the continent. Where they would go on landing was not
yet plain. Perhaps to the coastal cities Paul may have striven
vainly to reach during his Cilician ministry.

As they approached the Pamphylian coast they saw the
mouth of a river, the Cestrus or White River, and soon found
themselves sailing seven miles upstream to Perga. Cities had
been built inland where possible on this coast to lessen danger
from attack by sea. Perga's goddess was Artemis, a deity whose
devotees were to be among Paul's worst enemies years after-

ward. Her temple was on a height alongside the city, and here an important annual festival was held in her honor.

Paul felt no call to linger at Perga. He pressed his companions to go up with him through the mountain country into the interior. The Spirit would tell them when and where to start work.

Young John Mark, the kinsman of Barnabas, had been dismayed at the sight of Asia Minor from the sea. After talking with some townspeople, he looked scared. Up in those mountains there were panthers that might jump out of a tree on the passing traveler. One could hear them screaming in the night. Furthermore, this had long been a region terrorized by pirates.[1] And while the Roman general Pompey had destroyed their ships and their strongholds there were men who had escaped and lived by robbing wayfarers on mountain roads or plundering villages on the other side of the Taurus. John urged his relative not to go there. He was not so young any more—let him consider what it would mean to ascend those steep mountains that rose to a height of nine thousand feet, and then go through unknown country to the cities scattered along the thoroughfares running from east to west.

When Paul insisted on their departing, John refused to go along. He declared that he had shipped for a mission to Cyprus, not to Asia Minor.

Barnabas was caught in a dilemma. The Holy Spirit had been moving Paul. For Barnabas not to follow the leader would be to disobey the Spirit. His own will to lead under adventurous conditions was not great. He was content to follow, and may have sought to persuade John to do so too. But John had had enough. He was going to see about getting back home. Paul seems to have viewed this action as a military commander would view a desertion, but said nothing.

So up through the mountain country went Paul and Barnabas.[2] The way led through gorges, down which a torrent, overhung by great fir and cedar trees, came tumbling. It was a hard, fatiguing trip, and as they ascended it became uncomfortably cold.

After a climb of several days they reached the height of the land and then had to descend into the elevated country of inner Asia Minor.

The first city at which the missionaries paused to carry on their work was Antioch of Pisidia (*Yalovadj*).[3] Actually it was "near Pisidia" (as Strabo puts it) and lay in eastern Phrygia, for Pisidia was only a narrow strip of country on the north side of the Taurus, which they had left behind them. Seleucus I had established this Antioch to meet the need for a strong fortified and well garrisoned city to guard the southern route through Asia Minor in the area where it looped about the northern side of the great double lake called the Limnai. To the north lay the great mountain range that in modern times has been called Sultan Dagh, the pass over which is at least four thousand feet above Antioch. All this country being composed of crown lands, Seleucus had given some of it to this newly founded fortress that was to secure his control of the subjected Orientals. Since 25 B.C. it had become a Roman colony, which meant that retired Roman soldiers were officially granted lands and settled there. Some three hundred families or more were usually brought to such a colony, and each was given about 125 acres of land.

It was attractive to Paul to seek out such a Roman colony after his success with the proconsul at Paphos. He could cite his friendly reception by his namesake, Sergius Paulus, proconsul of Cyprus as a recommendation. Furthermore, he knew that there was a Jewish element at Antioch enjoying freedom of worship. This provided both a point of contact and a considerable protection, for since it was against Roman law to propagandize a new religion, Christianity could only spread by being a sect of the Jews. Wherever there was a synagogue,

there were Gentiles who had a basic knowledge of the mono-
theism taught by Judaism. This was a decided advantage.
Finally, it seems possible that Paul had met some people from
this city at the Olympic games of the preceding year, for it is
certain that both athletes and visitors went from here to
Antioch the Great at that time.

The Acts story attaches a special importance to Paul's de-
but at this city. The author regarded it as typical of many
similar occasions. As Jews, the missionaries went to the synagogue on the Sabbath. When the president of the synagogue
invited them as visitors to speak to the gathering, Paul arose
and, asking for attention with the orator's gesture of stretching
forth his hand, he addressed them. The speech attributed to
Paul (Acts 13:16-41) is an example of a typical synagogal
speech, but with a Christian twist.[4] The Jews liked to hear
the history of their people rehearsed. Paul's discourse reviewed
the period from Abraham to David, only to switch very suddenly at that point to the assertion that out of David's seed
God had sent to Israel the promised savior in the person of
Jesus, soon after John the Baptist had announced the im-
minence of his coming. Paul recounted the rejection of Jesus
by the people and the rulers because they did not recognize
what he was and did not understand the prophecies that are
read on the Sabbath in every synagogue. He said these leaders
had even helped to make these prophecies come true by delivering their Messiah to Pilate to be killed. They then had
taken him down from the "tree" and put him in a tomb.
But Paul could announce that God had raised Jesus from the
dead, and that he had appeared to those who had come with
him from Galilee and were now his witnesses. He declared
that forgiveness of sins through Jesus was being preached, and
that everyone who believed in his Messiahship would be justified by him of everything that was justifiable under the law.
Paul closed his discourse with a warning to his hearers not

to put themselves in the scoffer class and share their fate, as described in the prophets (Habakkuk 1:5).

The message thus brought to Antioch aroused great interest. At the conclusion of the meeting the people asked to receive more information about this new movement on the next Sabbath, and many, both Jews and proselytes, accompanied Paul and Barnabas. During the week they were besieged by interrogators and invited to houses. Even the heathen population heard of and saw these new teachers who had arisen among the Jews. Curiosity about them was so great that when the next Sabbath came the synagogue was full to overflowing.

This was not at all to the liking of the Jewish leaders, but under the circumstances they could not prevent the visitors from speaking. However, this time they began to contradict them. The clash waxed so hot that Paul, seconded by Barnabas, declared that since the Jews refused to receive the gospel they now felt entitled to bring it to the Gentiles in accordance with the prophecy, "I have set you to be a light to the gentiles that you may bring salvation to the uttermost parts of the earth" (Isaiah 49:6).[5]

Therewith they left the synagogue. As we shall see this is the first of three such declarations by Paul of going to the Gentiles, introduced at occasions of special significance by the author of Acts (14:16; cf. 18:6; 28:25-28).

It was a great experience for the Gentiles to feel that God was now turning to them, and that He was putting an end to the pretensions of the Jews that they had a monopoly on the divine favor. As has been suggested earlier, the Gentile had been both attracted and repelled by Judaism. No one could hear its sacred books read without being interested and instructed. Its prayers were simple, moving, and helpful. Jewish morality was high and stood out amid pagan immorality. The non-Palestinian Jewish communities had no sacrificial cult. That was being carried on exclusively in the Temple in far away Jerusalem. Only an annual atonement day was observed. But the ritualistic requirements of the Jews raised a barrier that few Gentile men cared to cross. They remained usually in the status of "god-fearers," who acknowledged monotheistic belief without taking the final step of integrating themselves in the Jewish community.

These people were now glad to form a Christian synagogue, containing and cultivating all that was attractive in Judaism, plus the new and wonderful message that the Messiah had come out of Israel and that belief in him and following his law of love were the only essential requirements.

The missionaries must have spent some time at this city, for Christianity was able to spread through the region.

The Jews, however, through some prominent Gentile women who aroused the leading men of the city, succeeded in starting a riot against Paul and Barnabas and drove them out of the district. The pair are said to have performed a curious ritual (which is also mentioned in Luke 9:5)—that of "shaking off the dust from their feet against them." But they were joyous nevertheless, over the success they had had.

Journeying eastward along a highway called the Via Sebaste, which had been constructed by the emperor Augustus, to connect the Roman colony of Antioch of Pisidia with another one at Lystra, they came next to the territory of Iconium (Konia).[6] This city lay considerably off to the north and they had to turn into a side road to get to it. Paul must thus have had a special prompting of the Holy Spirit to make this detour. Strabo calls Iconium only a small city, though a time was to come when it would attain great importance. The region in which it lay was known as Lycaonia. It had adjoined the kingdom of Galatia and in 37 b.c. the Romans had entrusted rule of this region to the king of Galatia, Amyntas. After his death, however, his entire kingdom had become a

kind of satrapy, embracing eight different areas of which
Galatia was the first and foremost.[7]

How refreshing it was for Paul and Barnabas to come to
Iconium. Like Damascus in Syria, Iconium lay in an elevated
plain, sheltered in the west by high mountains, from which
an abundant water supply came down and created a gar-
den spot. But as at Damascus, the river, having no natural
drainage, petered out to the east in the plain. In the Iconium plain mountains rise here and there like islands in the
distance.

The missionaries found that the deity primarily worshiped
here was a form of the Phrygian goddess Cybele and was
given the title "mother of the gods." The Greek element
of the population identified her with Athena, the Romans
with Minerva. But there was a Jewish element at Iconium,
too, though whether it had citizenship or only the status of
resident strangers is uncertain.

Paul and Barnabas again went to the synagogue on the
Sabbath and presented their message. Here, too, they had surprising success. But things went the same way as at Antioch:
the antagonistic Jews appealed to a particular group—in this
case the Roman—and poisoned its mind against the new-
comers. Even so, the missionaries stayed for a considerable
time in the city. But when a plot was made by both the
Jewish and the pagan faction to stone them, they fled.

The climactic experience of the whole journey took place
at Lystra,[8] which lay about eighteen miles south-southwest of
Iconium. Like Antioch it was a Roman colony. There were
no Jews there and so for the first time Paul and Barnabas
were concerned solely with pagans. The interest governing
the Acts story here seems to us to show how superstitious
these Gentiles were. Because of a faith-healing Paul performed, the people cried out in their native Lycaonian tongue,
"The gods have come down to us in the likeness of men."

They took Barnabas for Zeus and Paul, who was the chief speaker, for Hermes.[9] The missionaries did not understand Lycaonian and the situation did not become clear until the priest of Zeus, from the temple in front of the city, came with garlanded oxen to the gates and offered sacrifice to the supposed gods. This was terribly embarrassing and the description is almost humorous. According to the story, Paul and Barnabas tore their garments in grief and horror and rushed out among the crowd crying:

"Men, why are you doing this? We also are men of like nature with you and bring you good news that you should turn from these things to a living God." But they were hardly able to restrain the people from sacrificing to them.

The brief "evangelizing" of the missionaries is significant. The author of Acts is providing an illustration of how one should preach to such Gentiles. In the words attributed to Paul and Barnabas (Acts 14:15-17), there is nothing that goes beyond the Old Testament basis. In dealing with polytheists one must first teach them that there is only one Creator God. Otherwise there is no basis to talk about Jesus Christ, as there was when one spoke to Jews and to Gentile "god-fearers" who had already received such fundamental instruction.

The end of the mission at Lystra was a near tragedy. Hostile Jews came from Antioch and Iconium and persuaded the populace to stone Paul. No one laid hands on Barnabas— a fact suggesting that he had been less aggressive. A mob dragged Paul's body outside the city and left it lying there. Converts, made during the weeks spent at Lystra, gathered sorrowfully about their teacher. Among them no doubt was Timothy, whom he later was to call his "beloved and faithful child in the Lord" (1 Corinthians 4:18). To everyone's amazement Paul suddenly regained consciousness, arose, and reentered the city. Early on the following morning he and Barnabas departed.

The stoning at Lystra, incredible as it sounds, is confirmed
by Paul himself, when he says in the great resume of his hardships, "Once I was stoned" (2 Corinthians 11:25). Rather
surprising, however, is a report utilized in an epistle believed
to be post-Pauline, which paints a darker picture than Acts,
of Paul's experiences in the cities previously mentioned. "You
have observed . . . my sufferings, what befell me at Antioch,
Iconium, and Lystra, what persecutions I endured; yet from
them all the Lord rescued me" (2 Timothy 3:11).

The missionaries went next to Derbe, the true location
of which has only recently been established (Devri Shehri).[10]
This was an outpost of direct Roman rule on this route, for
the next city of consequence, Laranda (Karaman), belonged
to the kingdom of Commagene, whose king Antiochus I had
constructed the famous tomb on top of Nemrud Dagh. Under Claudius, Derbe received the honorary title of Claudio-
Derbe and thus must have been staunchly Roman in its
sentiments. An inscription mentioning the Claudio-Derbenes,
found at Kerte-Hüyük led to the rediscovery of the true
site. No doubt Greek was the official language of the city, and
was spoken by many. An old native god of the Heracles type
was worshiped there, and on its later coins the naked Heracles
is portrayed with mace in the right hand and a lion-skin
draped over his extended left arm. A bandit chief named
Antipater had gotten control of Derbe in 60 B.C. but had been
slain by the Galatian king Amyntas. The region south of the
point of departure toward the Taurus was known as Isauria,
and had been infested by robbers, until the Roman Publius
Servilius, surnamed Isauricus for his victories in this area, had
subjected them. The retired Roman soldiers of Lystra were
clearly put in this region for the maintenance of order.

For a man who had been stoned in such a way that he
was thought dead and dragged out of the city, this journey
from Lystra to Derbe must have been arduous and full of

torture. The damage done to his system may have affected his health permanently and even have caused the painful affliction of which he later spoke as his "thorn in the flesh" (2 Corinthians 12:7). It may have taken days for the bruised man to go this distance. What willpower Paul had. Yet once in Derbe he was again the missionary who sought to win men for Christ. Only one fact is reported from there: they made many disciples (Acts 14:21).

The season for travel in a land like Asia Minor was short under ancient conditions. Since Paul and Barnabas had to spend considerable time at each place to win converts and instruct them sufficiently in Christian convictions and in practice so that they would be able to continue by themselves, the winter season may have set in while they lingered at Derbe.[11] The two men had, of course, found employment and were actively engaged in that during the winter months. They intended to revisit the congregations they had established to give them more encouragement and guidance, but that had to await the return of spring. When magistrates ordered a man out of the city, as had happened at Pisidian Antioch, it was not possible to go back until new magistrates took office. At Roman colonies, this change probably occurred on January 1.

During the ministry in Derbe they gained one convert who became very much attached to Paul. His name was Gaius. We will hear of him at a later occasion (Acts 19:29, 20:4).

When spring came and the thaw was over the two missionaries said farewell to their kind friends at Derbe and retraced their course. They stopped at each city previously visited and spent some weeks in instruction and exhortation.

It thus may have been the next summer before they crossed the mountains again to descend to the Pamphylian shore. When they reached Perga, they preached the gospel there (Acts 14:25). Luke would hardly have mentioned this had not a Christian congregation arisen in this city at the time or some time afterward.

Hearing of a better opportunity to get a ship at Attalia ten miles to the west and on the coast—for only small vessels came up the river to Perga—the missionaries went to that harbor. Nothing is said of any preaching there. It may be that they made a connection so soon that there was no time for any missionary activity, or that the Spirit did not move them.

How restful Paul must have found it to be aboard a good ship again, carried along by the westerly breezes to the shores of Syria. For a time, the long weary marches were at an end. He could be satisfied with having planted Christianity in eastern Asia Minor and could be hopeful of its spreading by its own momentum in all directions.

10 THE CRISIS AT JERUSALEM

Then after fourteen years I went up again to
Jerusalem with Barnabas, taking Titus with
me. I went up by revelation.

GALATIANS 2:1 f.

THE CONGREGATION at Antioch in Syria had been in
much concern about Barnabas and Paul. The former's kinsman, John Mark, had arrived the previous summer by ship
from Attalia and brought news of the abandonment of the
mission to Cyprus after a hasty passage through the island.[1]
After delivering himself of this news John Mark had gone
back to his mother at Jerusalem. Since then there had been
no word of the missionaries. Whether they were dead or alive
nobody knew. So it was a great relief when a youthful runner
from Seleucia brought the news to Antioch that they had
returned. Leading men of the church went out to the city
limits to meet them, and greeted them warmly. They rejoiced
in the reception and promised to give a full report at a gathering of the congregation.

The report by John Mark that Paul had taken over the
leadership seemed untrue, for he deferred to Barnabas, who

105

now resumed his activity as the head of the Antiochene Christians. A service of thanksgiving was arranged and held. Barnabas recounted the passage through Cyprus, where the Spirit had led them to Paphos and given them the opportunity to present the cause to the proconsul; he told of the success they had had at Antioch in Pisidia, Iconium, Lystra, and Derbe, where four promising congregations had been founded. They had to thank God for some narrow escapes. Brother Paul had been stoned and taken for dead at Lystra, but an angel of the Lord must have watched over him. The great result of their journey was: God has opened up a door of faith to the Gentiles—not only to proselytes, but to absolutely pagan people. Antioch in Syria was not the only place where Gentiles were receptive. There was no limit to the appeal of the Christian faith.

Paul, in turn, spoke modestly and praised brother Barnabas for his understanding and support. Without his consent he could have accomplished little. They seemed, as the people of Lystra had thought, like the Greek gods Zeus and Hermes. He, Paul, was like Hermes, the messenger and speaker, while Barnabas was like Zeus, holding the power and possessing the dignity that impressed people.

It thus was clear that John Mark must have been wrong in describing Barnabas as dominated by Paul. The cordial relationship existing between them, each showing the other due honor and praise, gladdened the congregation and lifted a burden of anxiety from people's shoulders.

But the congregation was also much disturbed by the news from Judea. Since the death of Herod Agrippa I, it had again been under Roman governors, and was currently being governed by Tiberius Alexander, a nephew of the great Jewish teacher Philo of Alexandria, but an apostate from Judaism. The famine which had begun in Egypt had now struck Palestine (winter of 47–48), and there was great poverty and starvation. People remembered the prophecy of Agabus of hard times to come. The congregation felt moved to do something about relief for the Christian brethren in Jerusalem (Acts 11:29). Money was collected and Barnabas and some others were requested to deliver it. It is the first Christian relief undertaking on record, and as such remains noteworthy.[2]

The collection had been made and the Gentile members of the church had contributed generously. Then some men came from Jerusalem and caused a disturbance by telling the Gentile brethren that they could not be saved unless they followed the Jewish rite (circumcision) according to the custom of Moses (Acts 15:1). Paul and Barnabas, who had waived that requirement, opposed this interpretation. But Barnabas was instructed by the congregation to obtain a ruling from the apostles and elders when he went to Jerusalem.

Barnabas also had a third and important duty: to report about the mission work that he and Paul had carried on in the preceding season.

Though probably it was not at first planned that way, Paul accompanied Barnabas on this journey. He tells us, "I went up by revelation" (Galatians 2:2). He thus may not have been an elected delegate as Luke thought (Acts 15:2). We may assume that when Barnabas and his companions were about to depart, Paul informed Barnabas of the revelation given him that he was to go too,[3] and that he was taking along his young convert Titus.

Even revelations often had psychological presuppositions. Was Paul worried lest the new phase of missionary activity he had inaugurated by going into Lycaonia be disapproved? Would Barnabas be able to defend it successfully? He had consented to it and had stood up for it at Antioch, but would he back down if opposition were strong? He was a good man, but not skilled in argument. His mind had not been schooled as Paul's had been. Of even greater concern to Paul must

have been how his missionary message, which differed from
that of the Jerusalem group in important respects, would be
regarded. He knew that there had been considerable change
in the congregation since his departure from that city. Old
members had died or moved away and numerous Pharisees
had joined it (Acts 15:5). As an ex-Pharisee who had lived
in Jerusalem, Paul knew a great many men of this party personally or by name and reputation. He lifted his eyebrows
when he heard that this one or that one was now a Christian.
The whole attitude of the Church was bound to be affected
by this new constituency. He put the question up to the Lord
whether he, too, should go to Jerusalem. And so he had received the revelation.

Barnabas may have been surprised when Paul told him of
his intention to go with him. He would have liked it better
if he had been able to handle all negotiations alone, for he
anticipated that some very embarrassing questions might be
raised about his coadjutor Paul. It seemed to him an unnecessary complication, too, that the Gentile Titus was to go
along. But Paul declared that this was the revealed will of
God and that, of course, overcame any objection.

When they arrived at Jerusalem[4] Paul said to Barnabas,
"When you go to the apostles and deliver the collection, arrange a meeting for me with the leaders, I pray you. I would
like to confer with them before there is any public meeting."
He expected to stay at the house of his sister, while Barnabas
would find hospitality at the house of Mary, the mother of
John Mark. So they separated.

Had Paul presumed too much when he spoke of staying
with his sister? Would she receive him, after his father had
disowned him? When he knocked at the door and was admitted by a servant his sister came flying out, as she recognized
the voice. She kissed him and wept.

"Paul, my poor brother!"

"I have a young man with me, a Gentile, Titus. Where can he stay?"

"If he is your friend he shall stay with us."

If Paul was surprised at his sister's departure from Pharisaic fear of contamination by harboring Titus, he said nothing about it.

It must have been a happy reunion. Paul heard how his parents were faring. He was pleased with his sister's little children, especially with a boy of three. Thanks to the supplies sent from home, they had not suffered any need during the famine and were able to help others.

When his brother-in-law came, Paul heard about the import business and was glad to know that his father was not in any financial straits, but was maintaining his position.

Before long a messenger sent by Barnabas arrived. Paul would be received that night by James, the Lord's brother; John, the son of Zebedee; and Peter, who fortunately was at Jerusalem. They concurred in his wish that their meeting be private.

Due to Paul's connection with the Nazarenes, his brother-in-law had an interest in what was going on in the sect, and had picked up bits of information about the leaders. He reported that the present head, James, called "the Just," was a man of great piety, whom the Jews respected. Every day he went to the Temple to attend prayers and sacrifices. Peter (or Cephas as he was called in those days) had ceded to James his position as head of the community when he had escaped from prison. He was still honored and now that Roman rule was restored he could come and go at will. John, the son of Zebedee, was believed to be dissatisfied with James' legalistic standpoint, holding that Jesus had been much more liberal.[5] James was being backed by a Pharisaic element that was gaining influence in the church. This information was valuable to Paul as he prepared himself for the conference.

It was fully clear to Paul, as he went that night to the meetingplace, that much depended on this negotiation. He had to face the fact that he was in effect going to be on trial. Some years later when he wrote about it he indicated that he was aware that the outcome would show whether he "was running or had run in vain" (Galatians 2:2). If the heads of the church disowned him, it would damage his position and his usefulness. Instead of being in close harmony with the Jerusalem apostles, he would become the founder of a separate Christian sect—a doubtful honor. If he could win their approval, the unity of Christianity embracing both Jews and Gentiles would be upheld. That unity he desired with his whole being. But he could not sacrifice to it the mandate he had received from Christ or the clear insight God had given him into the nature of the Christian message. He must seek to prevail in the conflict he foresaw. He had the confidence that the Lord was on his side, and minimized what he could contribute personally. This humility is greatly to his credit, but cannot change the fact that Paul's natural ability, his total self that was the product of heredity, education, and experience, stood ready to be used by the Lord in that hour.

As Nicodemus had come to Jesus in the darkness, so Paul, too, entered the room in which the leaders awaited him.[6] In the feeble light of a burning wick hanging out of the snout of an earthernware lamp he saw the three leaders seated on the floor before him. They acknowledged his greeting of peace with a shelam. As Paul expected, the conversation was going to be in Aramaic, the only language James understood, though Peter and John understood and spoke some Greek. Paul had met Peter and James on his previous visit fourteen years ago, but he now met John for the first time. As head of the church James sat in the center, with Peter at his right and John at his left.

Paul waited politely for one of the leaders to open the conversation. Finally James spoke.

"You asked to speak with us in private, Saul. We are ready to hear what you have to say."

"As you know," Paul began, "a door to the Gentiles opened at Antioch, when some men from Cyprus and Cyrene first preached the Word there. You sent Barnabas to Antioch, and Barnabas sought me out at Tarsus to help in the work. We found a great readiness there to receive the gospel.

"But when it seemed that the congregation was well started on its way the Holy Spirit revealed to it that Barnabas and I should go forth on a mission to the Gentiles elsewhere. We went to Cyprus, then crossed over the sea and went to cities of Pamphylia, Phrygia, and Lycaonia.

"Again we were granted success with Gentiles, but the Jews refused to hear the Word and persecuted us. We preached as the Holy Spirit directed us to do. We laid no burdens of Jewish rites on the Gentiles, but taught them that if they believed in Christ they would be declared just in the sight of God for his sake.

"I asked for this meeting that you might understand what we are doing and to answer any questions that you might wish to raise as to our work."

After a brief silence Peter spoke up.

"I wonder, Saul, whether you are not too active in your quest to convert Gentiles. We Jews are the chosen people, and Jesus was sent to us as our Messiah. If Gentiles come to us of their own accord through having been god-fearers and so secondary members of the synagogue, that is one thing. But to seek them out and found Gentile congregations is another thing. Our Lord himself said, 'I was sent only to the lost sheep of the house of Israel'" (Matthew 15:24).

"Have you forgotten, Peter, that fourteen years ago I spent fifteen days with you and that you were fully in accord with

the mission I had carried out in Arabia? Were you not in
accord with the mission among the Gentiles when you sent
Barnabas to Antioch? Barnabas too was in accord with it
when he came to Tarsus to enlist my help in this work."

Peter was embarrassed, but James now spoke up weightily.
"How can we admit Gentiles to the church unless they obey
the laws given by God to Moses?" the interrogator demanded.

"It is not for us to trouble ourselves about such a question,
but simply to obey the Lord," Paul replied. "The Lord said
to me 'I have appeared to you for this purpose, to appoint you
to serve and to bear witness to that which you have seen
and that which will yet be shown to you. I will deliver you
from the [Jewish] people, and from the Gentiles to whom
I am sending you to open their eyes, that they may turn from
darkness to light and from the power of Satan to God, that
they may receive forgiveness of sins and a place among those
who are sanctified by faith in me.' "

Paul's features seemed illuminated by an inner light, notice-
able even in the dimness of a room lit by only the lamp wick.
A silence fell which was finally broken by John who had remained silent until now.

"The Holy Spirit is indeed with Saul, brethren. We dare
not refuse to admit it."

Paul now turned to him with a question.

"Do you not believe, O son of Zebedee, that the Lord meant
his teachings to reach all men?"

"He said so himself," agreed John. "Many shall come from
east and west and sit at table with Abraham, Isaac and Jacob."

"But our holy temple?" said James, "are not all the prom-
ises and prophecies of the future bound up with it, John?"

"Our Lord revised prophecy, as he revised the law, with his
'But I say unto you.' He declared to the woman of Samaria:
'Believe me the hour is coming when neither on this moun-
tain nor in Jerusalem will you worship the Father. God is

spirit and those who worship him must worship him in spirit and truth.' "

"Amen," said Paul enthusiastically. "You have expressed the real intent of the Lord as I understand it from the visions granted me."

Then, turning to Peter, he continued, "Did you not once tell me, Peter, that the Lord Jesus himself permitted you and your fellow disciples to break the Sabbath law and pluck ears when you were going through the grain fields?"

"Yes, it is so."

James seemed dazed.

"How could Jesus have departed from God's law? And if he did so, how can I condone departure from it? The people would drive us out of Jerusalem."

It was the despairing cry of a leader beset with changing circumstances difficult to master, but Paul answered him with measured words.

"It is your privilege, according to Christian liberty, to follow our Pharisaic customs here in Judea. But do not ask us who live in Syria-Cilicia to do so. That would be hindering the Spirit. The Lord called me to go to the Gentiles and with the call gave me the understanding of his gospel. I have no righteousness of my own based on law, but that which is through faith in Christ—the righteousness of God that depends on faith—that I may know him and the power of his resurrection, and may share his sufferings, becoming like him in his death, that if possible I may obtain the resurrection from the dead."

James closed his eyes and was silent for a time. He and his companions were not used to thinking about the Christian message in such terms. Finally he spoke.

"Do you agree, brother Peter, that we should let Saul preach freedom from the law to the Gentiles?"

"I agree."

"Do you, brother John, agree?"

"I do."

"Since you both agree I will consent, but the congregation will have to be persuaded to give its approval. Brother Saul will have to fight his own battle in the meeting."[7]

"For this I was sent, brethren," said Paul. "The Lord's will be done."

The first hurdle was over, and Paul's heart was filled with joy. He had contended with the leaders and, with God's help, had prevailed. He now looked forward to the second hurdle which, according to the remark of James, might be harder to overcome than the first.

The report of the arrival of Barnabas and others bearing gifts had caused a stir in the Christian community, and all came to the meeting the next day curious to see them. Apostles and elders were present. Barnabas presented the collection, and the community gave thanks to God and praised the brethren at Antioch for the grain that now could be purchased. Thereupon Barnabas gave a report of the work at the metropolis and of his and Paul's missionary travels. He told, too, how Paul had been stoned at Lystra, but had been miraculously preserved. When he had ended someone arose and asked what had been accomplished in Cyprus, where the Jews were so much more numerous than in Asia Minor, and why they had not remained there instead of going on into that vast, inhospitable land?

Paul saw young John Mark in the audience and suspected that the story he had told on returning to Jerusalem was behind the question.

Barnabas could only reply that the Holy Spirit had led them across the sea, and they had obeyed. And he related how Paul had overcome the sorcerer, Elymas, with his powerful words.

Then Paul, whose head still bore scars where the stones

had struck him, spoke of the friendly attitude of the proconsul of Cyprus, and of the wonderful prospects for winning Gentiles for Christianity. He called attention to brother Titus, a young Greek from Antioch, whom he had brought with him and who had abandoned worship of the idols to serve the Lord. He had great hope that Titus would become a valuable helper in future work among the Greeks.

At this point an ex-Pharisee asked whether in their mission they had made it clear to the Gentiles that they must obey the law of Moses? And first of all that they had to be circumcised?

Paul thereupon declared that neither Barnabas nor he had laid any obligations upon the Gentiles other than those which would arise from love of God and one's neighbor, for that, as Jesus had said, was the sum and substance of the law and the prophets.

Another ex-Pharisee now arose and said that they must insist that the young Greek whom Paul had brought along and introduced into their midst be circumcised.

This Paul rejected. When it was urged by others with some heat, Paul declared that faith in Christ was the sole condition of entry into the church, and baptism, by which one was admitted, was based on it. So firmly did he adhere to this position that all efforts to dislodge him from it were futile. Years later he wrote about this crucial hour, "We did not yield submission even for a moment that the truth of the gospel might be preserved for you" (Galatians 2:5).

Finally, the apostles present were appealed to as arbiters of the dispute. Peter expressed the opinion that the Gentiles should not be required to undergo circumcision. Mission work among them had now gone on for many years, since the church of Antioch was founded, and no such demand had been made upon them. To advance it now might lead some to withdraw from the congregation and would jeopardize its future growth. "As brother Saul has set forth so clearly," he said, "it is by faith in Christ as Lord that one is saved."[8]

The last word in the matter was spoken by James. It was evident, he held, that the Holy Spirit was putting the seal of his approval on the work of Saul and Barnabas. Who dared hinder the Spirit? He and Peter, however, were concerned with winning Israel for Christ. Let Barnabas and Paul go their separate way to the Gentiles in the service of the one Lord. He therefore bade the two come forward, and he, Peter, and John would give them the right hand of fellowship.

Barnabas and Paul then came forward as requested and took James' hand before the whole congregation, as well as the hands of Peter and John.

James then declared, "You go to the Gentiles and we to the Jews. But we have one request to make: remember 'the poor' here at Jerusalem."[9]

Barnabas promised further contributions, and Paul said he would do what he could once the new churches were firmly established.[10]

When Paul and Titus left the meeting the latter was curious to know what had been said, for he did not understand the Aramaic language sufficiently to follow the debate. Paul gave him an account of it.

"You see now why I had to take you along," Paul said. "It was to bring to a head the question of Jewish law and Gentile Christians."

Paul's leave-taking from his sister and her family affected him greatly. It made him realize how alone he stood. To see them was to think of father and mother and a world now barred to him. But the joy that he felt in the success of his mission offset the grief of this parting.

"Up and let us be going!" he said to Barnabas. On the next day they left for Antioch.[11]

11 THE BATTLE OVER SEGREGATION AT ANTIOCH

*But when Cephas came to Antioch I opposed
him to his face, because he stood condemned.*

GALATIANS 2:11

PAUL AND BARNABAS were able to return to Antioch
with the report that the Christian leaders at Jerusalem did
not require circumcision of converts. This was great news,
and with the anxiety over this question removed, the congregation could resume its vigorous and progressive life in the
great Syrian metropolis.

The rainy season was at hand and the time thus too far
advanced for any further foreign undertakings in that year.
With the arrival of spring, however, and the prospects that
the famine would soon be over as the new harvest drew near,
Paul became restless and eager to return to his mission field
in eastern Phrygia and Lycaonia. But just when he was about
to bring up the matter the news reached the congregation of
an impending visit of Peter to Antioch. The Jerusalem group
evidently held it advisable to take a more active interest in
congregations outside of Judea, and in view of the support
which Antioch had lent in the recent hard times, a visit by

117

the foremost of the twelve original disciples of Jesus must
have seemed particularly suitable.

The congregation felt highly honored. Had it not been
Peter who had uttered the first Messianic confession at
Caesarea Philippi? Was he not the very first to have been
granted a vision of the risen Lord? Had he not been the head
of the church until his arrest? When he arrived, with John
Mark as aide, a deputation was waiting for him at the city's
boundary. He was hailed and feted as no previous Christian
visitor had been.

That the disciple entered into the spirit of the Christian
fellowship at Antioch shows what a simple and kind-hearted
man he was. He ignored the taboos of clean and unclean
which were so important at Jerusalem, and he had no scruples
about attending the common meals. In connection with these,
the rite of the remembrance of Christ's last supper was held,
and it was a great thing for the congregation to have the man
preside who had sat at the right hand of Jesus at the original
occasion. He broke the bread and gave it to all of them, and
he blessed the chalice which then passed from one to the
other. So uplifted was Peter that he forgot all about the rites
of Judaism in the blessed fellowship of peace and happiness
in the Christian congregation. He brought forth from his
memory the treasures he had heard Jesus say or had seen him
do. The Lord's living presence was with them. No one needed
to have proof that he was risen from the dead. Of his return
Peter spoke with profound yearning and gave the slogan of
the Christians of Judea: *Maranatha* "our Lord cometh."

Then, unexpectedly, some other visitors came from the
Jerusalem church—Paul says "from James" (Galatians 2:12).
Apparently the Pharisaic party distrusted Peter's strictness and
wished a firsthand report by men of their own faction on the
observance of Jewish law at Antioch. When Peter heard of
their coming he sent word through Barnabas to the Jewish

Christians saying that they should no longer join in the common meal with Gentile Christians until the latter adapted themselves to the ritual law governing food and association. When no Jewish members turned up at the next common meal, Paul understood what was happening. He was shocked to note that not only did Peter not appear, but that even Barnabas was absent (Galatians 2:13). A pall settled over the occasion. The Gentile Christians felt themselves excluded from the more intimate fellowship with those whom they had considered friends and even had honored as blood brethren of the Lord Jesus, and whose part they had taken so often in the city.

Paul announced that on this night they would not celebrate the Lord's supper, for he saw the countenance of Christ filled with sorrow. But let them all be present at the next public meeting.

At this occasion Barnabas presided. The men sent by James were also there. In Paul's eyes the refusal of the Jews to associate with the Gentiles was "hypocrisy."[1] When he saw that they were not "straight-forward about the truth of the gospel" but were compromising it out of consideration or fear of the Jerusalem Pharisees, he spoke forthrightly to Peter before them all.

"If you, though a Jew, have lived like a Gentile and not like a Jew, how can you now compel the Gentiles to live like Jews" (Galatians 2:14)?

He declared that for days they had all eaten together and had had a glad fellowship with one another. Peter had been unconcerned about the ritual cleanness or uncleanness of the Gentile Christians. Now, all of a sudden, he was disavowing his previous role. If it was wrong in the first place, why did he do it? If it was right, why did he abandon it?

The embarrassment of Peter was very great. His inconsistency was exposed before the emissaries of James, and his

fear of them before everyone else. And Paul was even accusing
him of compromising the gospel of Christ!

This latter charge Paul explains in detail in his letter (Galatians 2:15-21). Both he and Peter believed in Christ in order
to be justified by faith. To make such things as avoiding ritualistic uncleanness essential to salvation was to reestablish justification by "works." Then Christ, whose atoning death was
the basis for Paul's faith, would have died in vain.

As Paul viewed it, Peter "stood condemned." He remained
silent and did not know what to say. But Paul is not able to
report that Peter admitted he was in error as to the understanding of Christianity. The difference between being brought
up in Judea and being brought up in the Greek world is manifested here. The Judean disciples, men of humble background,
could not develop their thought in a disciplined manner. They
could tolerate a dualism of law and gospel—stressing the one
at one time and the other at another time. Paul's mind required a single principle—either law or gospel. They had not
striven, as he had done with all his might, to attain perfection
in the law, or experienced such a collapse as his. He had found
deliverance in the way of faith—not in observing ritual laws
and doing prescribed good works. That discovery had been like
a great light shining in the darkness. To Paul it was the heart
of the Christian faith.

This debate marked an important point in the history of
religion. In retrospect one can see that when Paul and Peter
confronted each other at Antioch, Jewish Christianity and
Gentile Christianity stood at the parting of the ways. It was
due to what was made clear here by Paul that the worldwide
Christian community could come into being.

What Peter did was to confess having done wrong in associating with Gentile Christians.[2] His humility appealed greatly
to the Jewish Christian faction. "See what a great man he is,"
they said.

Some of those present took up the cudgels for Peter and assailed Paul. How could this onetime persecutor of the church show such disrespect to the Lord's foremost disciple?

The Gentile contingent was crestfallen. In a dispute such as this they could hardly speak, and they sensed that their champion would not for the moment prevail.

Barnabas now sought to calm the meeting and to bring it to a conclusion. He thought that brother Paul had assailed Peter too sharply. The authority of the head of the church, James the brother of the Lord, acting with the approval of the Jerusalem congregation, should be upheld. That was what Peter was attempting to do. True, he, Barnabas, had always held fellowship with the Gentile Christians ever since he had come to Antioch, and he had done so in the new congregations he and Paul had established in Asia Minor. But now that the Jerusalem church had spoken, he would abide by the decision of his superiors. He hoped that Paul would show the same deference to the authority of the mother church. It was essential that it be respected, else chaos would result in the churches.

Paul replied that he would support advice to the churches from Jerusalem when it was in the spirit of Christ, but he saw more evidence of the presence of the Spirit of Christ here at Antioch before this unfortunate attempt at segregation was introduced than he had seen at Jerusalem. Therefore he would remain free in principle with respect to what was not mutually agreed upon at the council in which he had participated.

Therewith the meeting terminated. A sharp cleavage had opened up, not only between the factions of the membership, but also between the leaders. Peter was so humiliated that he would hardly speak to Paul, and Barnabas was deeply offended.

Trying to bridge the gap between himself and Barnabas, Paul proposed to him that they again go on a missionary journey to visit the churches they had founded. Barnabas seemed agreeable to the idea but was going to think further about it. When they met again he said, "John Mark wants to go along as our aide."

Paul was taken aback, and asked, "Again?"

Barnabas seemed unusually testy.

"I need his services," he declared.

Paul's anger rose within him as he thought of the young man's desertion at Perga. He suspected, too, that "those from James" wanted John Mark to go along in order to report to Jerusalem what Paul was saying and doing. So he spoke sternly.

"The Lord said that he who takes his hand from the plow and turns back is not fit for the service of the kingdom of God. I can not agree to taking him along."

"And without him I will not go," replied Barnabas firmly.

Paul left the encounter in a depressed state of mind. It troubled him greatly as to whether he was to blame in the matter or not.[3] One thing was clear: the Jerusalem group which had hitherto contented itself with missions in Judea now was seeking to exercise control over the Jewish Christians outside of Judea, wherever they might be found. This was something new and in his belief ran counter to the agreement made with him.

Since Paul remained with the Gentile faction, he was not aware of what went on in the Jewish faction. At the next meeting of the latter it was announced that the congregation would send Barnabas and John Mark to Cyprus. The mission there, which had been prematurely broken off by Paul's insistence on going over to the mainland, would be resumed. It was a great field, for there were many thousands of Jews on Cyprus to whom the Word could and should be brought. Peter would remain at Antioch for a while and lead the congregation in Barnabas' absence.

It was clear that Barnabas was placing himself under Peter's direction as missionary to the Jews and, defecting from joint activity with Paul, would operate in the manner prescribed from Jerusalem.

Paul advised the Gentile Christians that on the following evening they should arrange to hold a common meal. In the meantime he was going to seek direction from the Lord. After a meeting place for the meal had been determined, Paul departed. He thought of doing what Jesus had done on several reported occasions—ascend a mountain to pray.

At the common meal of the Gentiles the next evening, it was apparent that he had communed with the Lord, for the radiance of it still lay upon him. Never was a celebration of the Lord's Supper more inspiring. It gave the whole group a great lift to see its leader so strong in the Holy Spirit. The pain of the dissension in the congregation could be overcome.

"Be of good cheer, my brethren," he said to them. "The Jews will yet turn to you for help and protection, and the differences of today will be swept away."

And then he announced that he was going forth to revisit the congregations of Lycaonia and Phrygia, and thereupon proceed to new territory, as the Holy Spirit would direct.

"But how will you go?" he was asked.

"I will go with your prayers and the help of the Lord," he replied.

Thus Paul was no longer a missionary sent out by the church at Antioch, but an independent one.[4]

As it seemed appropriate to take along an aide, he chose a man who was both a Jew and a Roman citizen. His Jewish name was Silas, but his Roman cognomen was Silvanus. It seems unlikely that he was identical with the Silas of Jerusalem (Acts 15:32 f.), but was a Jewish convert of Antioch.[5]

Titus was inconsolable at Paul's leaving.

"The next time I will take you along," said Paul. "But now Silas is the right man. Do you strive to hold together the Gentile Christians here at Antioch." Then he addressed them all. "Let not your souls be poisoned against the Jews. Be mindful of the words of the Lord: Father, forgive them, for they know not what they do."

Paul and Silas left Antioch the next morning. The little group of the faithful escorted them to the city limits. There was a tearful parting. Then the travelers, each carrying his bundle over his shoulder on a stick, went their way toward Cilicia, and neither looked back again.

12 THE SECOND MISSIONARY JOURNEY
From Antioch to Troas

> For though I am free from all men, I have
> made myself a slave to all, that I might win
> the more. To the Jews I became as a Jew, in
> order to win Jews. . . . I have become all things
> to all men, that I might by all means save some.
> 1 CORINTHIANS 9:19 ff.

FROM ANTIOCH THE way led northward past a fertile
plain dotted with villages and into the Amanus Mountain region. Soon the travelers came to a narrow pass—the so-called
Syrian Gates. The road led through it and into the coastal
plain. When they came to the Pinarus River (*Delichay*), they
saw the temple and altars of Alexander near the stream, and
beyond at Issus the great *quadriga* on which stood the statue
of Alexander as conqueror over the satraps of Darius.[1]

What cared these men for the history that had transpired
in this corner between mountain and sea? Yet their mission
depended on that history. For from Alexander's victory at
Issus had flowed the Hellenization of the Orient, with the

founding of a vast number of Greek cities and the creation of a common language—the language which Paul spoke and in which he thought and wrote his letters. And Rome, too, had made its contribution by taking over the western part of this empire, putting it under the reign of law, and building roads so that men could move about more freely and with greater safety than ever before.

Paul and Silas, after ferrying across the swollen Pyramus River (the *Jihan*) and circling the gulf of Issus,[2] came to Mopsuestia (*Missis*), "the hearth of Mopsus"—according to legend a city named after a famous seer of Apollo. Thence they went on to Adana on the Sarus River (the *Ceyhan*). If Luke is not just thinking of what lay ahead in Lycaonia when he says that "they went through Syria and Cilicia strengthening the churches" (Acts 16:41), they must have made a number of stops at churches founded by Paul during his Tarsus years.

The Adana road to the Taurus, which they now took, made a junction with the road coming from Tarsus twenty-eight miles from the latter city. From this point on a rapid ascent began to the pass of the Cilician Gates[3] which lies at an elevation of 3,750 feet above the sea. Originally just a gorge cut by the Cydnus River, it had been widened in a remote past to provide a passageway so that man and beast did not have to wade the stream.

It must have been around the beginning of June when Paul and Silas went through these Gates. At that season, the snow had just melted in the pass. It was rare that anyone ventured to make the trip much before that. A warm wind from the Cilician plain blew up as through a funnel toward the snow covered Taurus summits.

Many weary miles through mountain country and then across monotonous plains with occasional volcanic hills rising out of them brought them to Derbe, the farthest point east Paul had reached in coming from the opposite direction in the journeys made with Barnabas. Here at last, after the hardship of travel and of cold nights spent in bivouac, Paul and Silas found rest and refreshment in the bosom of the little congregation. Here, the youthful Gaius was eager to join him, but Paul did not yet regard him as sufficiently prepared.

At their next stop, Lystra, Paul received a real gift from heaven. The young man whom he had baptized on his first visit, Timothy, decided to accompany him. Though he had a pagan Greek father, who perhaps was no longer living, his Jewish mother, Eunice, and his grandmother, Lois, had shown a sincere faith, and Timothy had been acquainted from childhood with the sacred writings through attendance at a synagogue (2 Timothy 1:5; 3:15).[4] He now was highly regarded in the congregations of Lystra and Iconium.[5] Timothy was to become Paul's close associate and is later named as co-author of some of his letters. It is an indication of this helper's importance that in the second century, two letters believed to have been written to him by Paul were brought forward and came to be included in the New Testament.

No renewed visit to Iconium at this time is reported, but it would seem to be implied in the remark that Timothy was "well spoken of" there too (Acts 16:2). Nor is anything said of a visit to Antioch. But it seems clear that Paul could not have omitted revisiting this first congregation he and Barnabas had founded in Asia Minor.[6] His intention was to go on from there to "Asia" (in the narrower sense, used also as Roman provincial designation). In effect this meant Ephesus, the chief city of "Asia" and the terminus of the east-west highway through Asia Minor. But he was compelled to abandon that plan, for according to Luke "they were forbidden by the Holy Spirit to speak the word in Asia" (Acts 16:6).

An illness proved to be a great hindrance to Paul about this time (Galatians 4:13 ff.). Perhaps that had been forgotten when Acts was written or was metamorphosed into what we now read there of a prohibition of the Spirit.[7] A belief that a happening preventing travel signified an advice of the Lord not to proceed further would be readily understandable and could lead to such a changed presentation. If that is so—and it is at least possible—Paul prayed to the Lord for liberation from this suffering but received no reply. However, the attack subsided.

One can only guess at what point the interruption in the westerly course came. In any case, Paul and his companion veered north—perhaps at Metropolis, an important road junction west of Antioch.

It must have been a disappointment to Paul not to go to Ephesus, Smyrna, and other famous Asian cities. But the Holy Spirit's ways are not the ways of man. Paul was led on a course in which he would encounter Galatians—people whom he would have left to one side. The Spirit willed that the "barbarians" (non-Greeks) should hear the gospel too, from the lips of the apostle of the Gentiles and should later be the recipients of a letter from him that was to give their name an abiding place in Christian memory.

The only light on Paul's course, except for what can be inferred from the existence of an epistle to the Galatians, is to be found in the much debated words, "And they went through the region of Phrygia and Galatia" (literally, "Phrygia and Galatian country," Acts 16:6).[8] "Galatian country" is apparently distinct from Galatia as such and means Phrygian areas inhabited largely by Galatians. Such districts were to be found west of the Galatian border. There is no need of supposing that Paul went into Galatia itself and to such cities as Pessinus, Ancyra (Ankara), and Tavium. This would have taken a long time—too long for him to accomplish the travel subsequently mentioned for that season as Ramsay properly points out, and it is uncertain whether enough Greek was understood there to make such a journey worthwhile for a Greek and Aramaic speaking missionary. But in the rural region adjoining Galatia proper on the west, with proximity to Hellenistic cities, the Celts would certainly have been bilingual. One may assume, therefore, that Paul's new objective was Dorylaeum (*Eski-Shehir*) from where he could pass over into Bithynia.

Paul would not have stopped to preach to the Galatians had it not been for his illness. Perhaps, if our surmise is right that a first attack of it occurred on the road down to Ephesus, it was a second attack that befell him in "Galatian country" and was taken by him to be a warning of the spirit not to go into Bithynia.

What was Paul's illness? He himself once says of it, "A thorn was given me in the flesh, a messenger of Satan to harass me" (literally "to buffet me," 2 Corinthians 12:7). The suffering was evidently painful and an obstacle to his restless desire to press forward, yet was not permanently incapacitating. The idea of being buffeted has suggested epileptic attacks and the strongest argument in favor of that supposition is that Paul says in writing his Galatians (4:14), "Though my condition was a trial to you, you did not scorn or despise me" (literally "spit out before me"), for epilepsy was the particular disease before which one spat out, possibly with the superstitious idea that this would counteract peril of infection. Another possibility is that Paul's illness was a migraine disease particularly affecting the eyes. This theory would help to explain why Paul says of the Galatians, "For I bear you witness that, if possible, you would have plucked out your eyes and given them to me" (Galatians 4:15). However, that may just be figurative language, meaning they would have done anything to help him. Ramsay thought Paul suffered from malaria.[9] But there are other possibilities such as arthritis, or consequences flowing from old physical injuries. So it must remain a mystery just what Paul's affliction really was. This leaves everyone free to liken his own particular thorn in the flesh to his.

Paul received the surprise of his life in finding that these "barbarians" were capable of such kindness. He testifies that they received him as an angel of God, yea as Christ Jesus himself (Galatians 4:13-14). Among his own people there was little sympathy for the afflicted. They were regarded as being justly punished by God, and one was more concerned with raking over their sins after the manner of Job's friends, than in helping them.

We may assume that Paul prayed a second time for deliverance from his affliction and again received no answer. But the attack passed by, and he could interpret that as an indication that he now was to go on in a different direction.

It was not easy for Paul to leave these kind Galatians. The good qualities of the Celtic race were theirs. Their religious devotion, their loyalty to family or friend, their bravery in combat were noteworthy. They were unsophisticated as yet, having absorbed but little more than the most superficial elements of Greek civilization, but they were willing to follow spiritual leadership much more readily than Jews or Greeks.

Instead of going on to Dorylaeum, Paul may have gone west to Cotiaeum (Kutahya). From Cotiaeum the road may have led Paul to Adramyttium (Edremit).[10] At either place he was close to Mysia, north of which lay his recent objective Bithynia. If the RSV renders "Passing by Mysia they went to Troas" (Acts 16:8), this probably should be changed to "when they had passed through Mysia they came to Troas."[11] At Adramyttium he would have entered Mysian territory, skirted the gulf of Adramyttium to Assos, and then gone on to "Troas." Alexandria Troas, as it was called formally, had been so named in memory of Alexander the Great in 300 b.c. by Lysimachus, one of the so-called successors of the conqueror. It had grown greatly since then and in more recent times had been made a Roman colony. Hence it had a leading element composed of retired Roman soldiers, and was now one of the most important cities in that part of the world.

Alexander, on successfully crossing over from Europe to

Asia, had visited the nearby Achilleum (the supposed tomb of Achilles) and decorated it with a garland, for the Homeric saga inspired him more than anything else in all literature. Paul and Silas knew little of this saga, though Timothy may have been better informed with respect to it since his father was a Greek.

At Troas Paul stood opposite the shores of Europe. Whither should he turn? Should he go eastward along the Propontis or Sea of Marmara? Cities like Cyzikus, Nicaea, and Nicomedia must have lured him. However, the last two already lay in Bithynia, which had been barred to him from the south.[12]

Did Paul's affliction still trouble him here and did he pray for the third time for liberation from it? Whenever it was, his third prayer received an answer that was both negative and oracular. "My grace is sufficient for you, for (my) power is made perfect in weakness," i.e., where the human agent is weakest there Christ's power shows its greatest strength (2 Corinthians 12:9).

Paul had received one great gift: forgiveness for his sins and assurance of God's love and grace. Let him ask nothing more for himself than that.

Paul felt no prompting of the Spirit at this time to preach at Troas. He stood forlornly at the shore and looked over the sea. Opposite him lay the island of Tenedos; beyond that the larger island of Imbros; and beyond that the still larger island of Samothrace (the Samos near Thrace as distinct from the Samos off the coast south of Ephesus), with its lofty height from which, according to Homer, the god Poseidon watched the battle of Troy. The islands were like a giant's stepping-stones over the sea; and Paul heard from sailors that after a large gap there was a fourth stepping-stone, the island of Thasos, from which it was but a short additional step to Macedonia and the continent of Europe.

That night, Luke relates, Paul dreamed he saw a man

standing on the distant shore and beseeching him, "Come over to Macedonia and help us" (Acts 16:9). To the Greek reader, who liked to hear of dreams and portents in connection with significant actions or undertakings of men, this made it marvelously vivid that Macedonia was in need of the gospel and receptive to it, and that Paul was directed by a higher power to go there.[13]

At this point in the Acts narrative the author introduces a first "We-section," with the words, "Immediately we sought to go to Macedonia" (16:10). That first person plural style continues for seven verses and then is replaced by third person narration. But it is found again several times, as we shall see (Acts 20:5-15; 21:1-18, and in parts of chs. 27–28). Many have inferred from this that Luke, the traditional author of Acts, joined the party at Troas, perhaps as a new convert. But that cannot be proven and is unlikely. It is more probable that the author of Acts at this point is copying out a succinct travel account written by a companion of Paul such as Silas or Timothy, who were with Paul at this time. Ancient writers appropriated from one another without feeling the need for acknowledgment.[14]

Since Troas was such an important city and there were many ships touching this port, it was not long before a vessel was found that would take Paul and his party over the sea.

What anticipation must have glowed in Paul's heart as he thought of bringing Christ to the Western world, and first of all to that area from which Greek language and civilization had been carried to the East three hundred years earlier. Once rich and powerful, Macedonia and Greece now were prostrate, poor, and thinly populated. Hope in renewed greatness had died. Here was soil properly prepared for the seed of the gospel. Paul's faith saw the fields already white for harvest.

13 THE SECOND MISSIONARY JOURNEY
Through Macedonia

> So we are ambassadors for Christ, God making
> his appeal through us. We beseech you on be-
> half of Christ, be reconciled to God.
>
> 2 CORINTHIANS 5:20

THE VESSEL THEY took brought Paul and his party—
with a stop at Samothrace—to Neapolis (Kavalla) in Macedonia in two days. Here was the terminus of the Egnatian
Way, that ran to Dyrrachium on the shores of the Adriatic,
from where one could ferry over to Brundisium in Italy. Paul
did not need to ask where to go first. He had only to follow
the paved Egnatian Way to the next place, Philippi, for
which Neapolis was the harbor town. He was jubilant. His
footsteps were on the road to Rome! So he may have thought,
but the objective that now arose before his mind was long
to be denied him. The Spirit first had other tasks in store for
him.

In going the eight miles to Philippi, Paul and his companions had to cross the Pangaeum Mountain which ran

parallel to the sea. Silver was mined in that range, and this had led Philip of Macedon, the father of Alexander the Great, to found the city. From the height of the land the travelers had a wonderful view both to the south over Neapolis and the sea, and to the north over Philippi and the plain in which it lies.

Philippi was now the capital of the first of the four districts into which the Romans had divided this important province. Augustus had made the city a Roman colony, because of the victory he and Antony had won here over Brutus and Cassius, the assassins of Caesar. It thus had retired Roman soldiers for its leading citizens, and Roman type law and administration. Rights granted included civil liberty, freedom from taxation by Rome—an inducement for those settled here to remain—and the same status as was enjoyed by cities in Italy itself.

Experience with Roman colonies in Lycaonia led Paul to take a cautious approach. The first task was to find out if there were any Jews in the city. The Alexandrian troubles under emperor Caligula and the recently reported rioting of Jews at Rome under the present emperor, Claudius, had put this people into disfavor in places sensitive to what went on in the capital. Paul did not make inquiries, but relied on his knowledge of Jewish habits to discover their place of meeting. He knew that they would gather on the Sabbath and, where there was no synagogue, would go to where there was water in order to perform the required washing of hands before praying.[1] So on that day Paul and his companions went outside of the gate to the nearest water, the stream called the Gangites, which touched the Egnatian Way about a mile west of the city.

Here they found some women assembled and learned that they were keeping the Sabbath. Since no men were present they were evidently Jewesses and "god-fearers" whose husbands were pagans. These women could scarcely do more than go through the motions of a ritual, for female education was not held to be worthwhile in those times. Among them was one who was called Lydia. That was not her real name, but rather a substitute for one that may have been difficult to pronounce. It was given to her because she came from Lydia in Asia Minor. Her native city was Thyatira,[2] which lay in the Hermus River valley between Sardis and Pergamum.

Lydia was a dealer in "purple." We may imagine her as selling dresses to women, for much of the weaving done was of whole garments rather than of goods by the yard. "Purple" (actually red) is mentioned merely because that color was in demand by the wealthy as a status symbol. She no doubt sold cheaper lines, too. Thyatira, whence she came, was the center of the dyeing industry in Asia Minor. It seems unlikely that Lydia had come to Philippi as an independent sales agent. She no doubt had come with a husband, and was either a widow carrying on her late husband's business, or aiding a husband still living. Since there were Jews at Thyatira, she had become interested in Judaism like so many other fine Gentile women who were repelled by pagan rites. Here in Philippi she met with a few Jewesses on the Sabbath in a rather pathetic loyalty to their dimly understood religion.

How glad these women must have been to find men of their faith joining them, and a teacher like Paul able to conduct a regular service. We can hear him recite by heart some of the great sections of Isaiah in Greek—above all the servant poem of chapter 53. And then he brought them the teaching of the new sect: that these prophecies had been fulfilled in part by Jesus of Nazareth, and that the rest would be fulfilled when he returned as the Son of man of Daniel's vision to establish God's universal kingdom. Lydia especially was delighted with this message. She at once invited Paul and his companions to be her guests. Her household included men and women, no doubt slaves employed in her trade and personal service. This entire household was convoked to hear the new teaching, and with the mistress already persuaded, her dependents followed suit. She and her household were the first of Macedonia to receive Christian baptism. This ceremony must have been carried out later at the river Gangites. Wearing simple linen garments, they had to immerse themselves in the water, and were helped to their feet by Timothy. The bedraggled group returning to the city may have occasioned some wonder, but their faces were radiant with happiness as they knew themselves lifted out of a sordid world into a fellowship with God through his Spirit.

On the succeeding Sabbaths, too, Paul attended and led the service at the riverside. No doubt he adhered to Jewish custom, and the Christian element came in through interpretation of Scripture. Thus even those who may not have been ready to join the new sect had some sense of satisfaction.

On one of these occasions a peculiar incident is said to have occured. A heathen slave girl, who was gifted prophetically, was seized by inspiration and cried out again and again as she followed Paul and his companions.

"These men are servants of the most high God, who proclaim to you the way of salvation."

Apparently she spoke in a different voice when making prophetic utterances, and regarded herself as possessed by a deity. To Paul this was a case of demon possession, and the story is reminiscent of some told in the Gospels of the healing of demoniacs by Jesus. No doubt Paul was embarrassed by being acclaimed in this manner. The words uttered drew too much attention to himself—a thing he was anxious to avoid in the Roman colony. Thinking that the girl could be stopped by exorcism of the demon, Paul commanded the latter in the name of Jesus Christ to come out of her. At this the supposed demon went forth from the girl, but with the consequence that henceforth she no longer could speak in this inspired manner. We regard demon possession as one of mankind's mere sinister illusions, which was especially prominent in the ancient Orient. But its truth was attested to by many people—even by such a knowledgeable man as Plutarch. When a mentally ill person believed himself to be "possessed," it must have had a terrible reality for him. His actions convinced others of it too.

The slave girl was owned by several men who were exploiting for money, her gift of prophecy in fortunetelling. When her ability to prophesy collapsed after the exorcism, the blame fell on Paul. This brought on the very thing he wanted to avoid—getting into trouble with Roman authorities. The men who were injured by the loss of income dragged him and Silas before the city magistrates. Timothy, as a mere attendant, was left untroubled.

The tribunal at Philippi was on the north side of the market place.[3] It was a podium with steps leading up to it from both sides. The charge brought against Paul and Silas was: "These men are Jews and are disturbing our city. They advocate customs which it is not lawful for us Romans to accept or practice" (Acts 16:20).

Roman magistrates in the "colonies" had great power during their one year term of office, especially when it came to maintaining order.[4] They could inflict indignities and punishment on persons and expel them from the city. In dealing with outsiders, the tendency would be to hold them guilty when accused by local residents, especially if they were Jews, a people who were notorious for unruliness. Paul and Silas were obviously of that origin. The first step would be to tear off their clothes and deliver them up to beating with rods. It was a barbarous punishment, which was carried out by Roman lictors. Cicero relates that during his governorship of Cilicia he never had a man beaten with rods or had the clothes torn

off him. The remark reveals his humanity but there were, no
doubt, plenty of beatings in lower courts of his province.

One must ask why Paul did not stop the proceedings at
this point by declaring that he and Silas were Roman citizens?
But one can see a very good reason why Paul would refrain;
it would have resulted in long detention and investigation,
by which his whole missionary activity might have been
jeopardized. It must have seemed easier to him to accept the
worst that the magistrate could do under the circumstances.
After the beating, the men were put in the stocks.

The book of Acts relates a story of the happenings that
night which the author may have gathered from popular
tradition prevailing among Christians at Philippi. It is told so
dramatically that we may quote it directly:

"But about midnight Paul and Silas were praying and singing hymns to God, and the prisoners were listening to them,
and suddenly there was a great earthquake, so that the founda-
tions of the prison were shaken; and immediately the doors
were opened and everyone's fetters were unfastened. When
the jailer woke and saw that the prison doors were open, he
drew his sword and was about to kill himself, supposing that
the prisoners had escaped. But Paul cried with a loud voice
'Do not harm yourself, for we are all here.' And he called for
lights and rushed in, and trembling with fear he fell down
before Paul and Silas, and brought them out and said, 'Men
what must I do to be saved?' And they said, 'Believe in the
Lord Jesus, and you will be saved, you and your household.'
And they spoke the word of the Lord to him and to all that
were in his house. And he took them in the same hour of the
night, and washed their wounds, and he was baptized at once,
with all his family" (Acts 16:25-33).

Luke included this story for its value to the readers
of his day, many of whom were being put into prison for
their Christian beliefs. For at the time of his writings, the

Roman authorities were seeking to hinder the spread of Christianity. Luke was telling Christians how to conduct themselves
in such a situation: to pray and sing, to be friendly to non-
Christian prisoners and to their jailers and thus put themselves and their religion in the best light. If it pleased God,
they might even win new converts for their cause under such
circumstances.[5]

In the continuation of the story, we find Paul insisting
on being taken out of jail personally by the magistrates and
thus receiving their apology for having beaten Roman citizens.
Whatever one may think of that, the story serves Luke's purpose to highlight the importance and value of Roman citizenship, which is going to have so great a bearing on the final
events of Paul's life. The basic, irrefragable fact is that Paul
and Silas were released in the morning and asked to leave the
city.[6] Apparently, however, before departing they were able
to go to the house of Lydia. Her grief at their suffering was
great, as was that of other converts who were gathered there.
But this only bound the little church that arose at Philippi
more closely to Paul.

Paul and Silas now quit the city accompanied by Timothy.
With backs bloody from the beating, and after a night in the
stocks they had to march on.

They first took the Egnatian Way westward. The road ran
through a pleasant valley in which flax and other plants were
cultivated. The Pangaeum Range towered above them on the
south, sending down numerous brooks. At length, having
passed by this range, they came out into a broad valley, down
which came the Strymon River. It flowed through a large
lake and at its foot—three miles from the actual mouth of the
river—lay the city of Amphipolis (*Ienikeni*). It was a free city
and the chief town of the first district of Macedonia. The
travelers saw a curious monument standing there by the road-
side, a statue 17½ feet high of a seated lion on a marble

pedestal.[7] It is still there and is thought to have been erected to commemorate some event of the fourth or fifth century before Christ. Paul felt no impulse to do mission work at Amphipolis and pressed on. The road soon ran closer to the sea and after twenty miles crossed the Arethusa glen, down which came the waters from inland lakes. Here they passed the tomb of Euripides,[8] whom Aristotle called the greatest tragic poet. It was considered a mark of distinction that lightning struck his tomb immediately after his body had been brought into it. Such a sign of heavenly approval had been granted only to one other mortal, that holiest man of old and favorite of the gods (in the Greek view), Lycurgus. Unquestionably, plays of Euripides were given in the theaters at Tarsus and Antioch, so that Paul knew of the poet, even if he had never seen a play of his. Actually, he had reason to honor Euripides, for though he may not have known it, the poet had helped to undermine the old Greek religion by fighting against the idea of gods who acted immorally, against fraudulent priests and seers, as well as against religious zealots like those who put Socrates to death for supposed blasphemy. Truly, among those who paved the way for Christianity in the Gentile world, he was a major prophet.

Eleven milestones farther they came to Apollonia (*Pollina*), situated on an elevation above the southern end of a lake. Here Paul was very close to Mt. Athos, where in future ages Christian monks, his spiritual descendants, were to preserve priceless manuscripts of classics that otherwise would have been lost to the world. It lay to the south, at the tip of a peninsula extending into the Thracian Sea.

Passing through the region known as Mygdonia, Paul reached some heights on the east side of the Gulf of Therme. From these he must have seen in the southwest, on the other side of the gulf, a massive, snow-covered mountain with several summits, timbered in its lower portion, and rising to a height of almost ten thousand feet. This was the Thessalian Olympus, famed as the home of the old Greek gods. But who in Paul's day still believed that the gods dwelt there? Men had climbed the mountain and had found that there was nothing up there but rocks and snow, and a grand view over the country.

In any case, Paul's interest was centered on the city before him, Thessalonica, the largest city of Macedonia. Rome had granted it autonomy, and it was a place where Greek life flourished without much interference, though the Roman governor of the province resided there. The city was governed by a council consisting of six magistrates who bore the title "politarchs" or city-rulers.

With such a setup, Paul had a better chance of a prolonged activity than at Philippi, and so again he sought employment in his trade. He had to feed not only himself but two dependents, though they probably would have sought work, too, wherever they could find it. He twice received financial help from the Christians at Philippi (Philippians 4:16), and this was indeed a blessing in his weakened physical condition.

It must have been hard for Paul to resume his missionary activity. The experience at Philippi had not, as one might think from Luke's account of it, given him satisfaction. He himself registers the impression uppermost in his mind, not many months later, in writing to people at this very city.

"Though we had already suffered and been shamefully treated at Philippi, you know we had courage in our God to declare to you the gospel of God" (1 Thessalonians 2:2).

He was driven to action by the necessity that lay upon him, to which he once alluded in the remark: "Woe to me if I do not preach the gospel" (1 Corinthians 9:16).

Having learned that there was a synagogue in the town, Paul went to it on the Sabbath and presented his message that

Israel's Messiah had come in the person of Jesus of Nazareth.
The great Jewish objection that Jesus could not be the Messiah because he had died on the cross was met by the assertion
that he had risen from the dead, had appeared to many, including Paul himself, and would return in glory as the manifest Messiah. He elaborated on this at two further Sabbath
services, with considerable success. Some of the Jews, notably
a man named Jason, and many of the prominent Greeks or
proselytes as well as some leading Gentile women who were
wont to attend the synagogue service, joined his cause.

The passing allusions of a letter written to this congregation months later provide deep insight into the unselfishness
and integrity of Paul's missionary approach. He worked night
and day that he might not burden any of them with his support while he preached to them the gospel of God. He exhorted them individually. He never used words of flattery or
sought any glory. His behavior toward them was blameless.
They in turn accepted the Word of God in faith.

Paul's success aroused great anger among the rest of the
Jews, and led to a mob attack on the house of Jason. The
purpose, no doubt, was as deadly as that of the mob at Antioch
in Pisidia had been. Fortunately, Paul and his companions
were not there. Jason had been forewarned, and in the night
had concealed them in a house elsewhere in the city. But Jason
himself and other converts were dragged before the politarchs
and accused of harboring men of seditious activities.

The charge against Paul and Silas is brought out with
greater sharpness and clarity than was the case in Pisidian
Antioch or at Philippi: "These men, who have turned the
world upside down . . . are all acting against the decrees of
Caesar, saying there is another king, Jesus."

Populace and authorities alike were disturbed. The politarchs were under the eye of the Roman governor, and the last
thing Macedonia could afford was the cry of another king.

Rome had ended the Macedonian kingship when its general L. Aemilius Paulus defeated King Perseus at the battle of Pydna in 168 B.C.

The politarchs took bail from Jason and the rest and then released them. Paul and Silas (Timothy, too, though he is not mentioned) were led away from their place of concealment during the night and fled from the city. This situation had potentials of peril for Paul like that at Damascus years earlier, when he was let down over the city wall.

When Paul referred to his stay at Thessalonica, he wrote, "We had courage in our God to declare to you the gospel of God in the face of great opposition" (1 Thessalonians 2:2). He told the Thessalonian Christians that they were suffering at the hands of their own countrymen as the Judean church did from the men of Judea "who killed both the Lord Jesus and the prophets and drove us out" (2:15). Thus it is quite clear that even if the Jews were instrumental in arousing pagan opposition against the Christian congregation, the chief suffering, as such, was caused by Gentiles.

Did Paul have another indication from the Spirit that he was not to travel farther on the Egnatian Way? The next city along this road would have been Pella, the old capital of Philip and of the Macedonian kings. The Acts narrative, however, takes Paul to Beroea, which implies that he turned off to the south from the Egnatian Way. Since the latter was the road to Italy, he might easily have been pursued, or warnings could have been sent to the authorities at Pella. There was greater safety in quitting this highway. When Paul some years later speaks of having preached the gospel "from Jerusalem and as far round as Illyricum" (Romans 15:19), it would seem that he has in mind the farthest point west reached by him in this second missionary journey. For Illyricum adjoined Macedonia in the northwest.[9]

Beroea (*Karaferia*) was a city of the third Macedonian

district. Its inhabitants worked in marble quarries or practiced agriculture. Paul longed to go back to Thessalonica, and twice was on the point of going, but felt hindered by a hostile agency (1 Thessalonians 2:18). This was evidently a very different feeling from being hindered by the Holy Spirit (Acts 16:6). Meanwhile, he tarried at Beroea, and since there was a synagogue there he and his companions visited it on the first Sabbath. The Jews here were of a higher class than those of Thessalonica. This probably means that they belonged to an older immigration and had become more Hellenized. The Jews of Beroea "received the word with all eagerness" and studied their scriptures daily to discover the truth. Many were persuaded, including some prominent non-Jewish adherents of the synagogue, both men and women. But when the Jews of Thessalonica heard of this they came down and tried to incite trouble in Beroea. In anticipation of such an outbreak, the converts sent Paul off to the sea, perhaps to New Pydna, which was a nearby harbor city. Those conducting Paul even went on with him by ship to Athens. Silas, however, stayed behind at Beroea.[10]

The voyage took Paul down the coast past Dion. Between that city and the mouth of the Peneios River lay great Mt. Olympus, of which Paul now had a nearer view than from the heights east of Thessalonica. The Magnesian region with cone-shaped Mount Ossa in the north and flat-topped Mount Pelion in the south then became visible—both famed from the ancient Greek myth of the giants who arranged to pile Ossa on Pelion in order to storm Olympus. The coastal vessel took the winding inside passage through the gulf of Euboea and the narrow straits, passed Marathon of heroic memory, and finally rounding the cape of Attica came to Piraeus, the harbor of Athens.

It was with anticipation and renewed hope that Paul set foot on the shores of Greece.

14 THE SECOND MISSIONARY JOURNEY

Athens, Corinth, and the Return

> *Men of Athens, I perceive that in every respect*
> *you are very religious.*
>
> ACTS 17:22

THE ATHENS TO which Paul came was no longer the city of the age of Pericles. It was the tomb of former greatness. What was left of the Greek aristocracy had perished with Brutus on the battlefield of Philippi, for he had enlisted its support in the cause of republicanism against the dictatorship trend established by Caesar. The city thus stood low in the estimation of the Julian emperors. Neither were there now any great intellectual leaders at Athens. Stoic and Epicurean philosophies, however, were being taught by lesser lights.

It still was fashionable for young Romans to go there to study, and many tourists visited it, attracted by its fame and its peerless works of art.[1]

The men of Beroea who had accompanied Paul to Athens no doubt had contacts there and found a place for Paul to stay. Perhaps the woman named Damaris, who became a convert, was the one in whose house he received hospitality, as he had in that of Lydia at Philippi. When the Beroeans departed, Paul decided to send Timothy back with them (1 Thessalonians 3:1) to join Silas in the work at their city, with directions that both should rejoin him later. They could find out where he had gone at the house of Damaris.

One cannot imagine Paul as thrilled by the Parthenon, or the statues of Phidias. Jews did not have much appreciation of art, notably of sculpture, since pagan gods and mythology were the chief subject matter. The commandment, "You shall not make for yourself a graven image or any likeness of anything that is in the heaven above, or that is in the earth beneath, or that is in the water under the earth" (Exodus 20:4), and the polemic in the second part of the Book of Isaiah (chs. 40–66) against idols and idol making had impressed themselves deeply on the mind and the soul of the Jew. Paul would just as well have seen all the statues of Athens smashed to pieces. Every man has his limitations, and Paul's prejudices were deeply ingrained.

Athens had a synagogue which Paul attended. Here as almost everywhere in the Gentile cities there were some interested proselytes. Paul "argued with them" at the meeting, or after it, and he also argued with them individually when he met them in the market place.

Such arguing in public is apt to attract bystanders. In this way it may have happened that some of the followers of the Stoic and Epicurean philosophies listened in and caught a few words. When they were asked by others, "What is this babbler saying?" they replied, "He seems to be preaching foreign gods." They had picked up the words "Jesus" and "Anastasis" (meaning resurrection), and evidently took them to be the names of a god and of a goddess.

This was very strange to them. Since the Athenians liked nothing so much as to hear about something new and different (as Luke observes), they took Paul by the elbow and led him away from the market place[2] to where they could hear more in private. If he had something new they wanted to have it first and for themselves. If it was worthwhile or interesting they would have the advantage of having something to talk about to others.

It has been suggested that the philosophers took Paul to the rear of the point where the ancient court had met, in the direction of the acropolis.[3] Since it is unlikely that Luke had ever been in Athens he may not have thought of any specific point, but merely staged the speech on the hill, the name of which, Hill of Ares (Mars), everyone knew and thought of when Athens was mentioned.

This is an extremely important occasion to the author of Acts. In a brief discourse at Lystra (Acts 14:15-17), he has already given one example of how Paul preached to the heathen. But here at Athens Paul is addressing persons on a higher level. This was the ancient center of human culture, and the speech put into his mouth here had to be one of distinction.[4] In formulating it, Luke was thinking not only of how Paul had spoken—for who could recover those words that the wind had wafted away nearly half a century ago on the hill of Ares—but how Christian leaders should speak in presenting their message to the upper classes. For Luke desired Christianity to do more than to win the poor and the ignorant, the slave and the handmaiden—he wanted it to win the wise and the influential as well, so that it might have standing and support in the world.

Paul addressed not only a handful of philosophers or of the philosophically minded, but the intelligent citizenry, when he began with the words: "Men of Athens."

He first complimented them on their being "very religious," and illustrated this by saying he had observed in passing an altar bearing the inscription, "To the unknown God."

Here he could make the easy transition, "What therefore you worship as unknown, this I proclaim to you."

This was indeed an interesting and clever way of starting such an address. One must suspect, however, that the exact text of the altar inscription was "To the unknown gods." Not only is such an inscription reported by Pausanias, from a place near Athens, but an archaeological example of one came to light at Pergamum.[5] The purpose of such an inscription would have been to make sure that no god was overlooked. But to gain a lead for a monotheistic address, Luke has modified the inscription very slightly. That the form of it given by Luke is not the original one was already asserted by the church fathers Tertullian (A.D. 200) and Jerome (A.D. 400), doubtless on the basis of inquiry at Athens.

The body of the address first deals with God as creator, and in that connection there are given two quotations—the first, "In him we live and move and have our being," is of uncertain origin; the second "For we are indeed his offspring," attributed by the speaker to "some of your poets," is a quotation from Aratus of Soli (third century B.C.). Its idea, which was quite acceptable to the Greeks, is then used to prove the absurdity of making images of the gods. The whole Gentile history thus becomes one of transgression. But, the orator points out, those were times of "ignorance," since the Gentiles did not have the revelation granted to Israel, and God has generously overlooked all this transgression. But now he commands repentance, because he has fixed a day on which he will judge the world in righteousness through a man whom he has appointed, and of this he has given assurance to all men by raising him from the dead.

Thus the oration skillfully makes a transition to the Christian message. The basic requirement of repentance (which would imply doing away with the idols) and the proclamation of a world judgment are purely Jewish. The appointed man

is "the one like a son of man" in the seventh chapter of
Daniel. Only the "assurance" God now has provided is Christian, and here the name of Jesus is omitted. Luke probably
leaves it out to give the impression that Paul was interrupted
at this point—before he could say who the man was.

The idea of raising someone from the dead allegedly
aroused skepticism and mockery on the part of the "philosophers." They had heard enough, and now gave Paul the polite
brush-off: "We will hear you again about this." However,
they did not leave him, but he left them, thereby giving some
the opportunity to follow him.

Paul's preaching at Athens was by no means a failure,
according to Luke. "Some men joined him and believed."
Dionysius, a member of the Areopagus council—hence a distinguished man—and Damaris are mentioned as Athenian
converts. No one with any knowledge of missionary work
would expect greater success than that in such a situation and
from a single effort.

The incident of Paul's preaching to the "philosophers,"
as described by Luke, has great symbolical significance. To
state Christianity in terms that will make it reconcilable with
the knowledge of the world of which philosophy is the high
level expression, is part of the task of theology from age to
age. From the side of philosophy, too, great syntheses with
Christianity have been attempted. And Luke is basically right:
the great process began with Paul, and his visit to Athens was
the appropriate point at which to make this plain. Paul—not
only the Paul reported by Luke in Acts 17, but the Paul
speaking in his own words in the letter to the Romans and
in Corinthians—sat at the table with the philosophers, arguing
with them, and they with him. It is a conversation that goes
on through the ages while the world waits to see who will
have the last word.

From Athens Paul went to the second focal point in

Greece—Corinth. By land the distance was some forty miles.
The road would have taken him through Eleusis, home of
the Eleusinian mysteries, and Megara, the city famed as a
seat of the Socratic philosophy after the death of Socrates at
Athens. Since nothing is said of cities, it is of course possible
that Paul went by ship to the isthmus of Corinth. This neck
of land was tremendously important in ancient commerce, for
in order to avoid sailing around the Peloponnesus with its
dangerous Cape Malea—of which a proverb said: "If you
circumnavigate Malea forget your house at home"—merchants
preferred either to haul smaller vessels across the isthmus on
a slideway or to transfer their cargoes. The western harbor
was called Lechaeum and the eastern Cenchreae. Not so long
after this, under the emperor Nero, an attempt was made to
dig a canal through this isthmus, but it was abandoned—
apparently on grounds of superstition—and not carried through
until 1881–93.

Whether by land or sea, Paul came to Cenchreae. Perhaps
the Isis mysteries were already being celebrated there is his
time, though the description preserved of them by the Latin
author Apuleius is of a later date. Close at hand was the area
sacred to the god Poseidon, where the Isthmian games were
held every three years. The apostle must have passed its
sacred grove.[6]

A walk of three hours brought Paul to Corinth.[7] This was
no longer the beautiful city of earlier days, the home of the
graceful Corinthian pillar. Ancient Corinth had been destroyed by the Roman general L. Mummius in 146 b.c. Its
priceless art treasures were carried off and distributed among
142 cities. Many were wantonly destroyed. Polybius, the historian, with his own eyes saw soldiers using some of the most
famous paintings as gaming tables. At Corinth and nearby
Sicyon, painting, sculpture, and other arts had been brought
to the highest perfection. The city had had an abundance of

able men, not only in the arts, but in the conduct of affairs of state. All these were either slain or sold into slavery in foreign lands. What a tragedy of history! What a loss to humanity! But the world goes on, and as it had done so for two hundred years since those days, one may doubt that Paul knew or had heard anything about ancient Corinth. The city of his day had been refounded by Julius Caesar who, with an eye to the importance of its location, decided to revive it and made it a Roman "colony." Thanks to its command of the isthmus it had flourished more than any other city in decadent Greece.

What first must have struck Paul's eye was the height of Acro-Corinth, the site of the acropolis of a former day. It once had borne among other structures a glorious temple of Aphrodite. Now, however, there was only a small temple of this goddess on the site. The remnants of destroyed buildings and the wreckage of the razed acropolis walls could still be seen. At the foot of the hill lay the city. It had the usual Greek installations with Roman improvements. It was governed, as Paul soon learned, by a proconsul appointed annually by the Roman Senate.

Paul arrived at Corinth in a state of the utmost depression. He writes about it later: "I was with you in weakness and in much fear and trembling" (1 Corinthians 2:3). He was alone and probably entirely destitute. Persons capable of such high exaltation as Paul, can readily fall into the other extreme emotionally. What he needed now was work with his hands. No doubt he carried in his traveler's bag the few tools he required for his trade. He sought out the commercial district of the city to find employment, if possible. Providence led him to an establishment recently opened by a foreigner named Aquila. When he offered his services he found out to his joy that the man was of Jewish stock and had recently come from Rome. Indeed it is very likely that Aquila was already a Christian, since no mention is made of Paul's converting him, and since it seems highly probable that the man had left Rome because of his Christianity.

The allusion to Claudius' expulsion of Jews from Rome (Acts 18:2) is confirmed by a Roman historian, who explains it as due to the fact that they were rioting, "the instigator being Chrestus."[8] Since the name Christ is sometimes written Chrestus, it is quite possible and generally held by scholars that this is an allusion to him, and that the Jews who were driven out were fighting about Christianity.

One can imagine Aquila embracing Paul with joy as a fellow believer and famous missionary, for certainly his name was now known to Christians everywhere. He took him to his wife, Priscilla, who welcomed him and insisted that he stay with them. She saw how much in need he was of friendship and loving care and gave it to him to the best of her ability. Rather strangely and contrary to ancient custom, this woman is usually named first when the couple is referred to. Her name is that of a Roman family, and it is quite likely that she was of non-Jewish origin and of higher social rank than Aquila. The latter may have been a freedman or ex-slave.[9]

Jews who had accepted Christianity could still go to the synagogue, and no doubt Aquila and Priscilla went there regularly.[10] Paul, as a stranger, received the customary opportunity to speak. Luke declares that he argued in the synagogue every Sabbath and sought to persuade both Jews and Greeks. His earliest converts were probably those to whom he refers as baptized by himself—the household of Stephanas whom he calls "the first converts of Achaia," as well as Crispus and Gaius (1 Corinthians 1:14-16; 16:15). For when he had a helper available, like Timothy, he permitted such a one to take care of the baptisms.

The "fear and trembling" to which Paul alludes shows the low state of his physical health. What he had experienced at Philippi must have undermined his general strength. That was a Roman colony, and now he was again in a Roman colony. Did he again have to face such terrors? Well might his nature have rebelled against such a prospect.

He readjusted the emphasis of his preaching, too, for he says that when he came to the Corinthians he did not come proclaiming God in lofty words of wisdom. "For I decided to know nothing among you except Jesus Christ and him crucified" (1 Corinthians 2:1 f.). This is hardly an admission that he had previously anywhere or at any time spoken in lofty words of wisdom. It is erroneous to assert that he had done so at Athens and had found this approach unsuccessful. How he actually spoke at Athens we do not know, for the speech given in Acts is formulated by Luke in the manner of ancient historians, as we have seen. Perhaps Paul is contrasting himself with Apollos, of whom we shall hear later. But his restriction of his message at this Roman colony to the theme of the crucified Christ may have been a well considered one. It was less subject to misunderstanding than that of the Christ who *reigns*. The perilous charge adduced at Thessalonica of his "acting against the decrees of Caesar, saying that there was another king, Jesus," was less likely to be brought.

The signal for again adopting a more active role came to Paul when Silas and Timothy rejoined him. They had learned at Athens where he had gone, and at Corinth they had located him through the synagogue or through trade channels. What a joyful reunion this must have been, and what new strength and courage it gave Paul to learn that the congregations he had established were continuing.

The report that Silas and Timothy had brought of trials undergone by the converts in Thessalonica led Paul to write the congregation a letter. It is the earliest preserved letter from his pen, and the oldest document of the New Testament, which thus may be said to have begun its development at Corinth.

The young congregation had had a difficult time of it after Paul had left. And, indeed, he had prepared them to expect that. But so great was his concern whether they had met the test, that he was willing to be left alone at Athens and he sent Timothy back to them to strengthen them in their afflictions. He had a fear that the tempter might have influenced them to apostasy. Timothy's return had relieved him of that worry.

Paul takes advantage of the opportunity afforded by his writing the Thessalonians to include some exhortation and instruction, and at the end makes sure that the letter will be read to all the brethren, and not merely to an inner circle that excluded the slaves. Tertullian, a Christian teacher of about A.D. 200, asserts that the original letter of Paul was still in existence in his time and was being read at Thessalonica. The brethren there, he says, thought they could recognize Paul's voice and see his facial expression when they read it. That almost sounds as though a portrait of Paul existed there, made by someone who had known him.

At the next synagogue service in Corinth, Paul came out boldly with the Christian message. This aroused bitter opposition, and the Jews started to revile him. He saw that there was no possibility of continuing in the fellowship of this synagogue and documented his exit by the act of shaking out his garment[11] and saying, "Your blood be upon your heads . . . I have done my duty by you. From now on I go to the Gentiles" (Acts 18:6). This is the second of the three ocasions at which Paul is described as making such a solemn declaration (cf. Acts 13:46). The third instance will be the climactic one. The repetition is meant to impress the point on the reader.

Paul had no need to search for a preaching place. He must have considered the eventuality in advance. Among those whom he had persuaded was a "God-fearer" named Titius Justus, whose house was next to the synagogue (Acts 18:7). Here Paul's converts, among whom was Crispus, the ruler of the synagogue, and his household, could hold their meetings. Paul may still have been suffering from the consequences of his trials in Macedonia and have been in need of encouragement. A visionary experience sustained him. According to the Acts reconstruction of it, the Lord said to him one night, "Do not be afraid, but speak and do not be silent; for I am with you and no man shall attack you to harm you, for I have many people in this city" (Acts 18:9-10). This assurance led Paul to settle down to a protracted stay.

The Jews were not disposed to accept meekly the damage done their synagogue attendance. However, they awaited the coming of a new proconsul, perhaps because the previous one's term was about to expire.

On a day when the new official, (Lucius Junius) Gallio,[12] seated himself on the tribunal, an open-air rostrum on the south side of the Agora or market place, the Jews seized Paul and brought him before the Roman. Perhaps they had to await their turn, and if so there were waiting-rooms with marble benches on three sides, to the right and left of the tribunal.[13]

It was a moment worthy of remembrance when Paul and Gallio measured each other. Of Gallio it could be said, "He was the noblest Roman of them all." So at least thought his brother, the philosopher Seneca, who said that no one could be as kind to a friend as Gallio was to everybody, and that he deserved to be shown the greatest affection. He was the very incarnation of the Stoic ideal. How Paul would have loved to have had an opportunity to speak before him in his own defense! But it was not to be. Gallio heard the charge of the Jews: "This man is persuading men to worship God contrary to the law." He dismissed this complaint on the ground that it was a matter of interpretation of their own Jewish law, not of Roman law. No civil offense, he declared, could be claimed, and he refused to be a judge in a religious quarrel. Let them see to this themselves. "And he drove them out from the tribunal," says Luke (18:16). This action gave the general public present at the occasion the idea that Gallio had little use for Jews. The new ruler of the synagogue, Sosthenes, was seized and beaten before the tribunal without Gallio's paying any heed. The Jews thus were completely frustrated and unable to undertake anything against Paul or the Christians without running great risks.

It is evident that Romans of high station were becoming disillusioned with the Jews to whom they had shown so much favor. Gallio, like his famous brother who wrote a treatise against them, regarded the Jews as a peril to the empire. The Romans had been greatly aggravated by the Jews of Alexandria in Egypt. A papyrus letter of the Emperor Claudius, found in Egypt and written in A.D. 41, gives stern counsel to the Jews and the threat, "if they do not heed all these things, then I will treat them in every way as such who are bringing a general pestilence upon the world."[14] Gallio was a man who would have intimate knowledge of these matters; hence his attitude.

Under such circumstances, Paul was able to continue his work in Corinth unhindered by the angry Jews. We are told that he spent a year and six months at this place.

Satisfied that he had the congregation well started on the way to self-government, Paul then decided to leave the city. His decision coincided with that of Aquila and Priscilla to go to Ephesus. It seems very likely that this couple made their move in preparation for Paul's anticipated ministry in that place, which was to become his most important field of activity. These good people hardly went for mere business reasons, for like all early Christians they expected the end of the world to be close at hand and were not bent on laying up treasures on earth or procuring luxuries.

The men of the Corinthian congregation escorted Paul to the limits of the town and the parting was hard for all of them. Paul knew how to speak the words that went to the heart and he must have done so at that occasion as at so many others.

At Cenchreae, where they had to await an opportunity to find a ship bound for Ephesus, Paul allegedly "cut his hair, for he had a vow" (Acts 18:18).[15] This is a curious report. The act is not in accordance with Jewish law, for the hair was to be shorn only at Jerusalem. Paul could have made a vow, and then gone to Jerusalem to fulfill it. But vows and their fulfillment belong to the religion of the law and the storing up of merits is their objective. Paul had left that kind of religion behind him. Is Luke, as author, conditioning the reader's mind for an event he intends to tell of later (Acts 21:23 f.)? Or did he, as a man of Gentile birth, assume the Jewish custom of religious haircutting was like that in vogue among his own people? A great deal of such haircutting must have been done at Cenchreae owing to its proximity to the temple of Poseidon, for it was customary among the Greeks to offer up one's hair as a sacrifice to this particular god for deliverance from danger on the sea. Such an act could thus be very easily ascribed to Paul at this place.

Accompanied by Silas, Timothy, Aquila, and Priscilla, Paul set sail on a vessel bound for Ephesus and Syria. The journey across the Aegean Sea took about ten days, for the ancient vessels did not sail at night if it could be avoided. Around the island of Delos alone, sacred as the birthplace of Apollo, there were many smaller islands through which the navigator had to pick his way. The views that presented themselves to the eye were of breathtaking beauty, and we may suppose that even these other-worldly travelers were thrilled by them. At last, behind the island of Samos, the mountains of Asia Minor appeared in the blue haze of the distance. Particularly prominent was Mt. Tmolus near Sardis. This whole coast was Ionia, where Greeks had dispossessed the older populations and had established cities in which unforgettable contributions were made to civilization. Here the Homeric Epics were sung; here Herodotus wrote his history; here such wise men as Pythagoras and Thąles had been born. Ephesus[16] lay at the mouth of the Caystrus River, into which one sailed to the harbor Panormus, whence a canal led to an inner harbor at the city itself. The scene that presented itself to the eye of the traveler was that of a natural amphitheater, with the city in the foreground. On the north, the east, and the south there were mountains—over the southern one, Mt. Coressus, one could see on the skyline the old fortification walls running along the comb. Immediately in the foreground were some of the finest buildings of Ephesus: the Gymnasium, the Forum, the marketplace. Up Mt. Coressus and over the hill called Pion extended the residential city, and northeast of the Pion was the famed temple of Artemis, one of the seven wonders of the world.

According to the Acts narrative Paul took a first step toward a future ministry here by visiting a synagogue on the Sabbath—presumably while the vessel lay over to take on freight. He argued with the Jews, arousing curiosity about the new movement he represented, and he promised to return "if God will."[17]

Why did Paul not remain there? What led him to go back to Palestine? The answer may be contained in the brief report of his trip. "When he landed at Caesarea he went up and greeted the church, and then went down to Antioch" (Acts 18:22). The Acts report thus asserts that Paul visited Jerusalem.[18] Was this possible after the break with Peter and with James' representatives? It was just as possible then as it was several years later. And it was necessary—not for an accounting of his work, for he felt himself accountable only to Christ, but for the preservation of the link with the mother-church. Paul, we may be sure, delivered a token collection that he had raised in his mission churches to aid "the poor" as he had promised. On that score he says some years later (according to the usual understanding of his words); "which very thing I hastened to do" (Galatians 2:10).[19] But Luke, who has no knowledge of Paul's charitable efforts on behalf of the Jerusalem church, reveals no motive for his going to Jerusalem and no details concerning his reception there. It may have been a brief, uneventful, or even a painful visit.

Paul then "went down" from the high country of Judea to the lower one of Antioch. Memories of the events preceding his last departure from Antioch must have troubled him, as he traveled toward the Syrian metropolis. He had, of course, learned at Jerusalem where Barnabas was and where Peter had gone. Of greater concern to him was the division in the church at Antioch, and above all, whether his Gentile converts were holding together and increasing in numbers.

Paul's Gentile friends were overjoyed at his return. The story of the founding of Christianity in Macedonia and Greece thrilled them. Paul told them, too, about the great field he was planning to visit next: the province of Asia, with its great commercial center, Ephesus.

For his part Paul heard something from his friends that was new to him, and which had not been mentioned to him at Jerusalem. Two messengers from there, Judas Barsabbas and another Silas, had brought a letter to the congregation soon after Paul's departure on his second journey. It was addressed to "the brethren who are of the Gentiles in Antioch, Syria, and Cilicia," as a communication of "the apostles and the elders" (Acts 15:23-29).[20] It disavowed as unauthorized the demands of certain Judean visitors to Antioch that Christians of Gentile origin be circumcised, but laid upon all "these necessary things"—that they abstain from what has been sacri-

ficed to idols, and from blood, and from what is strangled and
from unchastity." The allusion to unchastity in all probability
is not to sexual license. There was no need of any special directive against fornication, nor could such a one, if intended,
have been made secondary to the ritualistic ones. The allusion
is rather to the prohibition of marrying close relatives, for all
four points then appear in that same order in Leviticus (17:8,
10 ff.; 19:6 ff.), where furthermore they were declared to apply,
not only to Israelites but to "the strangers that sojourn among
them." The Jerusalem group held that Gentile converts were
such "sojourners in Israel," and thus had found a basis for the
decree in the Old Testament. The purpose of the decree
seems to have been to make possible the fellowship of Gentile
and Jewish Christians by requiring Gentiles to obey the same
ritualistic commandments that were laid upon "the God-
fearers" of the synagogue.[21]

Paul's attitude toward this letter must have been one of
dissatisfaction. The "unchastity" requirement he regarded as
self-evident (1 Corinthians 5), and the others he considered
to be within the sphere of Christian liberty—and not to be
prescribed or imposed (see Chapter 15). He was basically
against any ecclesiastical efforts to put the Christian public
under tutelage in matters unrelated to salvation in Jesus
Christ. Furthermore, Paul interpreted the accord he and Barnabas had made with James, Peter, and John as granting responsibility for the Gentile mission areas to Barnabas and
himself. Why should the Jerusalem group send instructions to
these churches? Paul had carried the gospel through inner
Asia Minor and to Macedonia and Greece and he considered
himself as the father of the churches of the Gentile lands.

Paul evidently spent the winter season at Antioch. The
Acts account has no mention of what he did. A sixth century
monk who wrote a history of Antioch preserves a scrap of information from early second century writers when he says:

"St Peter did not receive or love the Gentile believers, but leaving them went out from there. St. Paul, however, returned to Antioch the Great later, and having learned this about Peter, he removed all stumbling blocks and received and loved all equally and brought all to the faith, as the most wise historians Clement and Tatian have recorded."[22]

Perhaps, then, Paul succeeded in reuniting and strengthening the church at Antioch with the enthusiasm born of his successes in other lands.

15 THE THIRD MISSIONARY JOURNEY

Through Asia Minor to Ephesus

*A wide door for effective work has opened to
me, and there are many adversaries.*

1 CORINTHIANS 16:9

*And apart from other things, there is the daily
pressure upon me of my anxiety for all the
churches.*

2 CORINTHIANS 11:28

WHEN THE SPRING of A.D. 53 came into the land, the indefatigable traveler set out once more from Antioch to go to Cilicia and the Taurus pass.

There is no mention of any companion, but since Titus appears in his company in his letters he certainly went with Paul. For some reason the Acts narrative never refers to him. Timothy, too, was either with Paul or joined him later at Lystra, where he may have spent the winter.

Paul took the same route as on his second journey. How painful it must have been for him to bypass Tarsus and the

loved ones there. Fondly his eyes may have looked back upon
the city and the plain lying in the golden haze, as he ascended
toward the pass.

Once in the high country he went "from place to place
through the region of Galatia and Phrygia, strengthening all
the disciples" (Acts 18:23). On the second journey the matter
was put differently: he went through the region of Phrygia
and Galatia (Acts 16:6). But Luke's language here should not
be pressed.[1] There can be no intended difference, since Paul
was only revisiting churches previously founded. Luke may
have put the matter both ways because he was not clear about
which came first. Paul must have come to the Celtic community, for in the letter that he would write them a year or so later
he indicates that he had been among them twice (Galatians
4:13). When he refers to himself as "debtor to both Greeks
and barbarians" (Romans 1:14), may we suppose that his sojourn among the Galatians had given him this extended idea
of indebtedness and of his duty to repay both with his preaching? Did he learn from the Celtic saga that their people had
come from the west and had kinsmen in Gaul and Hispania?
Did this help to put into his mind the new goal of the last-
named country that he envisions in writing the Romans (15:
28)? At the crest of his insight he knew himself to have received through Christ grace and apostleship "to bring about
obedience of faith for the sake of his name *among all the
nations*" (Romans 1:5). Had he gone to the Iberian Peninsula, then Gaul, Germany, and Britain would have entered
successively into his field of vision.

In the midst of these Galatian people, we may be sure, he
again found refreshment and joy.

This time the Spirit did not hinder Paul from going
through Phrygia (the "upper country" of Acts 19:1) to the
region called "Asia" and its foremost city, Ephesus. To that
city the main trade-route from the Euphrates or the one from

the Cilician Gates now led, instead of to Sardis, as in earlier centuries. He thus would have passed Colossae and Laodicea and perhaps made contacts there. Arriving at Ephesus he found his friends, Aquila and Priscilla, from whom he had parted in the previous fall and was hospitably received with his companions.

According to the peculiar tradition adopted by Luke (Acts 19:1 ff.), Paul's very first contact was with twelve men described as "disciples" (meaning Christians) whom he suspected of not having received the Holy Spirit. And, indeed, he found that they had never even heard that there was a Holy Spirit and that they had only received the baptism of John. The matter was rectified by baptism in the name of the Lord Jesus and the laying on of hands. They now received the Holy Spirit and "spoke in tongues" and prophesied, i.e., gave utterance both in ecstatic speech and in edifying exhortation (cf. 1 Corinthians 14:2-4). In part the incident serves to prove that Paul, like the apostles (Acts 8:14-19), could convey the Spirit. But it also illustrates the absorption into the advancing tide of Christianity of part of the sect of John the Baptist.[2] This was an early Christian objective, which the introduction to John's Gospel makes particularly clear.

The supporters thus gained formed a valuable help for Paul when he entered the synagogue on the next Sabbath. There he pushed his message aggressively for three months, "arguing and pleading about the kingdom of God" (Acts 19:8). This delineation indicates no different slant in his preaching than had been followed elsewhere, but is used for the sake of variety or for giving the impression of continuity with the message of John the Baptist and of Jesus.

Since Aquila and Priscilla had remained within the synagogue, though holding Christian gatherings privately in their house, they cannot have put forward Paul's sharper positions. This he himself did now, with his teaching that obedience to the Jewish ritual law is unnecessary for Gentile converts. This teaching struck at the very basis of the missionary effort of the Jews to win proselytes from among pagans (Matthew 23:15) and aroused bitter opposition. In consequence a scene occurred, in which some spoke evil of "the (Christian) Way" before the congregation. Paul did as he had done at Corinth —he left the synagogue with his adherents (Acts 19:9).

Luke had prepared the way for Paul's first act at Ephesus by telling about a man who had been there in the meantime and had "taught accurately the things concerning Jesus" in the synagogue (Acts 18:24 ff.). It was Apollos, an eloquent Alexandrian, who was well versed in the scriptures and no doubt interpreted them in the intriguing manner of Philo. But he knew only the Baptism of John. Aquila and Priscilla "had expounded to him the way of God more accurately," and they and some other Christians had given Apollos a letter of recommendation to the church at Corinth. He was still at Corinth when Paul arrived at Ephesus. The twelve men whom Paul baptized on coming to Ephesus were evidently the disciples of Apollos. Whether or not the latter himself received baptism and the Holy Spirit remains uncertain.

Paul now rented a hall in which he could teach—the school of Tyrannus—and argued there daily. Tyrannus was probably a "rhetor" who taught from early morning until eleven o'clock (the usual hours for teaching). Paul then would have used the hall from eleven to four, the period in which all work—including his own trade activity—halted. Teaching at such a public place was an important factor in bringing about the progress of Christianity in "Asia." For many people from cities of the interior came to Ephesus, and to hear this new teacher and his "philosophy" at a public place had great attraction.

Other unusual source material, too, was incorporated by Luke in his account of Paul's activities at Ephesus. He was

regarded in some traditions as a wonder-worker. In consequence, his "handkerchiefs or aprons" were taken and carried
to the sick and effected remarkable cures (Acts 19:11-12).
This is somewhat like the story about Peter in Acts 5:12-16
and may have been told to show that Paul was as much of a
healer as Peter.[3]

This information is only introductory, however, to the incident concerning the sons of Scaeva—allegedly the seven sons
of a high priest (Acts 19:13 ff.). That term as we have previously seen, did not necessarily mean a reigning high priest or
even an ex-high priest, but was applied to anyone eligible for
the office. That apparently is the case here, as no name like
Scaeva appears in the roster of high priests given by Josephus.
These men went about practicing exorcism of demons. We
have heard of an occasion at Philippi where Paul exorcised a
demon in the name of Jesus Christ. The odd thing here is
that these sons of Scaeva made an attempt to exorcise by using the formula, "I adjure you in the name of Jesus whom
Paul preaches." This was a rather backhanded use of a name.
The demon speaking through the man had cried, "Jesus I
know, and Paul I know, but who are you?" The sons were
beaten and put to flight by the demoniac, who evidently
was violent—like the one of Mark 5:4. The incident which is
told in a secular manner and has no religious point[4] reflects
the awe felt for Paul and for the name of Jesus in certain
circles at Ephesus.

Another bit of early material stressed Paul's battle against
magic. Ephesus was famous for "the Ephesian writings," or
magical texts, with the help of which people sought healing,
injury to foes, and the like. Many brought their magical books
to Paul and these were burned (Acts 19:18-19). The value of
fifty thousand pieces of silver placed on these books, if not
vastly exaggerated, would suggest that some were highly prized
for their supposed effectiveness, for average book production

costs at Rome were only about five cents per copied page.[5] In including this item Luke, no doubt, had his eye on the Christian reader of his day. Magic played an important part in the lives of Gentiles, and converts needed to be taught to do away with superstition of all kinds. Unfortunately, this book burning later inspired some churchmen to burn books we would give much to have today.

Paul's success in his ministry at Ephesus must have been remarkable. The summary statement that "the word of the Lord grew and prevailed mightily" is unusually strong.

Among the things that kept Paul busy were conferences with visitors from the churches he had founded elsewhere, or writing to such churches in response to requests for instruction. It caused him much anguish to be concerned with human frailties and to smooth over difficulties. He exclaims about it, "Who is weak and I am not weak? Who is made to fall (or is offended) and I am not indignant" (2 Corinthians 11:29)? This aspect of his labors is brought home to us most vividly by some of his letters.

Of all those who sent to Paul for advice and counsel at Ephesus, the church of Corinth in Greece deserves first mention. In no field had Paul spent so much time prior to his coming to Ephesus. None in his estimation was more important. It was at the crossroads of the world of that day. Furthermore, since Corinth was a Roman colony, it was of prime concern to Paul that the Christianity of this church should be exemplary. He spared no effort to guide it. He had written the church a letter which has not been preserved (1 Corinthians 5:9). But various questions had arisen in the minds of the membership, and the congregation wrote him asking for instruction on these matters (1 Corinthians 7:1). Three men from Corinth delivered this letter, for in answering it Paul mentions how he rejoiced at the coming of a committee of three—Stephanas, Fortunatus, and Achaicus—"for they have made up for your absence" (1 Corinthians 16:17). Presumably they then carried his reply, the letter we know as 1 Corinthians, back home with them. These men were evidently loyal to Paul, and he stresses the fact that Stephanas' household were the first converts he had made in Achaia or Greece proper (16:15). He also seeks to bolster their position in the congregation, pointing out what they had done and asking for continued acceptance of their leadership. Paul was a skillful church leader, one can see, but there is no indication that he practiced insincere flattery. He was able to make diplomacy and integrity coincide.

After the letter's introductory greetings and thanksgiving to God for the congregation, Paul at once appealed for harmony. He had received news of dissension among them, not from the representatives who brought the letter, but from another source, from "Chloe's people" (1:11). The persons named may have been servants of a woman named Chloe, who herself may not have been a Christian at all. His informants had revealed to him that there were four parties in the congregation. One said, "I belong to Paul"; another, "I belong to Apollos"; a third, "I belong to Cephas (Peter)"; a fourth, "I belong to Christ."[6] (1:12).

Division in a church and over Christ's servants! "What then is Apollos? What is Paul? Servants through whom you believed as the Lord assigned to each." One can hardly escape the impression that the Apollos party was the main rival of his own. When Paul says that he laid the foundation at Corinth like a skilled master builder and warns, "Let each man take care how he builds on it" (3:10), this may be with an eye to Apollos. When he disclaims giving his message "in lofty words or wisdom," the antithesis may be to Apollos (2:1, 13). The latter, it is true, was back in Ephesus when Paul wrote, and Paul even says at the end of his letter that he had strongly urged him to visit the Corinthians again with the other brethren (i.e. Stephanas and companions), but that it was not the will of God that Apollos go now (16:12). Paul thus shows no jealously of Apollos. Whether Apollos resented Paul's taking over his disciples remains in doubt.

The Corinthian congregation was faced by numerous problems which arose out of the circumstance that its people were recent converts from heathenism and lived surrounded by heathenism. Even today all mission churches in heathen communities face difficulties, for Christianity permeates only gradually the habits and customs of peoples.

It is instructive to see how fundamentally Paul deals with some of the questions posed.

Paul boldly assailed the Corinthians over a case of immorality in their midst: that of a man living with his father's wife (5:1-13). The exact situation does not come out clearly. Was it marriage or a liaison? Was the woman a slave, perhaps set free by the father at his death? Was she a heathen, since no blame is placed upon her by Paul? Was she young? The congregation was indifferent to the whole matter, and that aroused Paul's ire. He called it immorality of a kind not found even among pagans. That may have been true on the level of the common people, but in the higher circles of society the records show that worse things happened. In Paul's handling of the matter, we have one of the indications that he had not studied to be a rabbi, for in the rabbinical tradition the marriage of a proselyte to his stepmother was tolerated, though for a Jew it was forbidden.[7] Paul judged on the basis of the Mosaic law (Leviticus 18:6 ff.). Evidently he considered this paragraph of it to be moral, not ritual law. And one must agree with him that such a relationship was not proper. But he goes to a terrible extreme when he demands that the congregation deliver this man to Satan for the destruction of the flesh (5:5). He is as ferocious here as Peter is said to have been in the case of Ananias and Sapphira

(Acts 5:1 ff.). However, Paul's verdict—whatever may have been the practical execution of it—was no irrevocable decree, if the man repented. Unfortunately, this drastic example of church discipline provided ecclesiastics of a later age with an excuse for death sentences and tortures. It also shows the zeal and anger of which Paul was capable. It was that spirit which possessed him when he persecuted the church in his young manhood.

Paul had some other matters to criticize in the church of Corinth. He held it improper that Christians seek to obtain rights in public law courts, saying that they should be able to adjust their difficulties before referees from among their midst, who were men of esteem (6:1-8). He found that his teaching of Christian freedom was being taken as an excuse for immorality by some. Prostitution was common at Corinth, and the Aphrodite temple still had its quota of harlots. Temptation thus was great. But Christians are in Christ and should not dishonor him or their own bodies, but glorify God in their bodies (6:12-20).

The congregation desired to know Paul's teaching about marriage (7:1-40). Some believed that celibacy should be the rule for Christians. When nations decline, as Greece had indeed done, and life no longer seems to promise anything, a spirit of this sort can well arise. Furthermore, since Christians were expecting dreadful calamities in the near future, prior to Christ's return, it seemed futile and a great source of grief to have children. Even on purely rational grounds, a philosopher like Democritus had pointed out that adoption was wiser. Paul was personally an ascetic—above all, out of a realization that marriage would be a hindrance to his undivided service of Christ.

He would have liked to recommend celibacy generally, but was too practical to do so. He was absolutely opposed to the break up of existing marriages, except in the case when the partner of a Christian was an unbeliever and desired its termination.

In general Paul did not want to disturb the status quo: everyone should remain in the social condition in which he was when he became a Christian. This would hold true for the circumcised, who therefore should not seek to undo their circumcision, and for the uncircumcised, who should not be circumcised, and for the slave who should not seek freedom. He even thought a widow might better remain one, but considered her free to marry if she chose, so long as she wed a Christian.

The letter from Corinth had asked about the eating of meat that had been sacrificed to idols (8:4 ff.). The meat sold in the markets came in part from that source. Should one always inquire into the origin of meat and avoid it if it was sacrificial meat? And how should one conduct oneself when among friends or family members who were Gentiles? Paul is surprisingly broad-minded in this matter. If one does not know that it is sacrificial meat it does not matter; but if one is told that it is, then it is better to refrain from eating it in order to give no offense.

Paul desires the strong not to insist on their liberty if their example does damage to the weak. The way in which he speaks about this matter indicates that he did not consider the so-called "decree of the apostles" (Acts 15:23-29), which commands abstention from what has been sacrificed to idols, binding upon him.

Paul was quite concerned about the image of Christianity in a place like Corinth, where Gentiles might drop in out of curiosity to see how this Jewish sect conducted itself. Women were assuming a much more independent role here than was customary among the Jews. One indication of this was that they had begun to take off their head-covering, or veil, in congregational gatherings (11:2-16). Paul found this improper.

He had the curious idea that the head-covering was a sign of woman's subordination to her husband, and viewed its removal in public as a symptom of emancipation. A further reason for the covering of hair was "on account of the angels," meaning evil angels. His pagan converts may have understood him to mean satyrs, of whose spying and designs upon women they had heard, and who would be tempted by the sight of the unveiled woman. His utterances on this subject have kept Western women wearing hats in churches, but rather ironically making themselves more rather than less attractive.

In another matter, too, the congregation needed to be called to order and taught Christian manners (11:17-34). It was customary to hold congregational meals, and those members able to do so brought food with them. But there were slaves and men coming from work who arrived late and were unable to bring food. Instead of waiting and providing something for the late arrivals to share, those who brought food and drink began to consume it themselves. On top of this, the rite of the Lord's Supper was to be celebrated!

In regulating this situation Paul took occasion to repeat the sacred story of the institution of the last supper (11:23 ff.). When he says, "I received it from the Lord," he hardly means directly, but rather through the mediation of those who had been present at the original occasion. He considers the supper as an *act of the congregation* with which it proclaims the death of Christ "until he comes." It is a noble thought which is hardly emphasized sufficiently in Christendom's celebration of the sacrament. When he speaks of the deleterious effect of the eating and drinking on the part of the unworthy, he yields to mystical ideas which, where accepted, have vastly exalted the holiness of the rite. He may have thought of his new interpretation, as obtained from on high.

Paul also saw the great need of discouraging too much practice of glossolaly or "speaking with tongues." To understand this one must forget about the story of Pentecost (Acts 2), in which the phenomenon has been idealized. Paul prepared the way for discussion of the subject by speaking first of the great variety of existing spiritual gifts and their having been granted for the common good, and of how improper it is to think too much of some and too little of others (12:4 ff.). As though reluctant to come to the point he takes time out to set up a most beautiful picture of the things one should aspire to above all others: faith, hope, and love—praising love as the greatest (13:1-13). If he had written nothing else this chapter of Corinthians would have made him immortal.

Among the spiritual gifts, Paul values prophecy, by which he here means clear Christian witness, most highly (14:1 ff.). He thus relegates speaking with tongues to the background. It is only an uttering of unintelligible sounds in a condition of ecstasy, much as is the case with a bird pouring forth its song in springtime. The individual doing it finds it satisfying and uplifting, but since others cannot know what he is saying, Paul does not think it profitable for the congregation. He insists that any such speech in tongues be followed by an interpretation of its meaning by one gifted to do so (just as some symphony may receive interpretation by a musicologist) and that the number of such performances be limited. He asserts that he can speak in tongues better than any of them, but that he would rather speak five words that are understood than ten thousand that are incomprehensible.

On that basis he outlines what he considers a proper order of service (14:26 ff.), and in passing he directs that women are to remain silent according to the practice prevailing in all the churches of the saints (i.e., the Christians of Judea).

Perhaps the most important topic dealt with in the letter is that of the resurrection (ch. 15). This was a very difficult teaching to take into the Greek world, for Plato's idea that matter is evil and that the body is a prison from which the soul yearns to escape to realms of pure delight, had become widely prevalent. Resurrection was understood to mean resurrection of the earthly body. Just as mention of a resurrection led the philosophers at Athens to cut off further presentation of Paul's views, so here there were some who denied that there was any such thing. But Paul would not compromise in this matter. The fact of Christ's resurrection was to him the guarantee of the resurrection of the Christian. But his idea of both differed from the Palestinian Jewish idea of resurrection.

One must be grateful to Paul for this discussion, because it gave him occasion to report about the appearances of the risen Christ. We must bear in mind that he is writing years before any of the four Gospels were written. Neither they nor the book of Acts tell us as much about the resurrection experiences as Paul does.[8] When Paul describes the nature of the future resurrection of the believer, he gives us a clue to what he conceived that of the risen Christ to have been. The latter's physical body had been metamorphosed into a spiritual or glorified body, yet was recognizable as his and not another's. The risen Christ was not flesh and blood, for flesh and blood cannot inherit the kingdom of God (15:50). Paul thinks nobly about the ultimate mystery of death, but the starting point is how he and others had seen Christ, when he manifested himself to them and called them to his service. His certainty of that rather than the conclusions he draws is the most important thing here for us. What he thinks about our final destiny is necessarily speculative. It is God himself who will speak the last word.

The letter closes on a practical note: the request that the Corinthians join in raising money for the saints at Jerusalem, and the announcement of his travel plans (ch. 16). He intends to visit Corinth after passing through Macedonia, and may even spend the winter with them before he goes to Judea to deliver the collection he is raising. But he wants to stay at Ephesus until Pentecost. He has an "open door" there, but also many adversaries. He is sending Timothy to them with their returning representatives, asks for him a kind reception and hopes for the speedy return of his helper.

It is all in all the letter that gives us the richest insight into Paul's missionary practice and his handling of the diverse problems that he had to face. It reveals Christian leadership of a high order and remains a guiding compass for missionary work and church management of Christendom for all time.

In one passage of this letter Paul refers to his being in peril every hour, yea of dying every day, and then cries: "What do I gain if, humanly speaking, I fought with the wild beasts at Ephesus?" (15:32). Later, this was taken literally. Further stimulated by the words, "So I was rescued from the lion's mouth" (2 Timothy 4:17), stories about Paul and a lion were circulated later through the apocryphal *Acts of Paul*.[9] However, as a Roman citizen, he could not be condemned to the arena. He must be speaking figuratively, just as the bishop of Antioch, Ignatius, was half a century later when he described his experience with the soldiers guarding him on his journey to Italy in the words, "From Syria to Rome I am fighting with beasts, I am bound by ten leopards."[10] In Paul's case the wild beasts were most likely hostile civilians.

Local legend at Ephesus calls a tower on a ridge, extending from Mt. Coressus north into the plain, "Paul's Prison." The tower is part of the ancient defenses of the city dating from 287 B.C.[11] Its traditional identification merely illustrates the fact that men have been intrigued since olden days by stories of Paul's imprisonment at Ephesus.

Some confirmation of such an imprisonment (presumably prior to the writing of 1 Corinthians) would be afforded by the letter to the Colossians, to Philemon, and to the Philippians, if these letters were written from Ephesus. They presuppose a captivity situation, and traditionally have been

thought of as written later in Rome. However, their origin in
Ephesus seems probable to many scholars today, and so we
will consider them here.

The road leading eastward from Ephesus reached the valley of the Maeander River and followed it up to the so-called
Gate of Phrygia. After passing through this defile, it came
into a broader valley and then followed the Lycus or "Wolf"
River, a confluent of the Maeander. In this area lay the cities
of Laodicea, Hierapolis, and Colossae.[12] Above Colossae rises
great Mt. Cadmus (Baba-Dagh) to a height of seven thousand
feet. It has been described as "the father of all the mountains
of western Asia, with gigantic woods, full of dark precipices
and preserving its snows all the year round" (Renan).

The Colossians were the Christians of the city of Colossae. The congregation was apparently a Gentile one (2:13).
But it was now being disturbed by the propagators of a heret-
ical cult, which cannot presently be identified very satisfactorily
since only a few of its peculiarities are mentioned.

Paul calls the Colossians back to basic Christianity as it
had been mediated to them by Epaphras according to Paul's
doctrine, and he takes advantage of the opportunity to include
valuable teachings about Christ as well as practical exhortation. The curious mention of the Scythians, as the very extreme of barbarian, in one noble passage (3:11), suggests that
this far-flung people, now dwelling chiefly along the shores of
the Black Sea and in the direction of the Danube, are entering his field of vision.

In his closing greetings (4:10 ff.), Paul sends regards from
his fellow prisoner Aristarchus, a Jesus Justus, and "Mark the
cousin of Barnabas," who evidently has found a way back into
Paul's good graces. He has already given (oral?) instructions
to the Colossians about the man—an item suggesting that
Mark was not yet fully trusted. The request "If he comes receive him," certainly lacks Paul's usual warmth and suggests

that there were reasons not to receive him which Paul is willing to overlook.

Generous praise is given to Epaphras, who is evidently staying with Paul. Not only has he worked for the church at Colossae but also for the Christians at Laodicea and Hierapolis. Laodicea apparently has a less vigorous minister, Archippus, whom Paul urges to fulfill his duties. A woman named Nympha, in whose house the Laodicean group meets, is especially saluted. The congregation at Colossae is urged to share its letter with Laodicea. But Paul has also written the Laodiceans, who are to share their letter with the Colossians (4:16).

Paul sent one of his aides, Tychicus, to tell the Colossians of his situation—it was evidently unwise to put it in writing—and with him went Paul's beloved Onesimus (4:7 ff.).

But Tychicus also carried a letter for an individual at Colossae named Philemon, which concerned the aforesaid Onesimus. The latter, as we learn from it, was Philemon's runaway slave. The man had in some way found Paul and served him. The Christian groups from the beginning contained many slaves and ex-slaves, and so Onesimus, too, may have been attracted. Paul now sends him back to his master, much as he wishes he could continue to enjoy his services during his imprisonment.

The letter, bespeaking a Christian reception for the runaway, is the finest private letter to come down from the ancient world. With a light touch Paul seeks to disarm the angry slave-owner, and to bring about an example of the equality and freedom that should exist where the spirit of God reigns in a congregation. Paul did not seek to end slavery, but to reorient it so that it remained a mere form of economic dependence, like that of most women in marriage. He told Philemon to receive Onesimus as a beloved brother in the Lord.[13]

A mission of Tychicus is again mentioned in the Epistle

to the Ephesians (6:21 ff.). Since in the best old manuscripts of this epistle, the words, "in Ephesus" are missing in the address, some have held that they are a later interpolation, and that this epistle is really the lost letter to the Laodiceans.[14]

To the Ephesian captivity (if there was one) some would also assign the Epistle to the Philippians.[15] Traditionally, it has been linked with the captivity at Rome. However, the remark of Paul that his captivity "has served to advance the gospel, so that it has become known throughout the whole *praetorium* and to all the rest that my imprisonment is for Christ" (1:12 f.), need not be a reference to the "praetorian guard" (as the RSV renders the word). In the other passages in which "praetorium" is used in the New Testament, it is the abode of the *praetor* which was one of the titles of a governor. There was, of course, a praetorium at Ephesus, where the governor of "Asia" stayed when he came to that city from his residence at Pergamum. Paul may be thinking of all the servants and allied personnel maintaining that establishment, for if he was imprisoned in Ephesus, it was probably in this place.

His imprisonment, so Paul asserts in this letter, has led most of the brethren to speak out their Christian witness more courageously. He admits that there are some who "preach Christ from envy and rivalry," and "thinking to afflict me in my imprisonment." He rises to a sublime height when he cries, "What then? Only that in every way, whether in pretense or in truth, Christ is proclaimed; and in that I rejoice" (1:15-17).

Paul is quite convinced that he will be delivered from his present state, even though he yields to the thought that so far as he alone is concerned, death would be a gain (1:19 ff.). He hopes to send Timothy to them soon, and lauds him in a manner which at the same time does not reflect too well on the rest of his helpers. He is only waiting to see how his case will turn out, and later expects to come to Philippi himself (2:19-24).

The Philippians had sent a man named Epaphroditus to minister to Paul in his captivity. In ancient time and until recently in some eastern countries, a prisoner had to depend on friends and relatives for food. Unfortunately, Epaphroditus had fallen ill. Paul gives credit to God's mercy for his recovery, and hopes to send him back soon (2:25-30).

Paul has high praise for this congregation, which had helped him from the beginning in his hard struggle in Europe. One misses mention of the Lydia of Acts. Since he names two women who are at odds, Euodia and Syntyche, some have thought that "Lydia" is identical with one of them. He asks an unnamed "yoke-fellow" or co-worker to help settle the conflict and says that the two women have labored side by side with him in the gospel, together with a certain Clement and others (4:2 f.).

The Ephesian captivity, we may assume, was not of long duration. We may suspect that the "Asiarchs," whom the author of Acts introduces in connection with the final events at the city, played a role in Paul's liberation. These officials might well have been consulted as to whether they saw any danger to the state-religion in Paul's activity. Perhaps they were enlightened men, who considered it beneficial that he had dealt a blow at superstition of the low sort represented by the "Ephesian writings." They would have been impressed by the earnestness and integrity of Paul if they heard him speak in his own defense, and utter such sentiments of loyalty to existing government as he sets forth in the letter to the Romans (ch. 13). The governor, we may be sure, found the charges made against Paul for subversive activity insufficient, and decreed his release. After a period of inaction, Paul was able to go forth to new labors until the next storm would break.

16 THE THIRD MISSIONARY JOURNEY

The Crisis in Paul's Career

For the weapons of our warfare are not worldly
but have divine power to destroy strongholds.

2 CORINTHIANS 10:4

A THREE-YEAR PERIOD of labor at Ephesus was drawing to a close. It had no doubt been interrupted by short
journeys, such as the one to Corinth, and others of which we
have no knowledge. It seems incredible that Paul would not
have gone to Smyrna or Miletus when he was so close to these
famous cities. But now new storm clouds were gathering for
Paul—not only in Ephesus itself, but in the East and in the
West—threatening his standing in the Church of Christ and
his very life.

Some of these troubles he had brought upon himself. Being the man he was he could hardly have acted differently.
He had attacked those at Jerusalem who had taken command of the church and were leading it back into the
very spirit of legalism and ritualism against which Jesus
had fought. Paul's stand had aroused the anger of those

at whom the attacks were directed. To what extent James, Peter, and John were involved personally in the opposition to Paul that now rose is obscure. But Paul's ironical allusions to them as "those who were reputed to be something (what they are makes no difference to me; God shows no partiality)"; or "James and Cephas and John, who were reputed to be pillars" (Galatians 2:6, 9) indicates that he did not consider them blameless in the matter. A determined propaganda was aimed against him. Agents went about visiting Paul's congregations and their daughter congregations and sought to undermine his position. He claimed to be an apostle? The Jerusalem church did not recognize him as such.[1] His preaching of freedom from the law was heresy. The law was given to God's people to be obeyed and this first duty of converts was to become members of God's people by circumcision. The agitators were thus standing pat on a position disavowed in Acts 15:24. The agreement made in personal consultation between the leaders at Jerusalem and Paul was being repudiated. Uncertainty and confusion were spreading among the Galatians.

One day a few men who had come from the Galatian congregations brought Paul a report about what was happening. They were, perhaps, the kind friends among whom he had tarried at the time of grievous illness on his journey through the provinces. They desired that Paul should come and counteract the effects of the hostile propaganda. But it was impossible for him to drop his work at Ephesus and spend months traveling those long distances. He decided to write them a letter instead.

Some things about this letter to the Galatians are mysterious. Paul gives no greeting from the church at which he is staying. Was he traveling at the time? He does not even name an associate, though in other letters of this period, Timothy is usually joined with himself in the opening words.

But this omission is very understandable if Timothy was absent on the trip to Corinth (1 Corinthians 16:10). Paul mentions beside himself only the vague "all the brethren who are with me." Ordinarily he addresses a definitely localized congregation; here, however, he is thinking of a number of churches. Galatia clearly cannot be the real name of the area in which Paul preached, according to the description of his travels in Acts, and considerations based on the time available and the distances involved. However, the Celtic people to whom he came may have considered their area a part of Galatia on ethnic grounds. The political separation no longer meant much under Roman rule. Or, perhaps, it is an instance of Paul's occasional grandiloquence which comes to the surface in the address of this letter, just as it does when he speaks of having preached the gospel as far round as Illyricum (Romans 15:19). He had come no nearer to Illyricum than he had to Galatia, but he may have had knowledge that his converts had carried the gospel into Galatia proper and by addressing the letter to the churches of Galatia he may already be counting on a Galatian church. The hellenized Celts near the border would be the natural leaders for the church of Galatia. The address of the letter, then, may be viewed as propagandistic rather than realistic.

The letter was written in great excitement, grief, and anger. The introductory words reveal the defensive posture: "Paul an apostle not from men nor through man but through Jesus Christ." He required no endorsement from anyone.

After a peace greeting, and without the usual thanksgiving found in his other letters, he jumps right into the actual situation. He is astonished at their deserting him and turning to a different teaching—a perversion of the gospel! Like two thunder claps come his curses on anyone, were it himself or an angel from heaven, who would preach a gospel contrary to the one they received from him.[2] For his gospel is not man's gospel but was received by revelation from Christ himself. Paul reminds them that he was following an entirely different conviction, that of Judaism, when this revelation came to him and summoned him to preach Christ to the Gentiles. He then relates the story with which we are already familiar, about his independent missionary work and the only two occasions on which he had contact with the church at Jerusalem in the first seventeen years of his ministry, and about his conflict with Peter at Antioch. He had insisted that men are justified by faith, not by works of the law, and that therefore no such works are to be imposed on Gentile converts.

Against this background Paul sets up his exhortation not to allow anyone to deprive them of their Christian liberty (3:1 ff.). The ritual law of Judaism is not for them. It never was or could be a means of salvation, even for the Jew. It served God's purpose as a disciplinary measure until Christ came. Even in the pre-Christian order there was something that ranked ahead of the law: faith. Paul's proof of that is striking. Abraham's faith was reckoned to him as righteousness (Genesis 15:6) before circumcision was commanded (Gen. 17:9 ff.). The latter, therefore, can be of no significance for salvation. Vivid, too, is his comparison of the life under the law, with the control exercised over the young boy by the pedagogue—the slave entrusted with instructing him and bringing him up. Clever, indeed, is his interpretation of the story of the two sons of Abraham as symbolical of the two covenants, that under which Israel lives and that under which Christians live. It was Paul who first brought out sharply this distinction of two dispensations and perhaps even injected the new covenant allusion into the communion rite.[3]

With all his power of persuasion, Paul tries to make his Galatians see for what a mess of pottage they are selling their birthright in allowing themselves to be influenced in any way by the propagandists for legalism. They themselves have re-

ceived the Holy Spirit. Faith has shown its power in their
lives. And now they would sink back into ritualism? Perish the
thought! In baptism they "put on" Christ, as one dons a new
garment. What a glory is this: all differences between men
disappear in Christ's presence. And Paul rises to one of his
most sublime utterances:

"There is neither Jew nor Greek, there is neither slave nor
free, there is neither male nor female, for you are all one in
Christ Jesus" (3:28).

Out in the world the differences remain. When they go
forth from the charmed circle of Christ, a man is still a man
and a woman a woman, a slave is a slave, a Jew is a Jew and
a Greek is a Greek. The world will not adapt itself to them,
for it is governed by different motives and within its system
they must live their outward lives. But in the fellowship of
those who love Christ, the common allegiance creates a unity
which for a brief moment stands before Paul's mind with
the glory of a snow-crowned mountain.

In a reminiscent mood, Paul reminds the Galatians of the
days when he was among them and of the love they showed
him. He mourns the fact that others have come between
them and exclaims, "My little children with whom I am again
in travail until Christ be formed in you, I wish I could be
present with you now."

The principle that he enunciates is: "For freedom Christ
has set us free." The duty is plain: "stand fast, therefore, and
do not submit to the yoke of slavery." If they accept circumcision they will be severed from Christ. He alludes to an untrue charge that he, too, has at times preached circumcision.
Perhaps the report about his circumcising Timothy (Acts
16:3) was used against him to prove this. He asks: why then
is he persecuted? If anyone preaches circumcision then the
stumbling block of the cross is removed; then one is saved
by circumcision. Overcome with anger at the thought, he

wishes ironically that those unsettling his congregations would mutilate—meaning castrate—themselves. If merits count that ought to be an even more meritorious operation!

But Christian liberty is no invitation to license. It is living by the Spirit and walking by the Spirit. Vividly he sets forth that this means subjugating the flesh. At the same time, however, they are to deal with those who fall into sin with gentleness and humility. Let them sow the good and they will reap accordingly.

Apparently Paul dictated the letter or had it copied by a better penman. But then he added a postscript in his own handwriting. He calls attention to his large letters, perhaps to warrant the authenticity of this letter to its recipients. As an afterthought he asserts that the promulgators of circumcision are putting this demand forward out of fear of the persecution that would befall them at the hands of the Jews if they preached only the crucified Christ. By this means they hope to water down the sharp contrast between Christianity and Judaism. Furthermore, he asserts, they are chiefly interested in being able to "glory in your flesh," i.e., being able to say that they have won proselytes for Judaism. Actually they are not so serious about the law. But Paul glories only in the cross. The essential thing to him is the new creation—the birth of the spiritual man.

But Paul is weary of the whole subject. He expresses the wish that no one trouble him about it in the future, for he bears on his body the "marks" of Jesus (which are like the brands put on a slave, and make him the Lord's property). By those marks he means the scars on his body from the stoning and the beatings he has received, with which he can prove that he serves Christ devotedly, whereas his adversaries deny the Spirit by sticking to ritual laws and seeking to evade such afflictions.

This letter, red-hot from the anvil on which it was forged,

shows us Paul's character with remarkable clarity. He was no stained-glass window saint. Essentially a kind and loving man, he was capable of anger when his basic convictions were at stake. The power of his words, charged as they are with feeling, has rarely been equaled. He was a formidable adversary, and one can scarcely doubt that his letter achieved its purpose of persuading the Galatians to drive out his opponents and remain loyal to the gospel he taught.

But another great worry came to Paul from the west—from Corinth. Timothy had returned from his mission to that city, where he had not only helped to regulate affairs in accordance with Paul's letter, but had started the collection for Jerusalem, which Paul considered so important at this time (1 Corinthians 4:16; 16:1 ff.). But now fresh news was received that strange teachers had come to that congregation and had made an impression with their teaching. Not only that, but they had aroused rebellion against Paul's leadership. The matter was of such concern to Paul that, contrary to his plan of going to Corinth later via Macedonia (1 Corinthians 16:5; 2 Corinthians 1:16), he made an immediate trip across the sea to that city (2 Corinthians 12:14; 13:1). But it proved to be one of the most painful disappointments of his life.

What really happened can only be surmised. It seems that one church member insulted Paul and accused him of being no apostle at all. They were so taken in by these men who sought to undermine Paul's authority, that Paul had to quit the field and return to Ephesus. He touched the depths of despondency at this time. Ingratitude and insult were the rewards for his sufferings and sacrifices.

From Ephesus he wrote the Corinthians a letter "out of much affliction and anguish of heart and with many tears" (2 Corinthians 2:4). He dispatched Titus to Corinth with it, hoping to hear that it would bring about a change of heart there (2 Corinthians 2:13; 7:6,13 ff.). This letter apparently has not been preserved, unless as some believe, it is to be found in the four chapters now standing at the end of 2 Corinthians. They come in surprisingly after that letter was ready for a conclusion at the end of chapter 9.[4]

In the midst of this tremendous emotional strain caused by the situation at Corinth, there descended upon Paul at Ephesus itself happenings which nearly cost him his life. According to the Acts version of the events, the great success of his work in the province of Asia injured the business of the craftsmen who made models of the temple of Artemis (the Diana of the Romans).[5] Visitors to her temple, notably those from other places, may have bought such shrines to take home; others acquired them to give to the temple as votive offerings. The head of the guild engaged in this trade was Demetrius, the silversmith. The author of Acts makes him the prime mover in the happenings. In a speech at a meeting of his guild this man foretold danger for the future of the temple and even the downfall of the goddess from her exalted station.[6] Artemis is grandly called "she whom all Asia and the world worship."

The words of Demetrius inflamed the guild. They raised the cry, "Great is Artemis of the Ephesians." This demonstration, which we may imagine as carried through the streets of the city, led people to run out of their houses. Two of Paul's co-workers, Gaius of Derbe and Aristarchus of Thessalonica, were recognized, seized, and dragged to the theater. This was the natural place for people to assemble when anything of public interest was at issue. The open air theater of Ephesus, still there today, could seat twenty-six thousand people.

Paul wanted to rush to the aid of his helpers, but according to the narrative was prevented by "the disciples" or local Christians. He also received messages from "some of the Asiarchs who were friends of his" not to go to the theater.[7] The Asiarchs were persons in the province of Asia who had the honorary position of looking out for the cult of the goddess Roma and of the deified Roman emperors. Since there were a number of such temples in the province, there was a corresponding number of Asiarchs. It is also probable that ex-Asiarchs kept the honorary title, and there may thus have been several such present at Ephesus—not only the one now in office there. Every reader of Acts would conclude that if the Asiarchs were friends of Paul he certainly was no man whom Rome needed to condemn.

At the theater a leader among the Jews named Alexander now mounted the platform and tried to speak in order to disavow any connection between the Jews and Paul. But so great was the tumult that he could not make himself heard. For two hours the cry continued to roll heavenward, "Great is the Artemis of the Ephesians!"

For the Gentiles there was no reason to differentiate very much between Jews and Christians. The latter were considered by them simply a sect of the Jews. In view of the rising anti-Semitism in the Hellenistic-Roman world, the whole thing threatened to become an anti-Jewish pogrom.

The town clerk ("the scribe," or secretary—the official who, along with the magistrates, was mainly responsible for governing the city) now appeared on the scene. When he addressed the crowd, the noise subsided. He pointed out that Ephesus was the city of Artemis and that there was no question of danger to this cult. If there were grievances of any kind then there were courts of law before which these should be brought. For anything beyond that there was the regular assembly. He warned that popular demonstrations might bring a charge of rioting by the provincial authorities. That—so he implied—could bring the Roman soldiery into action to quell the disturbances. The warning was allegedly effective and the crowd dispersed. Gaius and Aristarchus were no doubt released.

After the uproar ceased Paul is reported to have sent for

"the disciples," (i.e., his congregation), exhorted them, and then left the city.

Luke's story serves to highlight for the reader the impression that Paul's ministry had damaged the Artemis cult and aroused the hostility of the heathen element in Ephesus against him. The consequences of that will appear later. The decline of Artemis may have been even more obvious when Acts was written. Indeed, some decades later, under Hadrian, Rome tried to bolster the cause of this deity by issuing coins bearing the image and name of the Diana Ephesia.

A few words of Paul, written a month or two after he had left Ephesus, reveal that the situation there had been much more dangerous than the Acts account would indicate. Paul writes, "For we do not want you to be ignorant, brethren, of the affliction we experienced in Asia; for we were so utterly, unbearably crushed that we despaired of life itself. Why, we felt that we had received the sentence of death; but that was to make us rely not on ourselves but on God who raises the dead; he delivered us from so deadly a peril" (2 Corinthians 1:8-10).

If Paul had gotten off as easily as the Acts narrative relates (20:1), there would be no basis for such words. What then really happened? Did the story of Philippi repeat itself? Was he haled before the magistrates and was the charge the grave one that Luke has brought in only once thus far, at Thessalonica: "These men . . . are all acting against the decrees of Caesar, saying that there is another king, Jesus" (Acts 17: 7)? Was Paul driven out of the city or did he have a hairbreadth escape? Was it in connection with this crisis that Aquila and Priscilla did the service that he acknowledges that same winter in the words: "Greet Prisca and Aquila, my fellow workers in Christ Jesus, who risked their necks for my life, to whom not only I but also all the churches of the Gentiles give thanks" (Romans 16:30). Was it at this time that Androni-

cus and Junias "men of note among the apostles," who had
become Christians before Paul, were his fellow prisoners (Romans 16:7)—perhaps arrested when they were only passing
visitors? We do not know.

In whatever way he managed to do so, Paul escaped from
Ephesus. He says nothing about what he did, any more than
he tells of his course on leaving Damascus, but only reveals
that he went to Troas to preach the gospel of Christ, and that
a door had opened for him there (2 Corinthians 2:12). He
thus had success and was able to assemble the nucleus of a
congregation at this place. But he was too restless to linger
long owing to his deep concern about Corinth and the failure
of Titus to meet him. When he had sent Titus ahead to that
city, it was evidently with the understanding that he would
soon leave Ephesus himself and that Titus would join him at
Troas for the mission he wanted to carry out in this important
harbor town. So Paul decided to leave Troas and go on to
Macedonia in the hope of meeting Titus sooner (2 Corinthians 2:13).

On arriving in Macedonia, Paul visited all the churches.
Luke reports that he gave them much encouragement (Acts
20:2).

But Paul was not spared further harrowing experiences.
He says, "For even when we came to Macedonia our bodies
had no rest, but we were afflicted at every turn—fighting without and fear within" (2 Corinthians 7:5). The fighting no
doubt was with the Jews, who had by now been inflamed
everywhere in these lands against him and his activities. He
was never safe from personal assault and even assassination.
We can see the faithful men of his congregations forming a
cordon about him to protect him wherever he went. His nervous system was again shaken, as had been the case when he
first came to Corinth alone from Athens.

Would Titus come soon to report? What had happened

at Corinth to delay him? Such questions troubled Paul day and night.

At last there came a turn in all this misfortune. Titus arrived bringing good news (2 Corinthians 7:6 ff.). We may think of him as rejoining Paul at Thessolonica. He was full of joy, and Paul says that he rejoiced more over the joy of Titus than he did over the comfort which the report of Titus brought him.

The pride that Paul had had in his Corinthian congregation and of which he had formerly boasted to Titus was now vindicated. For the letter he had written them, the letter so full of tears and reproach, had struck like a thunderbolt and filled the congregation with mourning. They had, perhaps, meanwhile seen through the false apostles. When Titus had come they had received him with fear and trembling. Paul thought of their grief as a "godly grief"— the kind which produced a repentance that leads to salvation and brings no regret. Titus reported to him how eager they were to clear themselves, how they longed to have the fellowship with their old teacher restored, what measures they took to disavow the insulting treatment he had received during his interim visit.

Paul decided, however, to linger awhile in Macedonia. He had—already from Ephesus—urged all his churches to raise a collection for the Christians in Judea, who to Paul are always "the saints" (or "holy ones"), because they lived in the Holy City and were the nucleus of the holy people of the future. In the new letter which Paul now wrote to Corinth (our 2 Corinthians), he told, among other things, how the grace of God had been shown in the churches of Macedonia, where the people, in spite of their own poverty and the grievous affliction caused by discrimination against them in their communities, had begged earnestly for the favor of being allowed to take part in the collection (8:1-5). Titus, when he found the Corinthians so repentant, had urged them to begin contrib-

uting to it, and Paul was now sending him back to complete
this "gracious work." Let them see to it that they excel in this
respect, too, as much as they do in everything else—in faith,
in utterance, in knowledge, in all earnestness, and in their
love for him (8:6-7).

With Titus were going two men whose names must once
have stood in the text of the letter in 8:18 and 22, but have
since been omitted. One is praised as "famous among all the
churches for his preaching," and as "appointed by the churches
to travel with us in this gracious work"; the other is one whom
Paul has "often tested and found earnest in many matters."
Paul told the Macedonians of the intention of the Corinthians
to raise money and he was sending these men ahead lest, if he
come with some Macedonians and find that little has been
done, he be put to shame for having been so confident. But
while he hoped for generous giving, he wanted it to be entirely
voluntary "for God loves a cheerful giver" (9:17).

Second Corinthians is the most personal letter of Paul, but
at the same time also the most difficult. This is due to the fact
that we do not know circumstances and conditions which were
fully clear to the first readers, and can only guess what lies behind some of his sentences. Paul did not intend to write for
posterity, but only for the particular congregation he was addressing. His purpose in this case was to renew his former
relationship with the Corinthian church and to reestablish his
authority. The letter thus becomes a great apology of his
apostleship. At the same time it involves much polemic
against his detractors.[8]

From the very outset, he bears these objectives in mind
and skillfully addresses himself to them. What an impression
it must have made that he urged the congregation to forgive
and comfort the man who had offended him, lest he be over-
whelmed by excessive sorrow (2:5 ff.). How he must have
pleased them when he declared that, unlike his adversaries, he

needed no letter of recommendation, but regarded the Corinthian church as such a letter, written on their hearts to be known and read by all men (3:1 ff.).

He begins this characterization of his apostolate suddenly in 2:14 with an utterance of thanksgiving.

"But thanks be to God, who in Christ always leads us in triumph, and through us spreads the fragrance of the knowledge of him everywhere. For we are the aroma of Christ to God among those who are being saved and among those who are perishing, to one a fragrance of death to death, to the other a fragrance from life to life" (2:14-16). Paul's ministry is that of a new covenant which has a far greater splendor than that of the old covenant (3:4 ff.). What he preaches is not himself but Christ as Lord, with himself as servant for Jesus' sake. He has the treasure of the knowledge of the glory of God —as seen in the face of Christ—in an earthen vessel (i.e., his fragile body). That is ordained to show that the transcendent power belongs to God. To a man of such a conviction no defeat can be decisive. "We are afflicted in every way, but not crushed; perplexed, but not driven to despair; persecuted, but not forsaken; struck down, but not destroyed" (4:7 ff.).

The experience of a narrow escape from death at Ephesus, and the symptoms of his own physical decline of which he is conscious, lead Paul to think of his hope of eternal life (5: 1-10). He goes beyond 1 Corinthians 15, where his thought remained within the scope of the apocalyptic pattern of the coming of the Son of man, the resurrection, and the judgment. He now thinks in more individual terms of being clothed with the resurrection body at death. But he still carries along the older ideas, as his allusions to resurrection and judgment show (4:14; 5:10).

But Paul swiftly reverts again to his accounting of himself and of his actions. He dwells on the glory of the ministry of reconciliation with God that he is carrying on. He describes himself as servant of God in every way "through great endurance, in afflictions, hardships, calamities, beatings, imprisonments, tumults, labors, watching, hunger; by purity, knowledge, forbearance, kindness, the Holy Spirit, genuine love, truthful speech, and the power of God." He appeals to the Corinthians to widen their hearts toward him, in response to the love he has shown them (6:1-11).

He reaches the supreme heights of his self-defense in the four closing chapters, which so many regard as derived from another of his letters. Here the battle which was seemingly ended is fought all over again and with much sharper weapons. The detailed catalog of his sufferings and hardships (11:24-29), which we need not dwell on here as we have utilized it for the reconstruction of Paul's history, is brought in by way of contrasting himself with his adversaries who by their teachings have escaped the kind of sufferings he experienced at Jewish hands. The entire apology is given in an ironic vein. He is forced to boast, and repeatedly craves indulgence for speaking in foolishness. He calls his rivals "superlative apostles." "Are they servants of Christ? I am a better one—I am talking like a madman—with far greater labors, far more imprisonments, with countless beatings, and often near death" (11:22-23). He boasts, too, of things that show his weakness and which his detractors may have used to heap scorn on him, for instance, his undignified flight from Damascus (11:30 ff.). His culminating boast is of visions and revelations of the Lord. Here he relates as an example—and as though it were another's experience—his mystical journey to paradise (2 Corinthians 12:2-4) and views his physical handicap as imposed on him to keep him from being too elated on account of the revelations granted him (2 Corinthians 12:7-10).

On the basis of such an ironical recital, Paul then comes to a final reckoning with the congregation (12:11 f.). They are not behind other congregations, as the "false apostles" may have insinuated. Only in this are they different, that he did not burden them with supporting him when among them, but provided for himself by the labor of his hands. He is now planning to come to them for a third time and will again remain independent of them. And what he has said is not said for his own sake as defense, but for their sake (12:19 f.). He trusts that when he arrives everything will be straightened out, and that no unpleasantness will result. And he mentions in passing that he trusts he will not again be grieved by the existence of sins of the sort encountered when he wrote 1 Corinthians. When he does come, Christ's power will be with him. He bids them examine themselves, and hopes that he can use his prophet's might to upbuild rather than to destroy (13:10 cf. Jer. 1:10). It is like a final thunderclap after the storm has receded.

One marvels how this man can touch the heartstrings, can shame and humble, praise and encourage. He is the peerless example of the Christian shepherd of souls, in the capacity to stir, move, and manage groups of men. He had new tools of expression derived from Hellenistic popular philosophy and mysticism and could use them on people who were more open-minded and generous-hearted than the stiff-necked and narrow-minded adversaries with whom Jesus had to deal.

The significance of the Corinthian correspondence, like that of the Galatian, is enormous. Paul's struggle with the Galatians was the decisive battle of Asia; that with the Corinthians, the decisive battle of Europe. Thus the crisis was weathered and the flag of Pauline Christianity firmly planted on two continents.

17 THE THIRD MISSIONARY JOURNEY

Corinth and the Letter to the Romans

Our hope is that as your faith increases, our field
among you may be greatly enlarged, so that we
may preach the gospel in lands beyond you.
2 CORINTHIANS 10:15-16

THE MISSION OF TITUS and his companions at Corinth
was successful, and a substantial sum was realized for the
collection for Jerusalem. Paul, therefore, came to Corinth
with his aides and renewed his old relationship with the congregation.[1]

It was during these months at Corinth that he forged
new plans. His mind was now at peace with respect to his
churches, which were co-operating in an undertaking of Christian endeavor. He could think about what new enterprise he
should undertake when he had delivered the collection to
Jerusalem.

It was clear to him that he had done the work of planting
the gospel of Christ in Asia Minor, Macedonia, and Greece.
He was sure that from the centers the Lord had chosen, it

would of itself spread swiftly over the surrounding regions by virtue of the dynamic that was in it and the blessing of God that would attend it. The onrushing kingdom required haste of him in performing similar work where the message had not yet been heard. For he was a pioneer. He complains that he "no longer has any room for work in these regions" (Romans 15:23). His ambition always was to preach the gospel where Christ had not yet been named (Romans 15:20).

In thinking about this hope he had to rule out Italy, for the gospel had been brought to Rome by others. There remained the regions west of Italy. Traditionally, Spain was looked upon as the "end of the earth." There were the pillars of Hercules. To go there would be to carry Christ's message to the uttermost parts. Then Christ could come.

But Paul was also empire-conscious. Since his youth he had longed to visit Rome. As the main traffic between Spain and the East now passed through Rome, he would have to go to Italy. He would at least have to make a courtesy call on the congregation at Rome. Though it had been driven out or underground in the reign of the emperor Claudius, it had been revived after his death in A.D. 54. Paul thus decided to write the Roman Christians a letter. His recent experience with Corinth had led him to anticipate that the same kind of men who had caused disturbances there might go on to Rome to spread their lies. He wanted the Romans to have something in hand with which to judge him before he came, and which they could compare with what others were offering by way of Christian insight. In this way, in case he did not succeed in his plan of a Rome journey, his message would have reached this congregation which, as he foresaw, was the most important for the future of Christianity.[2]

Did Paul know any Christians at Rome? That question seems to be answered for us by the last chapter of the Epistle. It would appear that his friends from Corinth and lately of

Ephesus, Aquila and Priscilla, were in the city on the Tiber. He also greets Epaenetus, his first convert in Ephesus. Had all three fled from that city at the time of Paul's departure? And how could he know and greet so many others so far away? It must strike the reader that the letter seemingly reaches an end in 15:33.[3] Thus the theory that Romans 16:1-24 was not originally part of the letter that went to Rome, but rather was one sent to Ephesus where Paul knew many people, has gained considerable favor. Perhaps it was attached to a copy of the letter to the Romans that was sent to the Ephesian church. Such a supposition would make it understandable that it became part of Romans in the manuscripts.

Whatever the truth of the matter may be, never did a woman carry a more important document than did Phoebe, "a deaconess of the church at Cenchreae" (16:1), if it was this letter which she took to Rome or Ephesus. The significance of the letter may not have been realized by the recipients any more than contemporaries recognized the greatness of Lincoln's Gettysburg address. Time was to elapse and Christian reflection on the heritage of the past had to begin before the power of Romans was fully appreciated as a statement of Christianity by the greatest mind among the early Christian leaders.

We may describe the epistle as a presentation of the gospel of Christ for both Jews and Gentiles.[4] Like Galatians, which gives a preview of Paul's position, it stands in close relationship to the battle he had fought at Jerusalem and more radically at Antioch for the understanding of Christianity. And almost at the outset he formulates his great position in the celebrated words which brought the despairing monk Martin Luther new illumination in his monk's cell and led to the Protestant Reformation:

"I am not ashamed of the gospel: it is the power of God for salvation to everyone who has faith, to the Jew first and also to the Greek. For in it the righteousness of God is revealed through faith for faith, as it is written, 'He who through faith is righteous shall live.' "

The gospel as Paul understands it answers the question of how man can become righteous before God. His own experience has given him the answer that the Pharisaic-Jewish theory of achieving this state by one's own efforts must fail. Man can be accepted as righteous only through God's grace. But Paul sees that grace tied to the person and work of Christ. His own vision of the Lord and the call to become his apostle convinced him that Christ has the supreme place as mediator of salvation. Through him the divine grace is available for sinful man.

This is indeed the unshakable foundation on which Christian religious teaching must be reared. To teach the grace of God without connecting it with the person and work of Christ cannot satisfy Christian needs. This insight is a great contribution made by Paul. It is essential to the life of the church today even if one regards the structure Paul built on as made with materials of ancient thinking in need of modernization.

As he enters on his great discussion, Paul does not remain on the individual level but views the religious history of mankind from a lofty perspective. He first sets forth the unrighteousness of both Jews and Gentiles in their religious history and thus demonstrates that both are under the divine wrath (1:18-3:20). This was hard for Jews to swallow, though Paul is at pains to concede to them that they had a great advantage over the Gentiles in possessing the special revelation of God. Now, however, a new order has begun, in which all, both Jews and Gentiles, can be "justified" or declared righteous by God's grace on the basis of the redemption wrought by Jesus. Through his death on the cross God has made him the means of expiation for sin. This, however, is to be received only through faith (3:21-30). Over against Jewish-Christian objectors who accuse him of putting aside God's law (3:31 here used in the broad sense of "Scripture"), Paul proves again, as in Galatians, that justification through faith was taught before circumcision was introduced; the latter was given only as a seal. Abraham is the spiritual father of all, whether circumcised or uncircumcised (3:31-4:25).

He then sets forth the relation of justification to the Christian hope (5:1-21). The one who is justified can go through life at peace with God certain of his salvation (5:1-11). Thereupon, he gives as background a vaster perspective by developing a parallel between Adam, as first man, and Christ, as inaugurator of a new humanity.[5] As one man's trespass led to condemnation for all men, so one man's act of righteousness leads to acquittal and life for all men. To the Mosaic law he grants only a minor function in the divine plan. It has the effect of increasing sin, but thereby grace abounds all the more (5:12-21). The last assertion was sure to drive any Jewish Christian legalist to object that this was an invitation to sin (5:12-21). He then refutes objection to his emphasis on faith and teaches that the Christian has died to sin; how then can we still live in it? His proof for this operates with symbolical interpretation of the rite of baptism, the immersion representing death and the coming out renewed life (6:1-14). He rejects, too, the idea that if we are no longer under the law, we may do as we please (6:15-23).

Paul can now show that the old order of morality and the new Christian order are different (7:1-6). But here he has to defend himself once more against the charge that he is defaming God's law. In that connection, he develops a view of the tragic situation of the unjustified man, whose innermost self, which desires to serve the law of God, is thwarted by the flesh, which tends toward evil and which the unregenerate will cannot control (7:7-25). The final development of the theme is carried through by setting forth the glory of the life of the justified man, culminating in the mighty declaration:

"I am sure that neither death nor life, nor angels, nor principalities, nor things present, nor things to come, nor powers, nor height, nor depth, nor anything else in all creation will be able to separate us from the love of God in Christ Jesus our Lord" (8:1-39).

Therewith a great discussion is ended. Paul has by no means sought to set up a system of Christian doctrine, for he makes no attempt to deal with all the topics belonging under that head. He has rather given a treatment of a single theme viewed as central.

In the continuation of the letter he deals first with a subject close to his heart and of great interest to men of Jewish descent in the Roman congregation: the problem of Israel's salvation (5:9-11). He does not give up hope for the conversion of his people, though he sees it as taking place only after the predestined quota of the Gentiles has been attained. As he contemplates the mysterious historical process, he breaks out into his great adoration of the divine wisdom, terminating in a doxology:

"O the depth of the riches and the wisdom and knowledge of God! How unsearchable are his judgments and how inscrutable his ways! . . . For from him and through him and to him are all things. To him be glory for ever. Amen."

In the final portion of the letter (12:1-15:13), he gives exhortations for the Christian life, such as would naturally occur to an experienced teacher of men. They do credit to his vision of the format of Christian character which he was seeking to develop in his churches. Of far-reaching consequences was his directive to be subject to governing authorities (13:1-7). That he could enjoin such obedience and loyalty to a pagan state and have pride in his Roman citizenship, as we have seen manifested in the Acts narrative, is a cause for reflection. He can hardly have been under any illusion as to the basic conflict between Christianity and the state. His Jewish elasticity, the product of his people's long experience in anti-Semitic persecution, may have taught him wisdom and restraint. He would have held that if the state becomes hostile, one can but hope and pray that God will bring about a change in his own time. A letter containing his teaching on the state could only commend him to pagan Romans.

Paul had evidently heard of peculiar teachings that were causing difficulty in the Roman congregation. Some members were exponents of vegetarianism, others of the observance of certain days (perhaps fast days). Paul urges mutual tolerance with avoidance of judging or condemning the other in these matters. He regards all such things as belonging to the sphere of individual liberty, but considers each person responsible to God.

It would be difficult to estimate the impact on Christian history of all those thoughts which Paul set down during those winter days at Corinth. For this was no dictated letter; it was written thoughtfully and slowly by his own hand. It was carefully planned, and weeks must have gone into its preparation. Through this letter to the Romans, Christianity received an intellectual presentation which gave it a standing in the world for ages to come. It moved the Old Testament away from being exclusively a possession of the Jew and appropriated it for Christianity, while at the same time invalidating the ceremonial elements found in it.[6] Jewish Christianity as represented by James and the Jerusalem church could now decline and perish. And Peter only maintained his high place by the efforts of the generation that followed him to represent him as having spoken and thought like Paul and in effect to make him an apostle of the Gentiles.

Romans may be the last preserved letter from the pen of Paul—if one discounts the "Pastorals" (1–2 Timothy and

Titus) as only written in his name, and puts the captivity letters in the Ephesian period of his ministry. It could be regarded as his last word. The Paul of this letter is in a more tranquil mood than the man whom we see in the other letters, in which he is struggling for the souls of his converts, while under attack from foes and beset by privations. The ship of his life is temporarily in a quiet harbor. But to him this is only a halfway station. The sea is calling him to new travels.

The legacy of Paul's letters was indispensable to the church. The four Gospels require their support. It was Paul who told the world the meaning of Christ.

But the letters also have a place in the history of literature. For the first time letters that reveal a real man come to the fore in the Greek language. The writing of the period was artificial and stilted, bent on imitating models of a classical age long past. "At last," says a famous classicist, "someone speaks again in Greek of a fresh inner existence. That is his faith, and in it he is certain of his hope. And his love embraces all humanity: to bring it salvation he will gladly sacrifice himself. Fresh life of the soul sprouts forth wherever he goes. He writes his letters as a substitute for personal contact. The style is Paul—no one but Paul. It is not a private letter that he writes, and yet not a literary one; it is. inimitable, though often imitated. Paul cared nothing about literature; he had no artistic vein in his makeup. But all the more must one esteem the artistic effect that he nevertheless achieves."[7]

Let him who would see a cringing flatterer read Ovid's letters from his dreary exile in Pontus. Let him who would see a lawyer and statesman of the old world read the letters of Cicero. Let him who would see a servant of God read the letters of Paul.

18 THE THIRD MISSIONARY JOURNEY

The Return to Palestine

The God of peace be with you all. Amen.
ROMANS 15:33

THE WINTER AT CORINTH was over. Paul was going to Jerusalem to present the offerings. A delegation from his churches had come to Corinth and would travel with him. There was a representative of the church of Beroea, and one from Thessalonica, two men from Asia-province, besides his longtime followers, Timothy and Gaius of Derbe. It is strange that no Corinthian representative was added to the number. As the book of Acts never mentions Titus at all we are left to wonder whether he too went.

Navigation opened on the fifth of March. Since thousands of Jews wanted to go to the Passover once in their lives there must have been many sailings around that date from various ports. If the Passover did not fall too early, it was possible to make the trip from Corinth to Caesarea with the aid of the prevailing westerly winds in time to be there for the festival.

No doubt Paul originally wanted to go as a Passover pilgrim. But as he was about to leave, his friends learned of a plot of the Jews to kill him. He therefore decided to go by land through Macedonia.[1] At Philippi he sent Tychicus and Trophimus on ahead to Troas to find a boat for his party while he and the others stayed there for a few days. It is at this point that a second "We-section" of Acts (20:5-8, 13-16) cuts in. The author was one who traveled with Paul and may have joined him at Philippi.

Paul was able to spend the feast of "the Unleavened Bread" at Philippi. It evidently was not particularly associated as yet in the Christian mind with the resurrection of Jesus, for if it had been, one could expect mention of the fact. After the festival Paul and his companions sailed from Neapolis for Troas. On arriving there they found their companions who had, of course, been received hospitably by the local Christians, waiting for them.

In the story of the stay at Troas we get a first allusion in Christianity's history to a Sunday service (20:6). It was held in the evening, in the third and upper story of a private house, where it was airy and pleasant. The narrator notes that there were many lights in the room. It was the night before the intended departure for Jerusalem, which Paul hoped to reach by Pentecost.

In new movements, full of zeal and enthusiasm, long speeches are the order of the day. That Paul spoke until midnight thus was not unexpected or wearisome to his hearers.

A very secular-sounding report of a startling event that took place during this service has been introduced here by Luke (Acts 20:9-12). A young man named Eutychus, who had fallen asleep in the window-seat during Paul's discourse, fell out to the ground. He was taken up dead, says the narrative. However, Paul went down, and embracing him, said to those with him, "Do not be alarmed, for his life is in him." The upshot of it was that they were able to take Eutychus

away alive. It is left hazy whether this was a case of restoring
a dead person to life, or whether the youth had been only
unconscious. Luke probably believed the former to have been
the case and related the incident at this juncture, where Paul
is winding up his ministry as traveling missionary, to leave
upon the mind of the reader an impression of his wonder-
working power.[2]

Rather strangely, Paul did not board the ship at Troas
with the others, but went alone by land to Assos, where the
ship was to stop and receive him. He knew the route, either
from his initial visit to Troas or from his more recent one,
when he fled from Ephesus.

But what was his motive for this lone walk? Did he again
suspect that there might be an assassin on board and was he
giving his associates time to get fully acquainted with the
passengers and crew? Or was he just in need of being alone
for a while with his thoughts and his God? One can only
wonder. The distance was some twenty miles, which could be
covered in a day's march. At the promontory of Lecton the
road which had run westward circled to the east and kept
along the gulf of Adramyttium. On the left were the Mysian
Mountain ranges with the Mysian Olympus and out in the
sea was the lovely isle of Lesbos.

As he neared his destination, Paul saw before him a high,
cone-shaped hill, on which was situated the acropolis of Assos.
No city of Asia Minor could vie with it in beauty of location.
The acropolis was crowned by an ancient temple dedicated to
the goddess Athena. The city was surrounded by a wall nearly
two miles in circumference. The market place with a colonnade on its north side lay directly below the acropolis. Farther
to the south was the theater, from which the spectator's eyes
could wander over the coastline to Lesbos. Part of the very
gateway through which Paul must have passed in going to the
harbor is still there, as is the mole on which his feet must

have stood when he embarked on the ship and rejoined his companions.

Following the custom of the ancients in these waters, Paul's ship traveled only by day, and anchored in a cove or in the lee of some island overnight. The skippers making regular runs had their favorite stopping places, and secured fresh water and provisions from the local populations at some of these spots.

The ship went from Assos to Mytilene, where it anchored for the night. This was the largest city of Lesbos, the home of many famous people, but above all of the poetess Sappho, of whose lyrics only a few fragments have come down. Strabo says of her that in the whole history of thought there was no woman who could be compared with her for achievement in the poetic art. That Paul had heard of her can scarcely be doubted. She had sung of a friendship of women for each other, surpassing the love of men. Evil-minded detractors of the future twisted this to mean female homosexuality which then got its name of lesbianism from the island of Lesbos.

The second day they came opposite the island of Chios on which they could see the Heraeum, or Hera temple, famed for its marvelous sculptures and paintings. On the third day they made Samos, the home of King Polycrates, of the poet Anacreon, and of Pythagoras, whose sayings were as authoritative to his followers as those of Christ were to become for Christians, and were cited with the formula *autos epha*—"he said." On the fourth day they reached Miletus, home of Thales and Anaximander, the historian Hecataeus and the orator Aeschines. Two marble lions of huge size stood at the entrance of the particular harbor, which ships coming from the north would enter.

Why had Paul bypassed Ephesus? The author of Acts gives a reason: because he wanted to be at Jerusalem before Pentecost. But Paul sends from Miletus to Ephesus and summons the elders of the church to come there to see him. This was a more time-consuming arrangement than a stop at Ephesus would have been. We may safely assume that Paul could not risk entering Ephesus after the recent happenings which had compelled him to leave the city. He might have been arrested and his whole trip would have been in jeopardy. The safety of the money the party was carrying may also have been a factor in his decision.

Miletus lay at the western end of the great Maeander River valley. It was originally one of the most famous cities of Asia Minor, but since its destruction by Alexander the Great, in whose time it supported the Persians, it had declined to second rank. Traffic now went mainly through Ephesus. There were Jews there, of course. In the theater they even had a reserved section marked by an inscription that has been preserved: "Place of the Jews, who are also called god-fearers"[3]—evidently proselytes, who did not want to give up their enjoyment of drama.

How would Paul have gotten word to the elders of Ephesus, and how long would it have taken for them to come to Miletus? Sir William Ramsay figures out that a messenger would have left in the early afternoon taking advantage of the sea-breeze that arises at that time and sailed across the gulf to the city of Priene. From here he would have crossed the hills of the peninsula and taken the coast road to Ephesus. He could have reached the city during the night. The elders, he thinks, would have done well to have reached Priene by evening and to have sailed across the gulf to Miletus with the morning wind. Thus if Paul had arrived in Miletus on a Thursday, it would have been Sunday or Monday before he could leave.[4]

The scene of the parting at the harbor of Milctus is one of the most impressive in Acts and Luke wanted it to be that. It represents the close of a great chapter in Paul's life: his mighty mission work in Europe and Asia Minor. The narrator knew what Paul did not yet know, that his traveling ministry was over. It is for this reason that he here has Paul give a farewell address[5] to the elders of the church of Ephesus, which he regarded as Paul's most important congregation. He lets his own admiration for Paul and his knowledge of what has happened since that day enter into those stirring words. And as usual he adds a few bits of information not previously revealed in the narrative.

Paul reminds the elders of the way in which he had served the Lord in their midst with all humility and amid tears and trials which befell him, and how he taught in public and from house to house. He now is going to Jerusalem, bound in the spirit. He is under a higher compulsion; he must go. He does not know what will come to pass, but wherever he has recently visited a congregation since leaving Corinth, inspired men have gotten up and declared that imprisonment and afflictions were in store for him if he went to Jerusalem. This comes as a complete surprise, for no such prophesies have been mentioned at such suitable occasions as the stops in Macedonia and Troas.

The reader is shaken by the situation revealed here. What is this divine compulsion resting upon Paul to go, and the strange counteraction of the Holy Spirit through prophecy, seeking to deter him from going? It is a conflict of spiritual forces worthy of the pen of Euripides.

But Paul declares that he heeds not the external warnings. He follows an inner necessity. He brushes off the warnings by saying that he does not count his life as of any value or even as precious to himself. He lives only for a single objective: to accomplish his foreordained course and the ministry which he received from the Lord Jesus, namely, to testify to the gospel of the grace of God.

The elders of Ephesus will not see his face again. He has

given them the gospel fully and holds himself blameless if they deviate from it. He points out to them their responsibility before God. With prophetic anticipation that could remind one of Jesus speaking to his disciples of the fall of Jerusalem as he stood on the Mount of Olives, Paul warns them of wolves that will come into the flock from the outside and of men out of their own midst who will try to gain a following. This no doubt reflects what had actually come to pass at Ephesus by the time Acts was written. It filled Luke with grief to see the congregation for which Paul had labored and suffered rent with dissension.

In his address Paul mentions the duration of the Ephesian ministry: for three years he did not cease night or day from admonishing them with tears. He sought no profit. With his own hands he ministered to the necessities of himself and those who were with him. In all things he has shown them that by so toiling one must help the weak, remembering a saying of Jesus, "it is more blessed to give than to receive."

Thus the ministry of Paul stands before the mind in heroic proportions.

And now there comes the final parting. In the light of morning, as the breeze comes up, the ship is ready to depart. We see Paul kneeling there on the shore praying with them all. They wept as they embraced their beloved teacher, and they kissed him farewell. They were deeply moved by his words that they would never see his face again.

We see Paul embarking with his party. There was something knightly in his bearing. Had he worn shining armor he could have been no more of a soldier of God than he was in his teacher's garb. The sails were hoisted, the ship started to move out into the bay. The little group on the shore grew smaller. The grim lions at the harbor entrance said a menacing farewell.

At this juncture in the journey the third "We-section"

(Acts 21:1-18) is utilized. The next stop, we learn, was at Cos, memorable as the home of Hippocrates and his school of medicine. Opposite Cos was Halicarnassus rising in terraces from the sea. It gave the world the historian Herodotus. It had, however, been destroyed by Alexander the Great and had never regained its status of glory. There was a Jewish community at Halicarnassus and a decree of the Romans had guaranteed its freedom when that was threatened by the Gentile population.

The next day the ship made Rhodes, once one of the most glorious places of all time. The great city planner, Hippodamus of Miletus, had founded the new Rhodes of that day. It had the shape of a theater, and possessed three harbors. Its celebrated Colossus had been one of the seven wonders of the world. Doubtless Paul and his companions saw this immense statue of the sun-god lying prostrate like the statue of Dagon at Ashdod, tipped over by an earthquake and broken off at the knees. It had not been raised again owing to the advice of an oracle. Rhodes had once been famous for its naval power, its commerce, its just and efficient government, and for a citizenry that looked out for the poor in its midst.

From Rhodes they sailed to Patara, which lay beyond the mouth of a river that vessels could ascend to the city of Xanthus. Patara was the most important harbor of Lycia and had a noted temple of Apollo. In this bay in 182 B.C. the Rhodian fleet had paralyzed the fleet of Antiochus III the Great, which was commanded by Hannibal.

At Patara the travelers found a ship bound for Phoenicia and changed to it. Continuing down the coast they must have seen the "holy promontory" and the Chelidonian or "swallow" islands before it. Here Alexander's army had had to wade in water waist high in order to pass the headland. As the ship entered the Pamphylian Sea, where there was great peril if a south wind came up, they could see Mt. Solyma, lifting its snow-crowned head 7,800 feet into the sky. But soon the ship veered off—possibly after a stop at Myra—to take a course leaving Cyprus to the north and made directly for Tyre. They reached it in two days. At this famous city, which had long since recovered from its destruction by Alexander in 332 B.C., there was a Christian group. Paul and his companions were able to visit them, since the ship tarried for seven days to unload and take on cargo. Here, again, Paul was warned not to go to Jerusalem. When the ship was ready to continue its voyage, the congregation, including women and children, conducted the visitors to the harbor. And there they all knelt down and prayed and then bade one another farewell. The occasion is memorable for the mention of children, who have hitherto been unnoticed in the Acts narrative of Paul's ministry.

It took another day for the ship to reach Ptolemais, the Acco of an earlier age and the Acre of the Crusades. This appears to have been the final destination. From here it was a march of thirty-seven miles to Caesarea involving a crossing of the Carmel Range, and this certainly would have required an overnight stop.

At Caesarea they came to the home of Philip, "one of the seven" whom Acts described as "deacons." Philip had four daughters who were gifted with the spirit of prophecy. They no doubt foresaw that Paul's trip to Jerusalem would be disastrous for him. But Luke, perhaps deterred by some faint knowledge of Paul's dislike of female "prophesying" (1 Corinthians 14:34), prefers to have a man voice the warning. Agabus, who had already been introduced at an earlier occasion (Acts 11:27), came down from Jerusalem and, in the manner of an Old Testament prophet, performed a symbolic act with Paul's girdle or sash. He first wrapped it around his own feet and then around his own hands and declared, "Thus says the Holy Spirit, 'So shall the Jews at Jerusalem bind the

man who owns this girdle and deliver him into the hands of
the Gentiles' " (Acts 21:11).

It was a dramatic scene. We see Paul's companions and
the Caesarean Christians begging Paul not to go up to Jerusalem, but to send the representatives with the collection
while he stayed at Caesarea.

What should Paul do? He had acted under the Holy Spirit
in gathering money for the poor in Jerusalem. The same Spirit
had led him to ask the congregations to send representatives
with him to the Holy City. Should he, their leader, draw back
in cowardly fashion at the last moment? Should he send the
men and the money with Timothy acting as his substitute?
But he had felt some uncertainty as to whether the Jerusalem
group would accept the collection in spite of its poverty
(Romans 15:31). Misunderstanding and prejudice had been
built up. Timothy might meet refusal and Paul's congregational representatives might be disappointed. The whole status
of his life's work would be in peril. He did not even dare to
reveal this concern to the kind-hearted Gentile Christians
whom he was leading. He alone knew the situation and the
men at Jerusalem.

The pillars, James, Peter, and John, had committed themselves to a recognition of his work among the Gentiles with
only the proviso that he remember the poor of Jerusalem.
They had given him their hands in a pledge of agreement.
Neither Peter nor John were there now; James was the only
one on hand, the real head of the church. The whole situation
demanded that he, Paul, as apostle of the Gentiles, be at the
head of his group and meet James face to face. The Spirit
of the Lord had not forbidden him to go, but had promised
personal misfortune if he went. The same Spirit, he knew, was
driving him to go with inexorable force. There could be no
turning back.

Surrounded by those who loved him and wept at the

thought of misfortune befalling him, their great, irreplaceable leader, Paul cried out: "What are you doing, weeping and breaking my heart? For I am ready not only to be imprisoned but to die at Jerusalem for the name of the Lord Jesus."

Realizing that his purpose was unalterable, his friends desisted, and resigned themselves to whatever might come.

One must wonder why these same Christians did not in their prayers ask the Lord to preserve his faithful servant and spare him for his great work that he might carry the gospel to the ends of the earth. Paul had even asked the distant Roman Christians to pray for his deliverance from the unbelievers in Judea (Romans 15:31). Such a consideration will suggest that Luke, who knew the outcome when he wrote, has shaped the story in the spirit of a historical tragedy, like that of the seventh book of the great history of Thucydides.[6] The reader is made to feel that the onrushing fate will engulf Paul and to shudder in advance over what the future will disclose.

19 IN THE HOLY CITY

But their minds were hardened; for to this day,
when they read the old covenant, that same
veil remains unlifted.

2 CORINTHIANS 3:14

ACCOMPANIED BY A few of the Christians of Caesarea,
Paul and his party went up to Jerusalem. Some of his companions were worried after so many ominous prognostications.
Paul's serenity, however, soon led them to put these thoughts
out of their minds. With eagerness they looked forward to
reaching the goal of their long journey.

The idea of visiting Holy Places associated with the life
of Jesus had not yet arisen. There is no mention of their
noticing Golgotha, where had stood the cross about which
Paul had preached so much. For Paul the drama of Christ
had taken place on a high stage, the earthly background of
which was of little importance.

The visitors were taken to the home of Mnason (to Jews,
Manasseh) who is called "an old disciple," a Cypriote, and
thus a countryman of Barnabas. Here they were able to lodge,
and found a friendly welcome from others who had been em-

215

pire Jews but were now Hellenistic Christians living at the Holy City of their dreams.

Paul was aware that it might be unwise for him to stay at his sister's house, lest his presence in the city become known. But he sent her a messenger apprising her of his coming and expressing his intention of paying her and her family a visit after dark. He was happy to see them and he rejoiced over the eldest son, who had now grown to be a youth almost as old as Paul had been when he first came to Jerusalem. Soon he was going to Tarsus to stay with his grandparents.

Paul's brother-in-law was well informed about what went on among the Christians as well as among the Jews, and gave Paul helpful information. His sister wept, as she bade him farewell; her intuition told her that she would never see him again. From her point of view his life had been a misspent and tragic one.

Paul's most urgent task was to confer with James, and an appointment for such a meeting had been arranged for him by his host.

The very next day, therefore, he went, attended by his fellow travelers, and found James and the elders awaiting them. After greeting them and introducing his congregational representatives, Paul "related one by one the things that God had done among the Gentiles through his ministry" (Acts 21:19). The accounting he felt obliged to give shows the great importance he attached to this occasion. He was seeking to prove that he had acted in accordance with the agreement made with Peter, James, and John. One might think it was a masterstroke of diplomacy that he did not stress what he had done but rather what God had done through him; but this required no pretense on his part. It was always Paul's way to view God as the prime mover and himself as the instrument in every success. His recital was, of course, in the Aramaic tongue; hence his companions could only be dimly

aware of what he was saying from the mention of the names
of cities or regions.

Did Paul come to the point and quote the prophecies of
how the Gentiles would bring gifts to Jerusalem in the latter
days? Did he then have the representatives of his churches lay
down their bags of silver coin before the feet of James and
the elders? The Acts narrative has as yet not said a word
about the collection. So far we know of it only from Paul's letters. But this was certainly the occasion to present it. The
reader is left to wonder whether the tender would be accepted,
since Paul expressed such uncertainty about it.

James and the elders, as responsible men, would naturally
be reluctant to affront Paul's Gentile representatives, who
were paying honor to Christ and to the mother Church by
traveling over land and sea to deliver the fruits of sacrificial
giving.

The dire poverty of much of the Jerusalem church membership, too, recommended acceptance. Gentile money was
like a heavenly rain on a parched land. Yet the elders were
not disposed to accept it without exacting a price from Paul
that could seriously embarrass him in the eyes of his own ecclesiastical representatives. They would require him to prove that
he was a good Jew as well as a Christian.

Speaking with authority, James told Paul what the council
of the elders had already approved of in advance.

"You see, brother, how many thousands there are among
the Jews of those who have believed; they are all zealous for
the law, and they have been told about you that you teach all
the Jews who are among the Gentiles to forsake Moses, telling
them not to circumcise their children or observe the customs.
What then is to be done? They will certainly hear that you
have come."

Thus speaks the brother of the Lord, the Christian caliph,
whose kinship with the founder of Christianity gave him a

vast prestige in the church of that Oriental world. He implies
that the Christians of Judea detest Paul as much as do the
Jews. He speaks with inflated authority. What are Paul's hundreds against the Jewish Christian missionary achievement of
gathering in thousands?

But then James presents the suggestion that can rehabili-
tate Paul and make his presence at Jerusalem less obnoxious.
"Do therefore what we tell you. We have four men who
are under a vow; take these men and purify yourself along
with them and pay their expenses, so that they may shave
their heads.[1] Thus all will know that there is nothing in what
they have been told about you, but that you yourself live in
observance of the law."

It was either a demand that he adapt his personal life to
Jewish law and henceforth enforce the latter on those of Jewish extraction or an invitation to dissimulate for a momentary
advantage. As though the former were the objective, James
adds that he need have no worry for his Gentile converts.
Nothing is required of them except what was set forth in the
decree of the Apostles (Acts 15:23-29), mention of which is
introduced as though it were something new to Paul.

The author of Acts has carefully prepared the way for this
moment in order to veil the extent of Paul's embarrassment.
He has accepted and worked into his narrative two helpful
items: the circumcision of Timothy and the vow at Cenchreae
(Acts 16:3; 18:18). The reader is thus willing to credit the
idea that it was a slander if Paul was accused of teaching
Jewish Christians living among the Gentiles that they were
not obligated to keep the Jewish law.

Nor would he feel that Paul was acting inconsistently in
accepting the proposition James made to him. But this diplo-
matic history-writing veils the true situation of that day.

Actually, the report about what Paul taught the Jews in
his congregations was true. He recognized no Jewish nation-

ality in the congregation of Christ. All were one. The laws and ceremonies belonged to the pre-Christian order. If closed communities of Jews in Palestine wanted to keep them up out of habit, that was their privilege, but it had no bearing on salvation and could be no obligation for Jewish Christians in Gentile lands or in mixed congregations. "For in Christ Jesus neither circumcision nor uncircumcision is of any avail, but faith working through love" (Galatians 15:6).

What should Paul do in that instant when the eyes of all were upon him, and the brother of the Lord Jesus according to the flesh put the proposition to him as the bags of money lay as yet unaccepted at his feet? Should he consent to do what was asked of him? One can see a glint of irony in the eyes of one or the other of the elders, as they thought of how Paul had accused Peter of having acted hypocritically at Antioch. Would Paul not be a hypocrite, too, in agreeing to do such a work of the law that had the sole purpose of storing up merits before God? How would the representatives of his churches regard it? They could as yet hardly know what the proposition was, but it must have been evident to them that something was being urged on Paul that he did not like.

The time element, too, was most inconvenient. Paul was hoping to leave Jerusalem after celebrating the Pentecost. The sooner he got away the better it would be for him. He may have intended to visit Antioch to present his delegation to the brethren there. But if he yielded to the request of James he would be tied down at Jerusalem for a whole week.

In the split second available for a decision, a man can only fall back on his instinct. James had not yet accepted the collection. If Paul did not comply he might not do so. Paul could not afford to have the offering of his congregations rejected. The calamity that could be occasioned by a refusal on his part to accede to James' demand would have effects reaching into the future. Paul had taught the Corinthian church that idol sacrifices were really nothing since the gods they represented had no existence, but that one should nevertheless consider the weaker brethren who still regarded them superstitiously and refrain from exercising one's Christian liberty for their sake (1 Corinthians 8:4-12). In like manner, he now could regard such vows as devoid of value and his participation in their fulfillment as an act performed merely to avoid offending these narrow-minded Jerusalem Christians. His one goal was to win men for Christ. He had proclaimed it himself: he was a Jew to the Jew and a Greek to the Greek, as the circumstances required (1 Corinthians 9:20).

He extended his hand to James and James took it. The agreement was made. But destiny was at the helm. The decision was to cost Paul liberty and life; and for James, too, this hour was to have consequences that were hidden as yet from his eyes.

When Paul went forth from the meeting he had to explain to his companions what had taken place. The one most concerned was Timothy, who wanted to see Paul quit Jerusalem without delay. The others were content with what Paul had done, and as Gentiles were on too unfamiliar ground to see very clearly into the situation that had confronted him.

The next day we may suppose was Pentecost—a Greek word meaning "fifty." The Hebrew name of the occasion 'Asereth, or its Aramaic one, 'Asarta, meant "conclusion." The one-day festival actually marked the end of the season that began with Passover. It was a thanksgiving festival for the grain harvest. A loaf made of wheat flour was brought to God as offering by all who celebrated.[2] The sacrifice brought at the Temple was followed by a joyous meal at home.

The next day Paul must have gone with his four indigent wards to the Temple to establish the date of their payment of vows and to be told of the purification requirement resting upon him. This included the utterance of a formula by him such as "Behold the sin and guilt offerings of so and so shall lie upon me." To be a temporary Nazirite by means of a vow required a period of thirty days—if longer, the period had to be stated. The men must thus have declared their intention to fulfill a vow that much earlier. During that period a man did not have his hair cut. He was forbidden to touch wine and had to avoid defilement, especially contact with the dead. Since Paul came out of the Gentile world, he was too unclean to enter the innermost Temple court because it was to be feared that he had had contact with the dead. Even to get near a tomb was enough to defile a person according to prevailing teachings. It was well known that the roads near heathen cities were so lined with tombs that it was almost impossible to avoid them. Hence, it was necessary for Paul to purify himself before he could go with the Nazirites when they brought their offering. They too had to purify themselves for having contact with him. All this required seven days. During that time they had to go twice—namely, on the third and seventh days—to be sprinkled with water of purification (Numbers 19:9 f.). The sacrifices could then be offered and the hair of the four votaries shorn immediately after that last sprinkling.

Paul's Nazirites turned out to be very humble men. He wondered a bit why they had made their vows coincide so closely in expiration date with Pentecost. They declared that there were many visitors to the city at that time and that there were always some who were looking for an opportunity to do a charitable work. As they were simple men, he dealt with them kindly, as was his wont.

The passage of time until the seventh day must have been very trying to Paul's patience. James had not minced his words in telling him how hated he was, and so Paul had decided to be as careful as possible in keeping out of sight.

The first trip to the Temple on the third day to be sprinkled with holy water was made without incident.

At last the seventh day came, and if all went well he would leave Jerusalem on the morrow. He and his Nazirites again went to the Temple. At the steps to the court of the women, the inscription, that he had read when he first visited the Temple as a youth, met his eye. It suddenly loomed like a raised finger of warning. He paused for a moment, but his companions were pressing him forward. He was committed, and there was nothing to do but to go on. They went to the place where they were sprinkled for the second time and, then, after Paul had made the pledged payment, entered the innermost court, where the altar for the sacrificial ceremonies stood.

Here, unhappily, it occurred that Paul was recognized by Jewish pilgrims from Ephesus. They had met Trophimus, Paul's Ephesian companion, in the city, and so knew that Paul was there, too. To see this hated enemy in the sacred precincts gave them a golden opportunity to destroy him. The cry, "Temple violator," rang out—the accusation that he had brought a Gentile into the Temple. That it was untrue did not matter to these foes. A scene was thus stirred up, and Paul was dragged out of the inner court.

Pandemonium reigned in the Temple. The fanaticism aroused was like that which had prevailed at the temple of Artemis in Ephesus (Acts 19:28 ff.). The Roman sentry on the Antonia fortress, who could survey the Temple courts from his post, must at once have reported that there was a riot and the tribune and soldiers rushed to the scene. The Jews desisted from beating Paul, but he allegedly was arrested and bound with two chains—a vindication of the prophecy of Agabus (Acts 21:11).

The tribune's inquiries of the crowd brought only confused answers. He ordered Paul to be brought to the Antonia, while the crowd pressed on behind shouting "away with him." Paul, we are told, had to be carried up the steps by the soldiers "because of the violence of the crowd."

When Paul spoke to the tribune, the officer was surprised that he could speak Greek and asked, "Are you not the Egyptian, then, who recently stirred up a revolt and led the four thousand men of the Assassins out into the wilderness?"

He was alluding to an event which had happened recently in the governorship of Felix (about A.D. 55). A false prophet had gathered people out in the wilderness and then had led them to the Mount of Olives in the fantastic expectation that the city walls would collapse at his word. The Roman soldiers had slaughtered many, but the "prophet" had escaped.[3]

In replying to the tribune, Paul revealed where he was from and allegedly asked for permission to address the crowd. When it was given, he extended his hand in the orator's gesture and the crowd subsided.[4]

One would expect Paul to assure the crowd with solemn oath that he was wrongly accused of Temple desecration. Instead he launches forth into a general apologetic of his life. The steps leading down into the Temple must have seemed to Luke an especially appropriate point for such a discourse. For when he wrote his story, the Temple had fallen and Jerusalem was destroyed. Paul's speech thus was a last call to Israel. He spoke in Hebrew, which as previously noted means the Aramaic language. He addressed the audience as "brethren" and "fathers," requesting them to hear his defense.

Paul now reveals something of his personal history: his zeal for Pharisaism; his persecution of the Christian "Way"; his conversion and its sequel (interestingly varied from the first report). He relates, too, the completely new item about a vision he had had here in this very Temple and the word of the Lord given to him at that occasion that the Jews would not accept him but that he should go to the Gentiles.

Mention of the latter created a fresh outbreak and the cry arose, "Away with this fellow from the earth! For he ought not to live."

They waved their garments and threw dust in the air—actions which indicated their abhorrence of the man and of what he had said.[5]

The tribune ordered Paul to be taken into the fortress and to be examined by scourging—the ancient equivalent of our "third degree." A lower officer, a centurion, was to supervise the inquest. When they were tying him up preparatory to this procedure, Paul protested against such treatment on the ground of being a Roman citizen. The centurion had to report this to the tribune, who had to come again to verify it. It seemed incredible to him since he himself had bought this citizenship for a large sum. Paul now revealed that he not only was a citizen but had been born one. The man was greatly impressed and even worried over the fact that he had bound him. This exchange heightens further the reader's appreciation of the value of Roman citizenship, which had already been conveyed to the mind by the story of the happenings at Philippi. Paul, so the author of Acts indicates, was not in any way disloyal to Rome. He gloried in his empire citizenship and appreciated the long arm of Rome that enforced respect for its law everywhere. Presumably, a man's Roman name was the chief evidence of his citizenship, but verification of the claim must have taken place where a person's identity was not known.

It is rather strange that the tribune does not investigate the cause of the riot against Paul or ask him for an explanation of what had occurred. Actually, he must have done so, and the Acts story is vulnerable for failing to relate it. But Luke wants to lift the arrest of Paul to a higher plane in order to introduce another vivid scene: an appearance before the council or Sanhedrin, the governing body of the Jews.

Allegedly, the occasion is arranged by the tribune and is conducted in his presence—all for the purpose of finding out "the real reason of why the Jews accused him" (Acts 22:30).

This again is an impressive staging: Paul's case, like that of Peter and John and the other apostles (Acts 4:5 ff.; 6:27 ff.), was important enough to engage the Sanhedrin of the Jews (Acts 23:1-10). The entire ministry of Paul is to be judged from a Jewish standpoint.

Paul, apparently without waiting to be asked to speak, takes the orator's posture, "looks intently" at his hearers and says, "Brethren, I have lived before God in all good conscience unto this day."

The high priest, whose name is subsequently given as Ananias,[6] commands that Paul be struck on the mouth for his utterance. Paul thereupon assails him with a fury almost like that which he showed in speaking to Elymas, the magus (Acts 13:10).

"God shall strike you, you whitewashed wall. Are you sitting in judgment to judge me according to the Law, yet contrary to the Law (Leviticus 19:15) you order me to be struck?"

The initial prediction is given in part in Biblical language (Deuteronomy 28:22) but was evidently formulated with an eye to what had come to pass when Luke wrote the story, for the high priest Ananias was murdered in A.D. 66.

The bystanders are horrified at Paul's words and exclaim, "Would you revile God's high priest?" It was against the Law to do that (Exodus 22:27), and Paul excuses himself for not having known it was the high priest. He thus is shown to be law-abiding in intention but given to outbursts of temper.

Observing that the council is partly composed of Sadducees and partly of Pharisees, Paul—according to the Acts account—makes a bid for Pharisaic support. He declares that he is a Pharisee and the son of a Pharisee and is being accused "on account of the hope [of Israel] and the resurrection of the dead." This unleashes a bitter fight between the two factions in the Sanhedrin, since the Sadducees do not believe in a resurrection (Luke 10:27). The Pharisees become Paul's defenders, and some of their scribes declare, "We find nothing wrong in this man. What if a spirit or an angel spoke to him?" Thus they even rationalized Paul's Damascus vision. The tribune fearing that Paul will be torn to pieces, sends for the guard to come down from the fortress and extricate his prisoner out of the midst of the gathering.[7]

The story apparently caricatures everybody, including Paul himself. The occasion is without consequence since Luke can report no decision of the august body he ridicules. But the incident serves the purpose of illustrating the chaotic state of affairs at Jerusalem, and the riotous habits of Jews, so well known from Rome, Antioch, Caesarea, and Alexandria, and of putting the Pharisees on the side of Paul. The last point had apologetic value in Luke's day, when the rabbis were approaching the point of excommunicating the Christians from the synagogues.

Actually, Paul, after the pounding received at the hands of the mob, must have been bruised and depressed. As on several other important occasions, he is said to have been strengthened by a divinely given vision. The Lord stood by him on the following night and said, "Take courage, for as you have testified about me at Jerusalem, so you must bear witness also at Rome" (Acts 23:11).

Luke evidently considered the address to the crowd and Paul's utterances before the council sufficient "testimony." With the vision report he prepared the reader for further developments. Christ, he believed, gave Paul the task to bear witness in Rome. Hence, no matter what perils may intervene, Paul can be confident that he will get to the city on the

Tiber and crown his ministry with this climactic achievement. Paul was to have an immediate example of dire peril and divine deliverance. His sister's son visited him in prison and brought him the news that more than forty men among the Jews' had made a plot and vowed not to eat or drink until they had killed Paul.[8] They had enlisted the aid of some members of the Sanhedrin to provide them with a favorable opportunity for doing the deed. The tribune was to be advised that this body would like to consider Paul's case again. On the way to the meeting Paul would be killed. In the narrow streets and in the dark of night it would indeed be easy for so formidable a band to overpower the guards and to plunge a dagger into the prisoner.

Paul at once asked a centurion to take the young man to the tribune. The latter received him kindly, heard his story in private and instructed him to keep silent about the matter. He immediately ordered soldiery and mounted men to be ready to take Paul to Caesarea at nine o'clock, after dark. He composed a report in letter form, beginning with the writer's name "Claudius Lysias." The name shows that he must have bought his Roman citizenship under the emperor Claudius. The letter, which was addressed to "most excellent Felix," reports what had happened—though with the slight variation that the writer rescued Paul from death on learning that he was a Roman citizen. The salient point brought out is that Paul was only accused of violating Jewish law, and had committed no offense punishable under Roman law. Lysias' order to Paul's accusers to appear before Felix had certainly not been given when Paul was sent out into the night. But that order would have been given before the letter was received.

The escort was assembled at the north side of the Antonia. Its reported size of two hundred foot soldiers, seventy horsemen, and two hundred spearmen reveals how important the prisoner was considered to be and how great was the potential danger. When all was in readiness and the letter had been entrusted to the commander of the horsemen, Paul was led out, given a horse to ride, and the procession started. We can imagine Paul turning at Mt. Scopus to look back once more at the city. Above the gleaming helmets of the infantry following him he could see the temple courts, empty and peaceful in the moonlight. Did he foresee the dark days in store for Jerusalem, "the great tribulation, such as has not been from the beginning of the world until now" (Matthew 24:21)? Whether he did or not he had written Jerusalem off. His mind was on a more promising objective for Christ: the city on the Tiber.

20 THE CAPTIVITY AT CAESAREA

*He is a chosen instrument of mine to carry my
name before the Gentiles and kings and the
sons of Israel.*

ACTS 9:15

THE TROOPS CONDUCTED Paul to Antipatris in the
coastal plain, a march of twenty-five miles. No doubt a rest
of a few hours was made there and then the horsemen went
on alone with their captive, leaving the footsoldiers to return
to Jerusalem.[1]

When the escort bringing Paul arrived at Caesarea they
rode straight to the Herodian palace, which now could be
called the praetorium, because it was the residence of the
praetor or Roman governor in his function as judge. The
commander of the troops presented the prisoner and the letter
of the tribune to Felix. Twice Paul had stood before a proconsul, or governor of a senatorial province, but this was the
first time he had stood before the governor of an imperial
province, the representative of the emperor.

"A Roman citizen?" said Felix when the letter was read
to him. "From where do you come?"

"From Cilicia."

Felix gave Paul an appraising look. A Cilician Jew who was a Roman citizen must be a man of means.

"I will hear you when your accusers, whom Lysias has directed to appear before me, arrive," he said.

Dismissing the centurion, who could return at once to Jerusalem, the governor gave Paul into the custody of his own soldiers and directed that he should be kept for the present in the guardrooms of the palace.

There is no report of the reaction of Paul's travel companions to the news of his arrest in the Temple. They turned to James for help, but found him more concerned about possible trouble for the Jerusalem Christians than about Paul.[2] "He is in God's hands," he may have said piously. The elders seemed undisturbed about Paul. From Paul's sister, his friends finally learned that Paul had been taken to Caesarea. So Paul's travel companions departed as soon as possible and went to that city to the house of the deacon Philip.

Five days later the high priest Ananias and several elders came down to Caesarea to bring charges against Paul (Acts 24:1 ff.). It offended their dignity to speak personally in Greek so they had a "rhetor" named Tertullus with them. The defendant was brought in and Tertullus was permitted to speak for the plaintiffs.

He began with flattery for Felix, the governor, and promised to be brief. The Sanhedrin had found Paul to be an exciter of unrest in all the world,[3] a leader of the Nazarene sect. He had also tried to desecrate the Temple. If the governor examined him (under torture) he would find the charges to be true.

Paul now was granted the opportunity to defend himself (Acts 24:10-21). In this speech some fresh information is given. We learn that twelve days have elapsed since Paul had come to Jerusalem, and that he had come for the purpose of bringing his nation alms and offerings. This is the only allusion in Acts to the collection that was so important a factor in Paul's journey and for the first time gives the reader of Acts an inkling why Paul took so many companions along to Jerusalem. But for some reason Luke does not reveal that the money was "for the saints." One might think it was a case of a public benefaction, such as Greeks and Romans were familiar with.

Paul criticizes his opponents for not producing witnesses of his alleged Temple desecration. He demands what wrongdoing his accusers had found when he stood before the council, except perhaps that he had cried out that he was on trial with respect to the resurrection of the dead. Since the accusers were of the Sadducaic party, they might count that a misdemeanor, but since the Pharisees were the dominant sect and believed in that doctrine, how could it be?

Felix, the narrator notes, "had a rather accurate knowledge of the Way" (i.e. Christian teaching) and evidently did not want to listen to argument about religious differences. He thus put off any decision until the next time the tribune came to Caesarea. It was a postponement "to the Greek calends," as Romans were wont to say, since the Greeks had no name for the first day of the month (Roman "calends" on which debts were payable). Paul was to remain in custody but with a certain amount of liberty (*custodia liberior,* under Roman law), notably that of seeing his friends and having them look out for him.[4]

Paul's friends, when they were finally able to see him, found him bruised from the mauling he had received, but of good cheer and untroubled about the future. He advised them all to sail for their homes since he suspected that his case would be of long duration. Philip and the Caesarean Christians could be relied upon to do for him what was needed. We may imagine that after a time the visitors followed his advice—all except one, Aristarchus of Thessalonica, the representative of a congregation that was particuarly close to Paul's heart.

One day Felix sent for Paul because his wife Drusilla was filled with curiosity to see him. She was a sister of Herod Agrippa II, of whom we will soon hear. She had already been the wife of the king Aziz of Emesa in Syria, who had even submitted to circumcision to wed the pretty Jewess. With the aid of a Jewish magician from Cyprus named Atomos, Felix had gotten her away from her husband. Paul spoke to them of faith in Christ Jesus. But when he spoke of righteousness and self-control (sexual continence) and the coming judgment, Felix became alarmed at the possible effect this might have on his domestic tranquility and dismissed Paul, saying that he would hear him again some day.

The days passed slowly. Paul—if the usual translation of Acts 24:27 is correct—had to spend two years under Felix at Caesarea.[5] The governor often sent for him, but Luke insinuates that what he wanted was money for Paul's release. It seems very likely that Paul's friends offered to raise a sum to buy his freedom, but that he did not permit them to do so. The words he had heard in his vision kept ringing in his ears. He saw in his situation a possibility of an advantage he could never reach in any other way: of testifying to his faith before the emperor at Rome.

The remark about Felix's cupidity is the only adverse item about him in Acts, while the compliments which Tertullus and Paul uttered in their speeches could make one think well of him. What we hear about him from other sources, however, is none too favorable. He was an ex-slave. The emperor Claudius had put many such persons in prominent posts instead of the scions of old aristocratic families. Three freedmen even ran the Roman government and one of these was Pallas, the brother of Felix. The latter was appointed to this high office through Pallas' influence. When he arrived in A.D. 52, he was faced with much unrest by Jewish Zealots and is said to have crucified a great many. Going underground the Zealots became *sicarii* or assassins of the kind that wanted to kill Paul. They had murdered many of the Jewish aristocracy who were friendly to Rome—notably the high priest Jonathan, who had endorsed the appointment of Felix.

It was perhaps in June A.D. 57 that Paul came to Caesarea as a prisoner. The delay in the processing of his case may have been due to other reasons than Luke suspected. For during the biennium that Paul spent there, Felix had serious trouble on his hands, which indeed was to be his undoing. There was a bitter feud between Gentiles and Jews at this city. The Jews demanded control on the ground that Caesarea had been founded by their king, Herod the Great. The Gentiles based their claim to control on the fact that Caesarea was their old city "Straton's tower," and on the pagan temples and the generally Hellenistic-Roman character of the city. The Jewish leaders who sat in the city council tried in vain to restrain their people, but the Jews got out of hand and tried to seize control by force. Felix quieted the disturbance with native troops, including reinforcements from Sebaste (Samaria). Many Jews were slain or imprisoned and their houses pillaged. He called off army reprisals, however, and sent representatives of both factions to Rome. Complaints of the Jews against him led to his being recalled. In view of the circumstances thus faced by Felix, he would hardly have wanted to do the Jews a favor by leaving Paul in prison. We may assume that he simply dropped everything when he had to hurry to Rome, from where he was not to return.

The new governor, who may have arrived in the spring of 59, was Porcius Festus. Festus, no doubt, had much to do before he got around to unfinished judicial business. He first went up to Jerusalem to familiarize himself with the

place, consult the Roman officers, and meet Jewish leaders.
The latter called his attention to Paul and urged that he be
sent to Jerusalem for trial. Their plan allegedly was to have
him killed on the way. Though Festus, as a new governor,
was certainly inclined to please his constituency, he did not
commit himself. The commander of the Jerusalem garrison
may have told him that Paul was a Roman citizen and so
had been spirited away by night for his protection. Festus
directed those who wished to bring charges against Paul to
come to Caesarea.

About eight or ten days after his return to the latter city,
Festus took his seat on the tribunal and had Paul brought
before him. According to Luke the accusers from Jerusalem
"brought many serious charges which they could not prove."
Paul claimed that he had committed no offense "against the
law of the Jews, nor against the temple, nor against Caesar."

Festus now asked whether Paul wished to be tried on
these charges in Jerusalem. This was a request of the Jews
which he had rejected when at Jerusalem. Luke explains
Festus' change of mind by saying that he wished to do the
Jews a favor. But perhaps he had another motive.

Understandably, Paul had no desire to be tried in Jerusalem. James and the Christian congregation, too, would
be embarrassed by such a trial and there might even be an
outbreak against them for having harbored him. So Paul declined to be tried in Jerusalem. He declared that he was standing now before Caesar's tribunal where he ought to be tried.
Festus, he said, knew very well that he had done nothing
against the Jews. If he had done anything else of which they
could accuse him, he was prepared to stand trial on that here
and now. But if there was no basis to the charges of the
Jews, he could not be given up to them. He would appeal to
"Caesar" at Rome. The Caesar now was Nero (A.D. 54–68).

Festus, so Luke relates, consulted with his legal advisers and thereupon gave this decision:

"You have appealed to Caesar; to Caesar you shall go." The legal basis for the action of Festus is not made clear. Roman law required this basis, especially in dealing with a citizen. After unproven charges have been presented by the accusers and denied by the defendant, the latter should have been set free. One cannot see any great advantage for the Jews or for the governor in making Paul take the radical step of an appeal to Caesar to obtain his freedom. The essential fact is that Festus refused to release him. There must, therefore, have been some charge against him which left a doubt in the mind of the judge. It is most likely to have been the one that Paul denied in the words, "nor against Caesar have I offended at all" (Acts. 25:8). The mere suspicion or rumor of that kind of an offense required investigation which, if the supposed crime took place in some other province, could best be dealt with at Rome. One may, perhaps, suspect that Festus wanted to maneuver Paul into an appeal to Caesar, and that this was the motive behind his suggestion of a trial at Jerusalem.

Such an appeal was an expensive matter for the defendant. It was necessary that it be so if a Caesar was not to be unduly burdened with an endless number of cases. How could Paul, who hitherto has labored with his hands to support himself, suddenly afford such a luxury? Did the representatives of his congregations promise to raise money for his defense? Did his relatives come to his aid? Or did he fall heir to a portion of his father's estate around this time? We are not told.

Just as Paul's departure from his mission fields ends in an impressive and vivid scene at Miletus, so his departure from Palestine ends in a final vivid scene at Caesarea. The biographer has hinted that Paul was a chosen instrument to carry

Christ's name before Gentiles and kings. He has shown abundantly how he carried it before the Gentiles, but he still owes it to the reader to have Paul carry it before a king. This he does through a presentation of Paul before Agrippa II, who came to pay his respects to the new imperial governor of Judea. He was the son of the Herod Agrippa I who had been king of Judea A.D. 41–44, but on the death of his father had been considered too young to succeed to so great a realm. He was brought up at the court of Claudius and first made king of Chalcis in Syria in A.D. 50. More recently he had been given the tetrarchy of Philip. His residence thus was at Julias, near the lake of Galilee and his summer palace was at Caesarea Philippi.

With Agrippa came his sister Berenice. She was the elder sister, too, of Drusilla, the wife of Felix. The visit was more than a courtesy one. The state of anarchy in Judea was of as much concern to this Herodian as to the new Roman governor, and many questions of policy must have come up for discussion. Festus also discussed the case of Paul with him, and Agrippa expressed the wish to see and hear the prisoner. A semi-public occasion for the appearance of Paul was arranged for the next day.

The king and Berenice, who was no less curious to see Paul than her sister Drusilla, arrived with great pomp. Paul was brought in, and Festus, addressing Agrippa, stated the case and made known his desire that the king, after he had heard Paul, tell him what report he should send to Caesar about the prisoner. Agrippa presided from here on and gave Paul permission to speak. Thus for the first time in his career, Paul stood before an audience composed of a king, notables, and officialdom. He stretched forth his hand and began his defense.

He considered himself fortunate, Paul declared, to be able to defend himself before a man familiar with Jewish matters.

He first traced his own beginnings. In that connection, he noted that there were former associates of his in Jerusalem who could testify to his zeal in Pharisaism if they were willing. He insisted that he was standing on trial for the hope of Israel. Why should it be incredible to Agrippa or to any other Jew that God raises the dead?

He dwelt on his own early unbelief and opposition to Christianity. Here, too, some fresh details are provided: as persecutor he went even to foreign cities. Damascus was only one—seemingly the last one.

He then related his experience on the way to Damascus once more, varying the previous accounts. After his conversion, he allegedly had preached first at Damascus, then at Jerusalem, then throughout Judea, and also to the Gentiles.[6] His preaching had been a call to repentance and to performing of deeds worthy of it (Matthew 3:8).

Paul then declared that it was for this message that the Jews were trying to kill him. But until now he had divine help, and so he stood here today, testifying that he was saying only what was foretold by the prophets: that the Messiah had to suffer and that by being the first to rise he would proclaim light to both the (Jewish) people and the Gentiles.

Paul's emphasis on the resurrection doctrine was too much for Festus. He said in a loud voice, "Paul you are mad. Your great learning is turning you mad."

But Paul had not been speaking to and for Festus. His target on that occasion was Agrippa. So he fended off the accusation politely, and said that Agrippa knew about these things—including the rise of the Christian movement—"for this was not done in a corner." And addressing Agrippa pointedly he asked, "King Agrippa, do you believe the prophets? I know you believe."

The Herodian exclaimed, "In a short time you think to

make me a Christian!" He went as far as he could in conceding the persuasiveness of Paul's approach. The statement was not intended to be ironical, but was complimentary. If he had been exposed for any length of time to Paul's argument, he would be forced into a Christian role.

Paul rose to the occasion when he expressed the wish that before long not only Agrippa but all his hearers at this gathering would be as he was (i.e., Christians) except for the chains that bound him.

The king gave the signal which terminated the hearing, and as the crowd left, the general consensus was that Paul had done nothing which deserved death or imprisonment. Agrippa even went further. He said to Festus, and apparently with regret, "The man could have been released had he not appealed to Caesar." Evidently the act of appeal was irreversible.

Luke does not tell us whether Agrippa helped Festus to formulate the report on the case. He had achieved his purpose of making clear through Paul's speech, and the general reaction it elicited, that Paul ought to have been set free. There was no ground to send him to Rome. Furthermore, by having Paul base his defense throughout on his Pharisaic resurrection doctrine, Luke seeks to keep Christianity under the shelter of the Jewish religion and thus share in the legal recognition the latter enjoyed under the Roman state.

The governor commanded Paul's transfer to Rome, which was to be effected at the next opportunity, before winter.

21 FROM CAESAREA TO MALTA

*I mention you always in my prayers, asking
that somehow by God's will I may at last succeed in coming to you.*

ROMANS 1:9-10

IT WAS AN AUGUST day at the harbor of Caesarea. Paul,
chained to a soldier stood on the shore with some of the
Christians of the city, led by Philip, who had assembled to
take leave of him. There was a great gladness in Paul's heart
and countenance. The long period of inaction at Caesarea
was over. He rejoiced at the prospect of going to sea once
more and, especially, that he would have a chance to bear
witness to Christ before Caesar. This was to be the climax
of all the opportunities of his life. But his friends were deeply
moved, knowing that even if he were set free he would never
return to these parts again.

Paul may not have been the only prisoner to be put
aboard the vessel. There was a constant stream of convicts
going to Rome from everywhere to provide amusement for
the people of that city by fighting for their lives in the arena,
whether with man or beast. No doubt some of those who

239

were to sail with him were facing that fate. But Paul also had
two companions, who must have received special permission
from Festus to accompany him.[1] Only one is identified—
Aristarchus of Thessalonica (Acts 20:4). Since a "We-section" begins here (27:1) the other of the two evidently was
the one who wrote the succinct memoir of the trip upon
which Luke drew. It cannot have been the author of Acts, because he would have told the entire journey in the first person, would have mentioned some essential things that are
omitted, and would not have told one incident, of which
he would necessarily have been an eyewitness, in such a
secular manner. The identity of the unnamed companion
has been carefully concealed, like that of the second Em-
maus disciple of Luke 24:18, the second disciple of John
the Baptist of John 1:40, and the two "other" disciples of
John 21:2.

The officer in charge of the convoy was a centurian named
Julius. He is said to have belonged to the "Augustan cohort."[2]
Such names were not given to regular army units, but only
to auxiliaries recruited from the local populations.

The vessel which the group boarded was from Adramyttium, a flourishing harbor of Mysia, situated at the head of
the gulf on which Assos lay. The ship headed for its home
port on this its last voyage of the season. It thus would be
necessary at some point for Julius to transfer his party to another vessel that was bound for Rome.

Sailing ships had many problems. Winds and currents
were their furtherances as well as their hindrances. The prevailing wind was westerly and thus contrary to the course
Paul's vessel had to take. However, there is a current coming
from the Nile and running up the Syrian coast, of which a
ship could take advantage. Since the vessel put in at Sidon
the next day and the distance was sixty-nine nautical miles,
it must have made about three nautical miles an hour. At

this ancient Phoenician city Paul was allowed to visit Christian friends.

When the voyage was resumed they kept east and north of Cyprus. There, too, advantage could be taken of a westerly current and land winds. Even so a great deal of tacking was necessary. In this way—with nightly stops—the vessel got as far as Myra in Lycia in about ten days. This city, since ancient times, had been a place which had direct traffic with Egypt.[3] It lay on a river two miles from the sea, but had a harbor town named Andriake.

At Myra the centurion found an Alexandrian ship which was carrying grain and freight to Rome, and to this vessel he transferred his whole party. It must have been a very large ship, for we later learn that in addition to freight it had two hundred and seventy-six people on board.[4]

With some difficulty they got to Cnidus. There a ship bound for Italy, headed for Cape Malea at the eastern tip of Greece. But the northwest winds sweeping down the Aegean at this time made that impossible.[5] The owner and the captain (for the former was aboard too) were faced with the choice of waiting for a favorable wind or of being driven to the south. The wind now prevailing threatened to carry any vessel down on the north coast of Crete.

Owing to the lateness of the season it was decided not to wait but to try to get to the southern side of Crete and continue westward in the lee of that island. They succeeded in rounding Cape Sammonium (*Salmone*), on the eastern end of Crete, and reaching more protected waters. But even here it was difficult to make progress. They finally came to a port called Fair Havens (Greek *Kaloi Limnai*), a name still clinging to a small bay a few miles from Cape Matala.[6] This was the farthest point on Crete which an ancient ship could reach when navigating by the northwest wind. From there on the coast veered north and the advantage of weather protection ceased. Near Fair Havens was a city called Lasea (Acts 27:8).

Since the period from September 14 to November 11 was dangerous for navigation, the alternative of wintering in Fair Havens presented itself. The prospect was not inviting. The country round the harbor was high and rocky, with only some stunted trees and thorny shrubs. Farther along the coast, however, there was a better harbor at a place called Phoenix[7] and the idea of going on to it was tempting. But Paul, who had had so much experience with shipwrecks (2 Corinthians 11:25), urged upon the centurion that they proceed no farther.[8] In prophetic words he warned that if they did go on, ship, cargo, and lives would be lost.

The narrative alludes to the fact that the fast had already gone by. If this means the Jewish fast, i.e., Day of Atonement, the date (10 of Tishri) would have fallen in A.D. 59 on October 5. This was the time when commercial navigation stopped, though we hear of warships, which had oarsmen and were not wholly dependent on the wind, being active in the seas in the middle of winter.

A vote was taken whether to go on or not and the majority favored going ahead. So when a gentle south wind arose they weighed anchor and proceeded, keeping as close to the shore as possible. Suddenly a northeaster (Greek *Euraquilo*, the halfway point between *Eurus*, north, and *Aquilo*, east) coming down from the high mountains struck them.[9] The ship had to change its course, and was driven in the direction of the island of Cauda or Clauda (Gozzo).[10] No doubt the large mainsail was hastily reefed when they saw or heard the blast coming, but the small forward-leaning bow sail, without which there could have been no steering, was left up.

When the ship was caught in the gale it must have been near a small group of islands called the Paximades in the Gulf of Mesara. The distance from there to Cauda was about twenty-three miles. Speeding ahead the ship passed around the east end of that small island and hove to in its shelter with the right side to windward. The first aim of the crew was to secure the water-logged lifeboat which they were towing. The next job was that of undergirding or "frapping" the ship.[11] This was still done not so many years ago by passing a cable under a ship's center four or five times but, in view of the difficulty in doing that, it may be that Paul's vessel was only girded with a rope around it longitudinally. It may already have sprung some leaks, for every time the ship's center rode the crest of a swell while both ends were in the air over valleys, the weight of the cargo caused strain and even created the hazard that the ship's back might be broken. Whatever was to be done, it had to be done quickly for the ship could not hold itself under the island and was being borne steadily southward.

The next thing related is, "Fearing that they should run on to Syrtis"—the great sand bank on the north African coast west of Cyrenaica—"they lowered the gear" (Acts 27:17). This, perhaps, is an allusion to dropping the "drag" or sea anchor used to check leeward drift.[12] The small foresail had to stay up if the vessel was to be steered in a westerly direction instead of being driven helplessly to the south. The next day, being violently storm-tossed, they threw out cargo. The third day they cast over the tackle of the ship "with their own hands"—an allusion emphasizing how desperate they were; for the sailors to throw overboard mast, spars, sail, ropes was as hard a thing to do as it would be for a carpenter to throw away his tools.

The stormy weather continued day after day. The worst of it was that the only possibility for checking on their course or trying to figure out where they were was barred to them by the cloudy skies. For the ancient navigators of these seas, when out of sight of land, could rely only on the constellations to determine their location and direction. However, experience gave them some idea of rate of speed and knowledge of distances. It seems likely that the skipper kept steering as much to the west as the wind permitted, and that he was trying to hit the coast of Sicily.

The misery of seasickness as their lightened vessel bobbed up and down must have been indescribable. No one could eat without giving the food up again and the people were like walking corpses. A hopeless sense of doom overcame them.

In this situation Paul came forward with a message for his shipmates.[13] He reminded them of his warning: had they stayed in Fair Havens, as he had advised, they would not have incurred all this damage. But now he was going to make another prediction; perhaps they would believe it. He assured them that they would all be saved, though the ship would be lost. He told his heathen audience that a messenger (angel) of the God to whom he belonged and whom he worshiped had spoken to him in a vision of the night and told him that he should be unafraid. "You must stand before Caesar; and lo, God has made you a present of all those who sail with you." He bade them take heart, for he had faith in God and in the assurance given in His name. So conscious of special divine favor are the godly great! The fact that he was on board and that his God did not want him to perish was their salvation. He added, however, as his own supposition, that they would have to run upon some island.

On the fourteenth night as they were being borne along in the Adria—at that time a name for the seas between Crete and Sicily[14]—the sailors began to suspect that they were nearing land. The time and distance calculations could have suggested it, but more probably they detected the sound of the surf which at the place where they then must have been (off Koura Head) can be heard a mile and a half away.[15] Repeated soundings giving twenty and then fifteen fathoms revealed that they were getting into shallower waters.[16] They now heard the roar of waves ahead and were afraid of striking rocks. They let out four anchors from the stern—so as to be headed for the shore if these did not hold—and they prayed that the day might come.

An exciting incident now took place.[17] The sailors lowered the lifeboat into the water, ostensibly to take out the bow anchors. Merely to drop them from the forward portholes would have been useless, for the light anchors of those days held only when carried out. Paul—so the report states—believed that this was only a ruse on the part of the crew and that they actually wanted to abandon the ship. He interfered by saying to the centurion and the soldiers, "Unless these men stay in the ship you cannot be saved." Thereupon the soldiers cut the ropes holding the empty boat and let it go.[18]

Some nautical experts have criticized Paul sharply for his landlubberly precociousness. His suspicions, they claim, were unwarranted. The sailors would not have risked going off in the darkness when they could hear the waves crashing on the rockbound coast! Perhaps not. But once they had the boat in the water they could have slipped off at crack of dawn before anybody could hinder them. These Levantine salts were not the salt of the earth, and a man in whom the intuitive powers were as highly developed as in Paul, is not likely to have been wrong in his suspicion of their intentions. Casting off the boat had one great advantage: all were now in the same situation and would live together or die together. The crew would be at their stations and would work with a will when the moment came to act.

As the dawn drew near Paul exhorted all to partake of some food.[19] He assured them that not a hair would perish from the head of any of them. He took bread in hand and after giving thanks to God in the presence of all, broke it and began to eat. The others followed his example and munched the moldy hardtack they carried in their haversacks. Then they threw overboard the rest of the wheat cargo to decrease the draft of the ship.

At last the day dawned. Anxiously scanning the scene they saw ahead of them a bay—henceforth to be known as St. Paul's bay—with a beach. The place they had reached when they anchored may have been a quarter of a mile from the shore, upon whose rocks the waves were breaking with tremendous force. Had they gone on for a few minutes more they would have been wrecked in the darkness of night.

As they surveyed the shore for a place to land they saw a creek and a beach. The captain and ship owner decided to make for one or the other of these spots. The paddles with which the ship was steered were lowered—here the sailors were especially needed—the four anchor ropes were cut and the vessel with its foresail again hoisted leaped forward. But it did not make the shore, for it ran aground on a shoal. Its bow was stuck in the clay and the waves were pounding its stern, threatening to break it in pieces.

It now was necessary to abandon ship and swim or drift ashore on planks. At this juncture the Roman soldiers demanded the slaughter of the prisoners, lest they be held responsible for any escaping. The centurion, however, would not accede to this, not wishing to see Paul slain and apparently unable to enforce an exception. All, therefore, were able to make their way to land.[20]

The plight of the ship had been observed from the shore, and as the travelers landed the natives started a fire for them so that they could warm and dry themselves. They learned that the name of the island was Melita (Malta).[21]

Only a single happening of that day is related.[22] A serpent is said to have attacked Paul when he was gathering wood. He shook it off into the flames. Apparently everyone thought he was pursued by a divine nemesis and expected to see him die. When he remained completely unharmed the people decided he was a god. This is a peculiar anecdote, and is not included in the "we" report. Luke may have collected it from tradition.

Malta was under administration by the Roman governor of Sicily and presumably Publius[23] was his local deputy. If he is called "chief man of the island" this is no mere description, but a title that is vindicated by inscriptions found at Malta. For three days Paul and his friends, and presumably some others, were entertained at the nearby estate of Publius, and Paul was able to show his gratitude by healing the father of this man from dysentery by laying on of hands (Acts 5:12; 19:11). The narrator reports that many other sick people were brought to Paul and that he healed them.[24] Though no conversions are mentioned there can be little doubt that the author of Acts thinks of this as the occasion of the founding of Christianity on Malta. In this sketchy fashion much time is covered, for Paul spent three months, or a little less, on this island.

22 ARRIVAL AND CAPTIVITY AT ROME

*One thing I do, forgetting what lies behind
and straining forward to what lies ahead, I press
on toward the goal for the prize of the upward
call of God in Christ Jesus.*

PHILIPPIANS 3:13-14

THE VESSEL THAT had been shipwrecked was not the
only Alexandrian grain ship that had been blown off its course.
There was another which had succeeded in getting safely to
the harbor of Malta, no doubt the present Valetta, eight miles
southeast of St. Paul's Bay, and was wintering there.[1] The
skipper wanted to leave as early as he could to get his cargo
to Italy. Favorable weather may have made it possible to risk
the short run to Sicily even before February 7—the date given
by Pliny for resumption of navigation. It was arranged that
Paul and his party were to go with that vessel.

The ship had the "Twin brothers" or "Heavenly Twins"
(*Dioscuri*) as figurehead or emblem.[2] They were Castor and
Pollux whose constellations in the heavens served to guide
navigators, and who were considered saviors at sea. It may
be that their heads were painted on either side of the prow.

248

But this does not need to mean that the ship was named for them. Greek ship names were commonly feminine. A festival was celebrated for the *Dioscuri* at Ostia on January 27, which might have been an especially appropriate day for the departure of the ship.

It is strange that we hear nothing of the centurion Julius and his soldiers or of the other passengers and crew of the lost vessel. The narrator may have considered it self-evident that the rest of the shipwrecked group also sailed on the departing ship.

After a grateful farewell to the kind people of Malta who supplied them with whatever they needed (Acts 28:10), Paul and his companions went aboard the *Dioscuri*. The ship hoisted sail and made for Sicily with the aid of a favorable (southerly) wind. This was only a day's sail. A change of wind, however, forced them to spend three days in the harbor of Syracuse, which lay in the shadow of Mt. Aetna. From there they went "circuitously"—availing themselves of the ins and outs of the shoreline—and arrived at Rhegium at the toe of Italy. Apparently, they had to wait here for another south wind to come up before negotiating the Straits of Messina.

They were lucky to lose only a day at Rhegium. A twenty-four hour run then took them through the Straits and up the coast past Capri and with Mt. Vesuvius in the east, to Puteoli (*Pozzuoli*). Near here, at Cumae, according to Virgil's epic, Aeneas had landed. Guided by the Sybil, he had descended to the nether world with the golden branch in his hand to hear of the great future which fate had in store for him and his descendants. Paul, another Aeneas, is likewise coming to Italy to conquer, but with the sword of the spirit.

Puteoli was the great port of Italy. Through it went the trade of the world. True, Claudius in A.D. 42 had built a great harbor in the marshy plain near the mouth of the Tiber and named it *Portus*. It had an island before it, the nucleus of which was the sunken giant ship that had been built to transport to Rome the Egyptian obelisk now standing in St. Peter's Square. But in Paul's day traffic from the eastern Mediterranean was still glad to come to rest at Puteoli.

Paul's ship was the first of the season to arrive. Its coming occasioned great joy. The grain fleet from Egypt would not get there until late in May, since the voyage from Alexandria took fifty days or more. When that event was at hand great crowds would gather to celebrate.[3]

We may be sure that Paul's name was well known to the Christians at Puteoli, and that they had long since heard of his imprisonment at Caesarea. His arrival, because of an appeal to Caesar, was astonishing news. He and his companions were immediately invited to stay a week with them. It is strange that no mention is made of the centurion and his permission. It almost seems as though Paul enjoyed some kind of parole since the shipwreck.

But the time came to part from these new brethren. Paul and his fellow travelers took the Campanian Way to Capua, and there struck the Appian Way coming from Brundisium on the Adriatic. A march of a week was in store for Paul as the distance from Puteoli to Rome was 135 miles. His long captivity had weakened his muscles, but he attempted to regain something of that swinging stride that had taken him through the far-flung regions of Asia Minor, Macedonia, and Greece. It was good to be on the road again. The heavenly voice kept ringing in his ears, "You will stand before Caesar."

To the right and left of the Appian Way were the estates of wealthy Romans, some of whom had hundreds of slaves. Those Paul saw working in the fields were always guarded and were chained at night.

At Formia Paul must have passed the monument and

country house of Cicero. Probably he was familiar with the name and reputation of this great orator, for Cicero had once been governor of his native Cilicia. Hereabouts was one of the highest points on the entire road, with a view over the gulf of Gaeta. The sight of the sea under the bright sun was glorious. How different it had seemed on those stormy days in the Adria!

Getting out of the mountainous area they now came to the Pontine marshes, through which Augustus had built a canal. One could rent a boat and be towed by mules that walked along on the banks; Horace once described such a boat ride in humorous manner.[4] In that satire he uses the word "scoundrels" in reference to the innkeepers of the Forum of Appius which is the next place mentioned in Paul's journey. It lay at the forty-third milestone from the capital.

At this point, according to the present text of Acts,[5] Paul was met by a first delegation from Rome—no doubt composed of young men, who could walk rapidly. We can imagine that they greeted Paul with great deference. Escorted and engaged in pleasant conversation, Paul continued on his way with this band. At the forty-second milestone the travelers passed the country house of Seneca, whose brother, the proconsul Gallio, had shown Paul kindness at Corinth (Acts 18:13-17). Later apocryphal tradition was to relate that Paul met Seneca at Rome and that a correspondence passed between them.[6] At "Three Taverns," the thirty-third milestone from Rome, Paul was welcomed by a second Roman delegation, no doubt consisting of the older and more important men. Paul is said to have thanked God and taken courage.

On the following day—perhaps after an overnight stop at Aricia—Paul came to Rome. As they neared the city they passed through a long cemetery, for the road was lined with the funeral monuments of the great Roman families. When the road dipped down it passed through an area later called *ad catacumbas.* It was to be significant for Christians in days to come.

The Appian Way reached the city at the Porta Capena, over which passed an aqueduct. After going through the gate Paul soon had a glimpse on the left of the great Circus Maximus, which had room for 260,400 spectators. His destination was the Praetorian camp in the northeastern part of the city. The prefect was Sextus Afranius Burrus, a man who had great influence with the emperor. He was in effect the head of the imperial police. Whether it was to him or to a subaltern that Paul was delivered is not reported. In any case it was ordered that he have the mildest kind of detention. He was permitted to rent his own living quarters and to be guarded there by a soldier. Therewith the last "We-section" of Acts ends.

For his conclusion, the author of Acts chose or fashioned an incident that would be both symbolical of Paul's work as he saw it and prophetic of the future.

After three days, Paul called together the leaders of the Jews (Acts 28:17 ff.). He addressed them as "brethren," thus seeking to maintain his solidarity with them. He explained to them that, though innocent, he had been delivered as a prisoner from Jerusalem into the hands of the Romans. (In the report previously given, it was the Romans who took him prisoner.) When the Romans wanted to set him free the Jews objected (again not quite according to the previous account), and so he had appealed to Caesar. But he desired to make it clear that he had no charge to bring against his own people.

This stroke of diplomacy illustrates Paul's foresight, for Jews were certainly going to be called in when it came to a trial. If he made clear that he would not accuse their leaders at Jerusalem, he stood a better chance of their not exerting their influence against him.

Paul declared that he had asked the Roman Jews to come that he might inform them of the real reason for his present plight. "It is because of the hope of Israel that I am bound with this chain." He thus speaks more generally than he had done at Jerusalem and Caesarea, where he had stressed the belief in the resurrection of the dead as part of that hope (Acts 23:6; 24:2; 26:7-8). Perhaps he did not wish to offend non-Pharisaic elements likely to be found among the culturally advanced Jews at Rome. That Paul was arrested by the Romans for the Messianic hope must have intrigued his visitors and made them curious. This hope took on various hues in the eyes of different people; for some it was the day of Jewish world rule under a king of their own; for others it was the day of the acceptance of the Jewish religion by the Gentiles; for still others it was the supernatural arrival of the kingdom of God. But for all it had an appeal.

The Jews with whom Paul was conferring declared that they had received no letters from Judea, and that no Jews who had come from there had spoken ill of him.[7] They wished to hear from him what his views were, "for with regard to this sect we know that everywhere it is spoken against." Their admission that Paul's movement was a Jewish sect, even though widely condemned, is one of the important aspects of this story, for it fits in with Luke's aim to keep Christianity within the Jewish orbit, sharing in the privilege of being a recognized religion in the Roman world.

The visitors arranged with Paul for a meeting day, and since he could not go to the synagogue they came to him "in great numbers."

It was a day devoted to religious instruction and discussion, for Paul "expounded the matter to them from morning till evening." When he testified about the coming kingdom he could be sure they would be in agreement with him. But when he tried to convince them "about Jesus" on the basis of

Scripture proof from the Law and the Prophets there was diversity of opinion. Some believed and others did not, and they left in disagreement, thus illustrating once more that no entire Jewish congregation could be won over to Christianity. Paul's parting words for the unbelieving ones was that the Holy Spirit was right when he spoke to their fathers through Isaiah, "You shall indeed hear but never understand," and he closed with the announcement, "Let it be known to you that this salvation of God has been sent to the Gentiles; they will listen" (Acts 28:25-28).

It is the third time that Paul utters this thought of God's now turning from the Jews to the Gentiles; the first time was at Antioch of Pisidia (Acts 13:46); the second time was at Corinth (Acts 18:6); and now he says it at Rome. But here alone he gives the climactic prophecy that the Gentiles will listen. It thus is evident that the biographer wanted to make this the final note of the book. Prophetic words, indeed! When Luke wrote, history had taken its fearful course. Jerusalem lay desolate. Frightful destruction had befallen its people, and the Jewish Christians, of whose numbers James had boasted (Acts 21:20), had shrunk to a small sect in Transjordan and Syria. Jews were expelling Christians from the synagogues. Christianity's adherents now were increasingly Gentiles, and among them it was making rapid progress everywhere. The mother church at Jerusalem was gone, and the leadership of Christianity now passed to Antioch, Ephesus, Corinth, Alexandria, and Rome.

This closing scene epitomizes the meaning of Paul, as the author of Acts saw it. Paul made the transition from preaching to Jews to preaching to Gentiles, while at the same time affirming and striving to maintain an indissoluble connection with the Jewish past. The links with the latter were the sacred books in the Greek translation and the hope of Israel in the fully developed form marked by inclusion of the

Pharisaic general resurrection doctrine, which in Luke's and Paul's view also supported the resurrection of Jesus.

The story in Acts then ends with the final vignette of Paul preaching Christ at Rome "unhindered." The author's political purpose was to see reestablished in the Roman Empire the situation of tolerance toward Christianity that had been shown by the state—as he has been at pains to establish—before the sad events came about which his readers well knew and to which he did not need to refer. If he failed in his purpose, it was nevertheless a noble attempt, which, had it succeeded, might have been the salvation of the Roman Empire.

The latter, once established, needed a new religion to hold it together, and was in the process of creating the cult of the majesty of Rome as represented by the emperor as incarnate deity. But men so corrupt and immoral as these rulers were unable to command the respect in which a deity must be held. The idea was, as Ramsay says, "incapable of life, for it degraded human nature and was founded on a lie." Paul offered the empire an idea of far greater potentiality: to permit free competition of religion. Given the opportunity to preach the gospel unhindered, he would have converted half the world, and provided the state with a loyal supporting citizenry. In the end, his idea was to be accepted after more than two centuries of Christian blood and tears. Constantine and Licinius issued the edict of Milan in A.D. 313, whereby Christianity became a legally permitted religion. Its consequent swift rise to power with the help of an emperor no longer claiming to be God, according to the same author, "gave new life to the rapidly perishing organization of the empire and conquered the triumphant barbarian enemy. Had it not been for Paul—if one may guess at what might have been—no man would now remember the Roman and Greek civilization."[8]

The modern reader of Acts is dissatisfied with the ending

of the book. His curiosity has been whetted, and he would
like to hear what had taken place after the "two years." Did
Luke plan to write yet another book to carry the story further?
One must regard that as unlikely. His narrative is ended when
the gospel according to Paul comes to Rome. He could not
complete the account of the life of Paul, since the latter was
the victim of an emperor's whim—of a man who now was
worshiped as a god in the imperial cult. And he did not want
to set up any apostolic martyr: Christianity should have only
one martyrology of consequence—that of Jesus.

To illustrate Christian martyrdom, he chose the obscure
person of Stephen and told his story early in his book. But
he leaves no doubt about it, in the discourse of Paul to the
elders at Miletus, that the apostle's death was close at hand.
Since Luke undoubtedly knew when and how he died, his
witness makes it very difficult to maintain the reports of a
release of Paul, followed by new journeys and a second
captivity.[9]

23 BEFORE CAESAR

> For I think that God has exhibited us apostles
> as last of all, like men sentenced to death;
> because we have become a spectacle to the
> world, to angels and to men.
>
> 1 CORINTHIANS 4:9

AT THE END OF THE "two whole years" (Acts 28:30),
came the decisive new development which the Book of Acts
does not relate—Paul's trial. Whatever his life was to mean
for the world had been achieved. It is fitting that when his
work is accomplished a great man should die, and his death
should be in keeping with his character.

The judge to whom Paul had appealed possessed power
over life and death. There is always a personal factor in every
trial, and in great trials not only the man at the bar but the
man on the bench is on trial before the court of history.
Seen in the perspective of the ages, Paul's trial was one of
the greatest of all time, though the record of it is forever
lost, and we can only attempt to reconstruct it on the basis
of analogy.[1] What manner of a man was this judge?

Nero was born in 37, the son of a prominent Roman and

Agrippina, the sister of the emperor Caligula. Nero's father died when he was three years old. When his mother succeeded in marrying the emperor Claudius in 49, the latter soon adopted her son Nero, aged thirteen. The philosopher Seneca became the boy's tutor. Pallas, the brother of Felix before whom Paul had stood, had been one of Agrippina's chief aides.

Through Agrippina's machinations and with the help of Afranius Burrus, who had been given the command of the Praetorian Guard after the fall of Pallas, Nero became emperor when Claudius died in October, 54.

During the first five years of his reign, Nero was noted for his clemency, liberality, and kindness, but from then on his character took a different turn. In 58 he became enamored of a married woman, Poppaea Sabina, who set herself the goal of becoming Nero's empress. The growth of her influence led to the poisoning of Burrus in 62 and to Seneca's retirement from the scene. The evil Tigellinus, companion of many of Nero's infamies, became Burrus' successor as commander of the Praetorian Guard. Poppaea's objective was attained by inducing Nero to bring about the death of his mother and of his wife Octavia (daughter of the emperor Claudius). Poppaea now became formally married to him. Statues of her were erected and coins were struck in her honor.

It was, perhaps, after the death of Burrus in 62, that the change in Paul's situation came about. It then must have been Tigellinus who, in seeking to clear the court calendar of unfinished business, brought Paul's case to trial. In 62 Nero would have been a young man of twenty-five; Paul, according to our chronology about fifty-one.

Paul's Jewish enemies at Ephesus and Jerusalem naturally had made moves behind the scenes at Rome to influence the attitude of Nero toward this prisoner. The Jewish author, Josephus, shows us how a Jew could accomplish that at this time.[2] He relates that he went to Rome at the age of twenty-six (in A.D. 64), stirred by the plight of certain priests whom Felix had put into bonds and had sent to Rome to plead their cause before Caesar. At Puteoli, which he reached after escape from a shipwreck, he became acquainted with Aliturus, a play-actor of whom Nero—himself an amateur actor—was fond, but who was a Jew by birth. Through this man Josephus was introduced to Nero's wife, Poppaea, and as soon as possible entreated her to procure the liberation of the priests. He obtained this favor from her and many presents besides. The same avenue to Nero—through Poppaea—was no doubt open in 62, and it is reasonable to believe that other influential Jews knew how to find it.

The day came when Paul was brought to the so-called "free prison" until the emperor should send for him. Here he found fellow prisoners who were deeply discouraged as they anxiously awaited their day in court and their verdict. Paul saw in this situation a new opportunity to preach the gospel. We may be certain that he did not preach in vain.

One morning a new prisoner was brought into their midst. He seemed to be very dejected, but was particularly drawn to Paul and kept asking him questions. Paul suspected at once that he was a spy. When he tried to maneuver Paul into saying something against the emperor, the latter declared that the interrogator could say about Nero what he liked, he would not betray him. But as for Paul himself, if he had anything to say about the emperor, he would say it to his face.

The prison warden seemed to be favorably inclined to Paul and asked him whether he needed advice as to how to conduct himself before the emperor. Paul said that he had an adviser—the Holy Spirit. Jesus had given his followers directives for such occasions when they were brought before kings and governors. "When they bring you to trial and deliver you up do not be anxious beforehand what you are to say; but say whatever will be given you in that hour; for it is not you who speak but the Holy Spirit" (Mark 13:11).

"I am glad to find you so confident," said the warden. "Let not Nero's voice or his grim countenance disturb you, for his voice sounds harsh, even when he wishes to speak softly, and his brows overshadow glowing eyes."

On the morning of the fifth day, a scribe with four soldiers came to conduct Paul to the court. The sun had risen, and the nobles were allowed to enter the courtroom. It had been widely reported that Paul, whose alleged preaching of a new religion had caused many protests, would be tried, for the emperor desired a large attendance at such an occasion. The trial promised to be an an interesting one and would set an example.

One can imagine that all craned their necks when Paul was brought in. What manner of a man was he whom they had gone forth to see?

"Paul," says an old source, "was of short stature, bald, of gray head and beard, with a well-shaped nose and bluish gray eyes, of heavy brows, clear complexion, ruddy countenance, and a good chin."[3]

The prosecutor greeted him with scorn. He had a scroll in his hand and waving it said triumphantly, "This list of charges will be your undoing, O Jew!"

Behind the prosecutor Paul recognized an Ephesian, the freedman of a leading member of a synagogue. Obviously he was the sycophant or informer who had told the prosecutor lies about him. Paul saw, too, one from the guild of the Ephesian craftsmen.

"Only false witness can be brought against me," said Paul with dignity.

When the emperor came in, all rose to pay him homage. He seated himself on the dais and declared the court session opened, whereupon the prosecutor cried, "The voice of a god and not of a man!" All save Paul joined in endorsement of this flattery.

"Miserable Jew," the prosecutor cried. "Do you not revere the manifest god?"

Paul raised his eyes to the ceiling as in worship of him who made heaven and earth.

The prosecutor now requested the emperor to "measure the water" allowed to Paul in the hourglass, "lest he talk everyone to death."

The emperor fixed the time of the defendant at half an hour. He then commanded the prosecutor to proceed, and particularly to stress information given by the sycophant. He should put aside the rest as of no consequence.

The charges were formidable. Paul, the prosecutor alleged, had brought unrest into every city to which he had come. Where peace and harmony had reigned, people were now divided and contention was going on. Families were rent asunder.

He had damaged the worship of the gods; of the Ephesian Artemis; of the Corinthian Aphrodite, and others. He discouraged marriage, and allegedly encouraged immorality. It was suspected that in his churches they had secret rites in which they sacrificed human beings and ate their flesh. Worst of all Paul demanded worship for a fellow Jew named Jesus, who had been crucified as a revolutionary in Judea in the time of Tiberius by a Roman governor, Pontius Pilate. It was unthinkable that a state could endure in which such a religion became widespread. And Paul was the man chiefly responsible for spreading it. Even as a prisoner here at Rome he had gained a large following.

Nero then gave Paul the opportunity to defend himself against these charges. We may imagine the apostle as beginning by praising Nero's just government. But he expressed his regret at finding the freedman of a Jew from Ephesus acting as informer. Ephesian Jews had falsely charged him of violating the Temple at Jerusalem by bringing into it a disciple named Trophimus, and this had led to his arrest and trial. He requested that he be set free, as this charge was entirely false. Trophimus was here and could testify that he had not been in the Temple. He then denied the other charges of the prosecutor, and asserted that his enemies among the Jews were the ones who were guilty of fomenting disturbances. If they would but hold their peace, and go their own way, there would be no unrest. The accusations of his favoring immorality or of human sacrifice at cultic meals were wholly malicious and untrue. His message concerned a belief in the resurrection of the dead, which was a tenet of the popular Jewish party called the Pharisees. Paul and his sect held that this resurrection had already begun with that of a man named Jesus whom God had sent to his people but who had been killed by them at Jerusalem (1 Thessalonians 2:15). He had appeared to many, including Paul himself, and had instructed him to carry the message of redemption from sin and death to all men. Paul and his followers were awaiting the return of this Jesus to earth, and at his coming the resurrection would take place. But until heaven itself interfered, the state was secure.

The hourglass, Paul noted, was running low, so he terminated his defense.

Nero now seemed overcome by a fit of anger. Glowering at Paul he asked,

"Did you or did you not call this Jesus 'king'?"

"We call him 'Christ' which is a word for 'king' because our ancient kings were anointed at their accession. So when our people hoped for a king of the future they called him 'the anointed.' "

"Do you expect this king to come soon?"

"When God appoints the day and the hour."

"Will he acknowledge the supremacy of the emperor of Rome?"

"All earthly kingdoms will end. All men will be judged by him, and there will be only one kingdom, a kingdom of God, of which Christ will be the earthly ruler."

"Do you pray to this king?"

"We pray to God and to him, for he is God's son."

The emperor went on, "The Roman empire of which you are a citizen has a state cult. Do you pray to its gods, to Roma, genius of our city, and to the divi—Divus Augustus, Divus Gaius, Divus Claudius?"

"As Jews we cannot do this. The foremost of our laws, one which all of us would rather die for than disobey, says 'You shall have no other gods besides me.' Our people have shown this more than once—most recently when Gaius commanded his statue to be set up in our temple."

"If you will go now to the Roma temple and worship her and the Divi you can go free."

"I am a born Roman citizen and loyal to Caesar. I am willing to do everything for him that is not against conscience, but this I cannot do."

The hourglass had now run out.

"It is Christ or Caesar," said Nero fiercely. "No man can serve both."

The emperor waited a moment, but Paul remained silent, with bowed head.

Then addressing Tigellinus, Nero commanded sternly, "Have him taken out of the gates."[4]

The verdict, which meant death, found vociferous approval from an audience composed of Nero's retainers. A great precedent had been set. All these Christians must be brought to trial as enemies of the state. The Ephesian freedman grinned sardonically; the Ephesian craftsman jeered, "Great is the Diana of the Ephesians."

Paul was led forth by the soldiers through the city's southern gate. He was followed by the downcast Timothy who soon was joined by other friends. The procession passed the pyramidal tomb of Cestius, which still stands there as a witness of the event, and turned into the road heading for Ostia. On the right Paul saw the valley of the Tiber and on the left was the Appian Way by which he had come to the imperial capital.

What a medley of thoughts and emotions must have passed through his soul. He remembered how in the midst of the storm in the Adria he had been reassured by a divine vision, "Fear not Paul thou shalt stand before Caesar." And now, after two years of a ministry of preaching the gospel in chains, he had stood before him. God had brought him here—not to be acquitted but to bear witness to Christ as the king before whom every knee must bow, including Caesar's. Nero had to hear that message, and now he had heard it. Henceforth, this young man of twenty-five was filled with rage against Christ's followers. With prophetic vision Paul saw what storm clouds were gathering for the Christians. But Christ would prevail.

Tramp, tramp, went the footsteps of the marching soldiers on the pavement blocks of the highway. Clank, clank, went his chains. The sounds awakened Paul for a moment to the significance of these passing minutes. Yes. He was going to his death. Well, what was that?

Memories rushed in upon him. He was back in Tarsus. He saw the buffaloes lying up to their necks in the Cydnus River in the suffocating heat; he saw as clearly the parting scene at the harbor when he first went to the Holy Land. He thought of the sin that tortured his mind so often in the night when he could not sleep, how he had persecuted the humble followers of Jesus. Suddenly, there came to mind the awesome hour before Damascus, when he had seen Christ and was called by him to be his apostle. Had it not been revealed to his first mentor, "I will show him how much he must suffer for the sake of my name"? What labor had been performed by him, that he could say, "I have worked harder than any of them" (1 Corinthians 15:10). There were those thousands of miles of marches. Often he had had nothing to eat but the bulblike root of the asphodel, which was the food of the poor. There were the cold nights of Asia Minor in which darkness overtook him and his companions, and they had to huddle together by a small fire. He thought of all the hindrances that were put in his way; of the struggle with Peter and James; of the false apostles who had sought to destroy his congregations; of the treachery and ingratitude he had experienced. But he brushed those memories aside and thought with thanksgiving of the loving friends of Thessalonica and Philippi, of the loyal aides he had had—above all Timothy and Titus—who had never disappointed him. They would carry on his work.

Tramp, tramp went the footsteps of the soldiers. Clank, clank went his chains. Never mind. When that noise would stop his hour would have come.

The travail of his life stood before him, as he had once summarized it: he had been a better servant of Christ than the false apostles "with far greater labors, far more imprisonments, with countless beatings and often near death." He thought of the roar of the sea—the sea that had lured him with its fascination in his youth, so that he had dreamed of being another argonaut, sailing to the setting not to the rising sun. He had experienced its fearful power, had seen it in its rage. Four times he had suffered shipwreck. Vividly it came to his mind how he once had spent a night and a day floating about on wreckage before he was saved. But Christ did not let his servant perish because he still had use for his services. And so it had been throughout the years—in one desperate situation after another. Even in that crucial hour of the night off Malta he had come forth alive when all hope seemed lost.

Tramp, tramp went the footsteps on the pavement. Clank, clank went the chains.

There was so much he still would like to do. He once had wanted to go to Bithynia, but the Spirit had hindered him. There were the fair cities Nicaea, Nicomedia, and beyond was Pontus with Sinope and Amisus. But no matter. The Gospel would spread to them from his congregation at Troas. He once had dreamed of going to the pillars of Hercules, to Gades, with its many heathen sanctuaries or altars, including one unique in all the earth, dedicated to "Death." But others would go there from the converts he had made. His captivity had aided the cause of Christ by enlisting the sympathy of his congregations and arousing fresh zeal. The conviction came to him clearly: his death for Christ would win more men for him than he had been able to persuade in all his life.

Suddenly, a command rang out and the tramp of marching feet ceased. They had come to a swampy depression, the so-called *Aquae Salviae* at the third milestone from the city.[5]

Looking back he saw a little band of disciples following the soldiers and behind them was the throng of the curious bent on seeing the execution that was sure to take place when someone was being led out from the gates.

A soldier relieved him of the chains he had worn so long.

Paul turned to the east and raised his liberated hands once more to utter a brief prayer in the direction of Jerusalem. He spoke in the language of his childhood, beginning with *Abba* "O father" and ending with *Maranatha* "Our Lord cometh."

Gruff was the command of the officer. "Bend forward."

The horror-stricken group of Paul's friends saw Paul obey; saw a soldier's uplifted sword flash for a moment in the morning sun; heard a slight thud as the head fell; saw the body lurch forward and collapse on the ground.

A command rang out. The soldiers turned and marched away. Killing was their business, and they thought nothing of it. The public departed, laughing and jesting. One Jew less. There were too many in the city anyway.

Paul's friends came and stood about his body. There, to one side, lay his head. There was a pool of blood and the red stream was still oozing slowly from his neck. He had written to the Christians of Philippi that even if he was to be poured out as a libation upon the sacrificial offering of their faith, he was glad and rejoiced with them all (Philippians 2:17).

When the blood had ceased to run the disciples wrapped Paul's head and body in his mantle and bore it to a place two miles distant—to the country place of a Roman matron named Lucina, where they dug a simple grave.[6] Here they placed the remains, and covered them over. Ashes to ashes, dust to dust.

The disciples carried the news abroad as swiftly as possible: Paul is dead. There was mourning in the churches of Greece, of Macedonia, of "Asia," of Galatia, Phrygia, and Lycaonia. They were bereft of their father. But the mourning was tempered with a holy gladness. He had borne witness and was with Christ the Lord.

What epitaph could be more appropriate for this fallen leader than the words: "I have fought a good fight, I have finished my course, I have kept the faith" (2 Timothy 4:7)? Thirty years later Clement of Rome declared over Paul's ashes, "He gave his testimony before the rulers, and thus passed from the world and was taken up into the Holy Place—the greatest example of endurance."

Chronological Table*

	LIFE OF PAUL		REIGNS OF THE ROMAN EMPERORS
A.D.			
11	Birth of Paul	14	Death of Augustus
28	Paul comes to Jerusalem	14-37	Tiberius
30	Crucifixion of Jesus. Founding of the Church		
31	Martyrdom of Stephen		
32	Conversion of Paul		
32-34 (35)	Sojourn in Arabia and Damascus		
34 (35)	First Jerusalem Visit, to meet Peter		
34 (35)-44	Paul in Cilicia	37-41	Gaius (Caligula)
44-45	Paul at Antioch	41-54	Claudius
45-47	First Missionary Journey		
48	Second Jerusalem Visit. Council of the Apostles.		
49 (48)	Peter at Antioch		
49-52 (48-51)	Second Missionary Journey		
49	Expulsion of the Jews from Rome		
51-52 (49-51)	Paul at Corinth		
52 (51)	Return to Palestine and Antioch		
53-57	Third Missionary Journey: Ephesus	54-68	Nero
57	Paul arrested at Jerusalem		
57-59	Captivity at Caesarea		
60	Arrival at Rome		
62	Trial of Paul (death or release?). Martyrdom of James the Just at Jerusalem		
67	Persecution of Nero; death of Peter (and Paul?)		

* Tentative. See discussion on p. 272.

The Sources

Paul's Letters and the Book of Acts remain the primary sources from which his story must be reconstructed.

Since it was customary in antiquity to write letters in the name of some famous man, by way of bringing one's own ideas forward, some letters ascribed to Paul are suspected of having been written by later Paulinists. The letters to Timothy and Titus are believed by some to be of this nature. Some also have questions about 2 Thessalonians and Ephesians. The main weight for a picture of Paul must be carried by the remaining letters, especially the one to the Galatians and the two to the Corinthians. Here we have Paul revealed most vividly.

The Book of Acts is invaluable for the information it has preserved. It has come to be much more clearly understood in recent years. Many have wrestled with its details. But for an understanding of the author's methods and procedures, as seen in the light of the historiography of his time, no one has done as much as Martin Dibelius. Like Eduard Meyer he still took Luke to have been the author but evidently not one who was very close to Paul or an eyewitness of anything he related. From this conclusion Ernst Haenchen, in his masterly commentary, has gone further and denied Lucan authorship. It is very clear from this Acts research that the author of Acts (whom we continue to call "Luke" in a noncommital sense) has built up his history out of slight first hand resources. Furthermore, he wrote primarily not from a desire to record history as we understand it, but to serve the need of the church of his own day—which may have been close to the end of the first century A.D. He has therefore been silent about many things of which we hear in Paul's letters. The story of Acts thus must be corrected by the epistles in reconstructing the life of Paul.

For the rest the sources of Jewish history and Hellenistic-Roman history, as well as of early Christian history come in for occasional use.

Abbreviations

A few abbreviations will be used for reference to books as follows:

Beginnings. (Jackson, F. J. F. and Lake, K. ed. *The Beginnings of Christianity,* 5 vols., 1920–23)

Bible Atlas. (*Rand McNally Bible Atlas,* Edited by E. G. Kraeling, 2 ed. 1962)

Dibelius, *Studies.* (Dibelius, M. *Studies in the Book of Acts,* 1956)

Haenchen. (Haenchen, E. *Die Apostelgeschichte,* 12th ed. of the H. A. W. Meyer series; 1959)

Historical Atlas. (Rand McNally, *Historical Atlas of the Holy Land,* Edited by E. G. Kraeling)

Meyer. (Meyer, Ed. *Ursprung und Anfänge des Christentums,* vol. 3, 1923)

Ramsay, *Cities.* (Ramsay, W. M. *The Cities of St. Paul,* 1908)

Ramsay, *St. Paul.* (Ramsay, W. M. *St. Paul the Traveler and the Roman Citizen,* 1898)

Schürer. (Schürer, E., *Geschichte des Jüdischen Volkes im Zeitalter Jesu Christ,* 3 vols. 3 ed., 1903)

Str. Bill. (Strack, H. L. and Billerbeck, P. *Kommentar zum Neuen Testament aus Talmud und Midrasch,* 5 vols. 1922–28)

271

The Chronology

It is perhaps better to speak of chronological assumptions, for certain basic questions of chronology cannot be settled with the means presently at our disposal.

The only nearly certain date in Paul's life is his appearance before Gallio at Corinth (Acts 18:12 ff.). Thanks to an inscription from Delphi, this official's one year term can be dated as either from mid 51–52, or 52–53. Either in August 51 or 52, therefore, Paul left Corinth after spending eighteen months there (Acts 18:11). The later date suits the chronology of Paul better. We will accept it and first proceed from that point and then work back from it.

1. THE THIRD MISSIONARY JOURNEY
AND THE CAPTIVITY

An uncertainty enters here as to when Paul began the third journey, for Luke says only that he left Antioch "after spending some time there" (Acts 18:23). Meyer 3, 41 assumes he did not leave Antioch until the spring of 54. We suspect that he does this on account of the date he accepts for the recall of Felix (cf. below). It would seem preferable to suppose that Paul left on his third journey in the spring of 53, reaching Ephesus by late summer. He spent three years there (Acts 20:31). That would take one to the summer or fall of 56. He then spent the following winter in Corinth as we know from 2 Corinthians; Luke gives him three months in Greece (Acts 20:2). In the spring of 57 he sailed for Palestine, was taken a prisoner and brought to Caesarea. Uncertainty exists as to when the recall of Felix, the governor of Palestine took place. Some date it in 55 (cf. Lake, *Beginnings*, 5, 466) and then must readjust the Pauline chronology to fit. Others (e.g. Schürer, *1*, 579; Meyer 3, 54) in 60 or 61. But 59 seems equally possible. In the former case the words of Acts 24:27 "when two years had elapsed" are understood by some (e.g. Haenchen, 60) as applying to Felix's history rather than to Paul's. We believe that they apply to Paul's history and give him a two year period of captivity, extending from the summer of 57 to that of 59. In the fall of 59 Paul would have started for Rome, but not have arrived until the spring of 60. Two years of captivity (Acts 28:30) would put his trial in 62.

2. THE SECOND MISSIONARY JOURNEY AND THE PRECEDING INTERIM

Paul may have arrived at Corinth at the beginning of 49 or of 50. He must then have left on this journey in the late spring of 48 or of 49.

At this point the question of the journey to the so-called Council of the Apostles (Acts 15) is important. It is quite generally identified with the second Jerusalem journey and conference with three apostles mentioned by Paul in Galatians 2:1. Here the problem is: did the council or conference precede or follow the first missionary journey? It is generally held that it followed, for the simple reason that this tallies with the order of the Acts narrative, though good arguments can be brought forward for the other view, which was proposed by Eduard Schwartz. For the present purpose we take the Acts order to be the most acceptable solution and so infer that the council took place late in 47 or early 48. The visit of Peter to Antioch then came in the late spring of 48 or in 49 and soon after it Paul may have started on the second journey.

The years 46–48 were famine years. It can be shown from other sources that Luke has dated the famine too early in Acts 11:27 ff., for Herod Agrippa, in whose reign he seemingly puts it, died in the spring of 44. In view of Paul's assertion in Galatians 2:1 that he made only two visits to Jerusalem, it becomes attractive to assume that the relief journey (Acts 11:30) and the journey to the council (Acts 15:2) are identical and that Luke was mistaken in separating them.

3. THE FIRST MISSIONARY JOURNEY AND EARLIER EVENTS

The date and duration of the first missionary journey are obscure. If Paul and Barnabas returned in the late summer of 47 and if one gives them two years for this journey as does Ramsay with his unrivaled knowledge of Asia Minor travel, they would have left in the spring of 45.

As Paul is given a year's ministry at Antioch (Acts 11:26), he may have come there in the spring of 44. He then would have been present there at the time of the newly reconstituted Olympic games, for which permission was obtained in 43–44. As these were always held in Julian leap years thereafter, it can be safely inferred that they were held in October, 44.

Paul's second Jerusalem visit took place fourteen years after his first (Galatians 2:1). If the second occurred in late 47 or early 48 the first must have taken place in late 33 or early 34. However, when whole years are not specified the figure may be overestimated by nearly a year. The year then could be 34–35. Since we do not include the three years spent in Arabia (Galatians 1:18) in the fourteen of Galatians 2:1 (as some do) the conversion of Paul would on this basis take one to 31–32. If three years is only a fraction over two years one could have a figure of 32–33.

Still working backward the question here is when the death of Jesus and the founding of the church took place. The generally favored date is 30, though some would go back as far as 28.

Allowing a year for Paul's persecution activity one can put the death of Stephen in 31–32. Some time would seem to have to be allowed for the development of the Church up to that point, though it is a well known fact that new movements can develop very quickly.

The tightness of the schedule would be relieved if the earlier date for the crucifixion could be counted on, or if one include the three years of Galatians 1:18 in the fourteen of Galatians 2:1.

As to when Paul came to Jerusalem and how old he was when he became a persecutor, the conclusions depend on very flimsy suppositions. Some argue that Paul must have been thirty years old before he could start persecuting. Against this stands the Acts account which makes him a young man (see note 9 on Ch. 1). Some scholars (Ramsay, Deissmann) hold that Paul may have been about seventeen years old when he came to Jerusalem. We have accepted that view here.

If we assume that he came in 28 at age seventeen he would have been born in 11.

On the chronology cf. Lake in *Beginnings*, 5, 445–467; Haenchen, 53–64; Meyer, 3,. 37–54; Knox, J. "The Pauline Chronology," Journal of Bibl. Lit. 58, 1939, 15–30. Cf. also Finegan, J. *Handbook of Biblical Chronology*, 1964, 515.

Notes and References

CHAPTER 1. A TARSUS BOYHOOD

1. See *Bible Atlas*, 423 f.; for full account see Ramsay, *Cities*, 85 ff. For Cilician "atmosphere" read Mary Gough, *Travel into Yesterday*, 1954.
2. Roman citizenship and Names. See Cadbury, H. J. *The Book of Acts in History*, 1955, 65–82.
3. On Tribal associations and the necessity of Jewish adaptation see Ramsay, W. M. *Letters to the Seven Churches*, 1914, 146 ff.
4. Aramaic. Josephus too quotes Aramaic words as "Hebrew," as does the New Testament. On whether Paul understood Biblical Hebrew, see ch. 3 note 7.
5. On "tent-maker" see Zahn, Th. *Die Apostelgeschichte* 3 ed., 1922–27, 633. The idea that Paul was a weaver is most improbable. It was a despised occupation and forbidden to a rabbinic student; see Jeremias, *Zeitschrift für die neutestamentliche Wissenschaft*, 30, 1931, 299. It should not be ascribed to Paul by those who think he was one.
6. See Strabo, *14*, 5, 12 f.
7. Some Jews sought to "remove the marks" of circumcision. See 1. Maccabees 1:14 f.; Jos. *Ant.*, *12*, 5, 1.

8. See Plutarch, Antony, 26.
9. The incident is, of course, imaginary, but some reason for Paul's going to Jerusalem must be presupposed. The age at which he went is also uncertain. Acts 22:3 as rendered in the RSV seems to suggest that he came as a child. But if so, neither his father nor he could have been Tarsian citizens—only incolae; see Ramsay, W. M. St. Paul the Traveler, 31 f. This is just stock biographical pattern; cf. the Dutch treatise of van Unnik, A. C. Tarsus of Jerusalem, 1952. Acts 26:4 suggests that he was a youth when he came to Jerusalem. Ramsay, W. M. The Teaching of Paul, 2 ed. 1914, 40 ff. (or The Expositor, 1911, 470 ff.) and Deissmann, A. Paul, 1911, 92 think Paul, judging from his Hellenistic outlook, came to Jerusalem at age seventeen. See also Haenchen, 554 n.

CHAPTER 2. GOING TO JERUSALEM

1. See remarks on chronology.
2. A fictional figure. Paul father's commercial relations with Jerusalem are an invention.
3. A year's engagement is to be assumed in the case of a marriage with a young girl. See Str. Bill. 2, 373 ff. and my The Clarified New Testament, vol. 1, The Four Gospels, 121.
4. On Paul's sister cf. Acts 23:16. Her age relative to his is unknown.
5. On Caesarea see Bible Atlas, 419 f. Ant. 15, 9, 6, 16, 5, 1; B.J. 1, 21, 5–8.
6. This is said of the present inhabitants of the country. See M. Gough, op. cit. 93.
7. River of Life. Ezekiel 47; Revelation 22. The incident is invented.

CHAPTER 3. THE QUEST

1. See Bible Atlas, 399–401 on the Temple tour; Josephus, Ant., 15, 11.
2. See Avi Yonah, M. and Kraeling, E. G. Our Living Bible,

1962, 322 for a color photo of one of these tablets that has survived. For tr. see *Bible Atlas*, 400, or Barrett, C. K. *The New Testament Background: Selected Documents*, 1956, p. 50.

3. See *Bible Atlas*, 415 on the synagogue and an inscription that may come from it. Cf. Barrett, *op. cit.*, 51.

4. Nearly everyone assumes that Paul studied to be a rabbi. This is improbable for the son of a Tarsian Roman citizen, and is made doubtful by the insufficient understanding of rabbinic teaching that he displays. And where but in Jerusalem and Babylonia were there rabbis? These were not like the rabbis of today, who are a counterpart to the Protestant clergymen, but legal scholars, bent on handing down the legal tradition, which was in Hebrew, based on the Hebrew Bible. A Hellenistic youth would have a hard time catching up with fellow students. And where should he make use of knowledge in which there was no livelihood? What the people in the Hellenistic synagogues needed to know about the decisions of the leading teachers was communicated to them from Judea. See the examples in Schlatter, A. *Geschichte Israels von Alexander bis Hadrian*, 3rd ed. 195, p. 439, n. 269. Paul, in our view, was sent to Jerusalem to study Jewish "philosophy," just as Roman youths went to study Greek philosophy at Athens and elsewhere.

5. The association with the Sadducees is assumed on the basis of Josephus' description of his own "philosophical" studies, given in *Life*, 2.

6. The meeting with Caiaphas is imaginary; but see Acts 9:1.

7. Paul nowhere reveals knowledge of the Hebrew Scriptures. His Bible was the Greek translation. Had he known the Hebrew original he would certainly have considered it authoritative, and could not have used the Greek version in the manner in which he does. But that being the case he lacked the equipment to be a regular pupil of Gamaliel. Goodspeed, E. J., *Paul*, 1947, 223 f. modernizes the situation and goes astray here. Even the leading Hellenistic-Jewish commentator on

the Law of Moses, Philo, knew no Hebrew. See Schlatter, *op. cit.* n. 43, p. 395 f.

8. Cf. stringing Biblical quotations, as in Romans 9-11 and the Rock of 1 Cor. 10:4.
9. See Str. Bill., *1*, 250 f.; *4*, 3-21.
10. On conscience as a concept derived from Hellenism see Feine, P., *Theologie de Neuen testaments*, 3rd; 1936, 290 f.
11. Paul's interest in Essenism is modeled on that of the young Josephus; see note 5. That he visited the community seems probable.
12. The Essene community, as rediscovered at Qumran, furnishes the setting for our narrative here. See *Bible Atlas*, 369 and 390 f.; *Historical Atlas*, 5 f. The books of M. Burrows, *The Dead Sea Scrolls*, 1956, and *More Light on the Dead Sea Scrolls*, 1958 can help the reader further.
13. The incident is imaginary.
14. On Bannus see Josephus, *Life*, 2. But it is uncertain whether he was on the scene in 28-30.
15. The grove of willows is indicated on the Mosaic map of Madeba by the Aramaic name of the tree. See *Historical Atlas*, 70, upper left hand corner, where the words are "Ainon; there now *Sapsapha*." Arabic has the same word, *Safsaf*, "willow."

CHAPTER 4. THE PERSECUTOR

1. The two year stay with the baptizer is modeled on that of Josephus, whose studies had the aim we also attribute to Paul of finding the right "philosophy."
2. Having Paul at the Jordan has the advantage of explaining (of course, only hypothetically) how he could have been in Palestine without seeing Jesus or witnessing the crucifixion. (2 Corinthians 5:16 should not be taken to mean that Paul knew Jesus.) Of course, if Jesus had been crucified in A.D. 28 as Meyer, 3, 171 and 205 f. holds (cf. also H. Braun in *Die Religion in Geschichte und Gegenwart.* 3 ed. vol. *1*, 1957, 1963), Paul could have come to Judea after that event.

3. That Paul was encouraged by members of the high priestly party, hence by Sadducees, is indicated by Acts 9:1.

4. That Paul describes himself as a Pharisee suggests that he is thinking (in Greek manner) of "doctrine." In practice the Pharisees were not given to such activism as Paul displays in persecuting Christians. Acts 5:34 ff. depicts the Pharisaic attitude quite well. Paul stood close to the Zealots (as he betrays by referring to his zeal, Phil. 3:6). He may not have been a member of the party (which was Pharisaic in doctrine) because it was anti-Roman, but he was drawn into similar illegal conduct.

5. We have departed from that part of the account of Acts 6:8–7:1, in which Stephen is brought before the council. This is Luke's dramatization and is effective. But it is improbable here since the matter ends in a mob scene in 7:54 f. The laws governing trial and stoning are not observed (Str. Bill. 2, 685 f.). How impossible a death sentence and "regular" stonings were when a strong Roman governor was at the helm is made plain by the story of the stoning of James the Just, *Ant.* 20, 9, 1, which took place after the death of a governor and before a successor had arrived, and then led to an investigation. After a legal stoning, furthermore, no lament was permissible such as Acts 8:2 relates, Mishnah, *Sanhedrin* 6, 5, 6. The true course of events is discernible in the mob violence element of the account. We have reconstructed according to that cue.

6. Most of the discourse attributed to Stephen is a sermon rather than the defense of an accused man. This is because Luke desires to give the episode a broader significance for his book as a whole. His purpose in this speech is to make clear that the whole Hebrew history was one of resisting the Holy Spirit. Dibelius, *Studies,* 167 f., Haenchen, 240 f.

7. Luke has dramatized this story. When he wrote little can have been known about how Stephen conducted himself more than half a century ago.

8. The Acts account has made Paul's role more effective by hav-

ing him cast no stones himself. The laying down of the garments (they were a hindrance when one wanted to throw stones) is referred to again in Acts 22:20 as a *keeping* of the garments. Luke thus implies that there was a danger that they might have been stolen. He is thus willing to believe the worst of the Jerusalem mob. However, he has probably confused this laying aside of garments with the customary taking away of the garment of the man who was to be stoned (Mishnah, *Sanhedrin*, 6, 1 ff.).

9. See Plutarch, *Lucullus*, 1 for the priest's remark.
10. It is inconceivable that the reigning high priest would have been directly involved in this illegal business.
11. The foreign cities of Acts 26:11 may be a generalization of the Damascus visit.
12. The coming of Paul's sister and husband and what is told about them are imaginary. All we really know is that many years later his sister was living at Jerusalem and had a son who was a young man (Acts 23:16).
13. In Acts 9:1 (cf. 22:9; 26:13) Paul is going to Damascus to bring any Nazarenes that he might find, both men and women, to Jerusalem as captives. Luke here shows himself unaware of the legal difficulties that would stand in the way of such action. The involvement of women in such an arrest is wholly un-Jewish. Luke's assumption, however, permits him to give Paul an accompanying police force that would enable him to carry out the supposed deportation plan. But once the plan is recognized as unhistorical the need for such a company falls away. What was a secret venture of Paul to carry his terrorism to Damascus has been elevated to public status by the narrator. This magnified Paul's role as persecutor and also provided witnesses for his Damascus experience. That in turn had apologetic value. But that value was and is illusory. Faith must stand on its own legs, and not use the crutch of rational proof. We have sought to imagine Paul's trip in more plausible circumstances, in agreement with our belief that his activities were secret.

14. The route presupposed is only one of several possible ones.
15. Since we consider the presence of others at the vision experi-
    ence incredible, we have chosen this way of providing privacy
    for Paul.
16. Sir William Ramsay—in so many respects extremely conserv-
    ative—says that he gained more understanding of Paul's ex-
    perience from a fiction story than from any scholarly treat-
    ment (thus implying that Luke's account is far removed from
    reality). See his *Pauline and other Studies*, 1906, 326. He
    quotes the relevant portion of that story in *The Education of
    Christ*, 1902, 8 ff. We have made some slight use of the
    story's idea, but have fused with it a further idea. Cf. the next
    note.
17. This is drawn from an experience related by Thomson, W.
    M. *The Land and the Book*, 3 (1885), 432. That author and
    a companion nearly perished in early May in riding from Da-
    mascus to Sa'sa'—the same stretch in which Paul's experience
    must have taken place—when a chilling blast from Hermon
    descended on them. This becomes understandable in the
    light of a *Wind Chill Table of the U.S.* Army, according to
    which e.g. a thirty-five mile an hour wind at 39 F. has the
    effect on exposed body surfaces of a windless 38 below zero.
    We have told the story in that manner, since it had to be
    told in some more credible way. There is, of course, no possi-
    bility of knowing what actually took place. Paul's words in
    Galatians 1:16 seem to point to an experience of a more mys-
    tical type, that had no external dramatic situation such as
    Luke sought to give it.
18. How far removed from reality the Acts account is may be
    seen from the fact that according to it Paul saw only a daz-
    zling light, whereas Paul testifies that he saw the risen Lord
    in person, 1 Corinthians 9:1; 15:8. The variations in the two
    further rehearsals of Paul's experience (22:6-11; 26:12-18)
    suggests that Luke does not feel tied down to any one pre-
    sentation. He therefore was composing freely in each case.
    All he really knew was that Paul had had his vision of Christ

on the way to Damascus. He narrates it in the manner of Hellenistic storytelling. Compare the vision of that would-be temple-robber Heliodorous (2 Maccabees 3:22-30), which also takes place before witnesses.

19. The Hebrew name form (transcribed Saóul) is used in addressing Paul—not the Hellenized Saulos (7:5,8). But the Lord probably spoke Aramaic. In the eastern Aramaic (Syriac) Bible translation the rendering is: mānā radeph at li?

20. At this point Paul must have received his commission as apostle of the Gentiles (Galatians 1:15-16). Luke has chosen to withhold that here and have it revealed to Ananias (9:16), but in the account given in 26:12-18 the Lord gives Paul the commission at this occasion.

21. A compromise between the idea that Paul rode to Damascus and Acts 9:8. In art representations of the experience he is generally portrayed as riding a horse.

CHAPTER 5. ARABIA AND DAMASCUS

1. The association of Paul and Ananias has been described in an imaginary manner.

2. In Acts 9:16 Paul's Gentile missionary task is revealed to Ananias privately and coupled with a task for Israel. Luke makes it appear that Paul at first devoted himself to conversion of Jews (until the situation of Acts 9:29; see 22:17 f.). This is partly because he wants to give Peter the credit for the origin of mission among the Gentiles (cf. especially Acts 10:11-18), and partly because he wants to keep Paul in the Jewish sphere until he goes to Antioch.

3. The idea that Paul retired to Arabia for contemplation and there developed his theology is modern sentimentalism. Thought develops with action. Paul leaves no doubt about it that he received his task when called. The assumption that he followed the divine command promptly has everything in its favor. That he does not stop to tell us what he did, corresponds to the fact that he is silent too about what he did in

Syria and Cilicia (Galatians 1:21). But the point he was trying to make in Galatians was only that he carried on his work
independent of the Jerusalem group. Elaboration on the work
itself was out of place there.

4. Bostra and Adra'a were called Bozrah and Edrei in Old Testament times.

5. For the Nabataeans see Starcky, *The Biblical Archaeologist*,
18, 1955, 84 ff. The historical material is covered most fully
in Schürer, *1*, 726-44.

6. On Hagra see Musil, A. *The Northern Heğaz*, 1926, 299 f.

7. Aretas IV ruled ca. 9 B.C.–40 A.D. On his daughter's escape see
Josephus, *Antiquities*, 18, 5, 1.

8. The order of Aretas is only my assumption.

9. The mission work of Acts 9:19b-22 must belong after the return from Arabia. Luke has no knowledge of the three years
spent there.

10. We must reject the idea implicit in the RSV rendering that
Aretas was given the government of Damascus by the Romans. This immensely important outpost for the control of
the East would not have been relinquished. The word trans-
lated "governor" is *ethnarch* and this can mean the head of
the foreign community of Nabataeans at Damascus, see Meyer, 3, 246. In any case under Tiberius the coins show Damascus to have been Roman, and our chronology puts the incident in his time.

11. Paul's sister and brother-in-law have been brought in by
imagination only.

12. That Paul sought contact with the local Christians but that
they were suspicious of him (Acts 9:26 f.) does not fit with
the fact of his mission work, of which they certainly had
heard and is ruled out by the nature of his visit (see next
note). But we have retained the mediating role of Barnabas.

13. Luke's account of Paul's preaching at Jerusalem (Acts 9:28-
29) is contradicted by Paul's words (Galatians 1:19-24). His
visit was secret. If he refers to the Jews driving him out

(1 Thess. 2:15) this may have been from Damascus. It affected his status for all Palestine as well.

14. This vision is probably an echo of the one described in 2 Corinthians 12:2-4 which, however, belongs to a later date; see ch. 6. Assuming that he previously spoke chiefly to Jews, Luke has used it for the revelation to Paul of his task for the Gentiles. But this construction is not to be trusted.

CHAPTER 6. THE HIDDEN YEARS

1. The narrative of this chapter is necessarily imaginary reconstruction.
2. A break with his family is virtually a necessary assumption. See Ramsay, *St. Paul*, 36. The account of it is imaginary.
3. It is unthinkable that Paul, having received his task from Christ, sat in Tarsus working at a trade until the time reported in Acts 11:25. Cilicia provided him with a great field. That we hear nothing about his work there from the author of Acts is not surprising. For him this was a forgotten chapter of Paul's history, like the three years in Arabia. This field may have come under the control of the Church of Antioch and then under that of Jerusalem after Paul's break with Peter and Barnabas (see Acts 15:23).
4. J. Knox, *Chapters in A Life of Paul*, 1950, 54 ff. identifies this experience with Paul's Damascus vision. But the "fourteen years" of 2 Corinthians 12:12 and those of Galatians 2:1 demand no identification. Paul, as generally held, wrote the Corinthians in A.D. 57. This would take the incident back to 43 or 44, too late for his Damascus vision. There is a vast difference between seeing the Lord and a visionary trip to paradise.
5. On the events under Caligula see Josephus, *Antiquities*, 18, 8.
6. Acts 12:4 connects the events with the Passover season, which, however, fell very late in 44.
7. See the next chapter. It is, of course, problematic when Barnabas sought out Paul, but 44 A.D. fits our chronology and permits bringing in these games.

CHAPTER 7. ANTIOCH THE GREAT

1. *Bible Atlas*, 427 f.; *Historical Atlas*, 76 (photo); Metzger, B. M. "Antioch on the Orontes," *The Biblical Archaeologist*, 11, 1948, 70 ff.; Downey, G. *Ancient Antioch*, 1963.
2. Malalas 10, 243-245. An English translation from the Church Slavonic version is available, Spinka, M. and Downey, G. *Chronicle of John Malalas Books VIII–XVIII*, 1940. It notes differences from the Greek, which for Books IX–XII is given by Stauffenberg, A. Graf von, *Die Römische Kaisergeschichte bci Malalas*, 1931.
3. Malalas 10, 242, 10 ff.
4. Kraeling, C. H. "The Jewish Community at Antioch," *Journ. of Bibl. Lit.*, 51, 1932, 130 ff.
5. See Meyer, 3, 165 ff.
6. This is a popular story-motif. Josephus has a different version of the story of Herod's death, likewise of popular origin, *Ant.*, 19, 8, 2.
7. The story of Titus given in this chapter is imaginary.
8. Plutarch, *Moralia*.
9. Downey, 90, 103 ff.; see Stauffenberg's chapter "Die Antiochenischen Olympien," *op. cit.*, 412-413.
10. Polybius, 31, 3-4; cf. Downey, 59 f. For want of contemporary information we have retained in what follows numerous items from the games of Antiochus.
11. Stauffenberg, 419.
12. 1 Corinthians 9:25.
13. Some scholars put the Jerusalem journey of Galatians 2:1 ff. before the start of any missionary journey. See Meyer, 3, 169 ff. They then can date the Jerusalem meeting before the arrest of Peter in 44. This has certain advantages but it remains a hypothesis, and there is no compelling necessity to accept it. We therefore have adhered to Luke's order of reporting the first missionary journey before Paul's second Jerusalem visit since his conversion.
14. Renan, E., *St. Paul*, tr. by I. Lockwood, 1869, 212.

CHAPTER 8. THE FIRST MISSIONARY JOURNEY

Cyprus

1. Mark's age is merely a guess, based on his assistant's role.
2. On Jews in Cyprus see Cassius Dio, 68, 32.
3. Aphrodite, Odyssey, 8, 362 f.
4. Sergius Paulus. See *Beginnings*, 5, 465 f.; Ramsay, W. M. *The Bearing of Recent Discoveries*, 1911, 150 ff.
5. On the Magus see Nock in *Beginnings*, 5, 164 ff.
6. Luke's explanation of the name Elymas is unlikely. It is Aramaic *'alima* and means "the servant." The word occurs in that sense already in the fifth century B.C. Aramaic papyri.
7. On the trouble caused by Simon Magus see Eusebius, *Ecclesiastical History*, 2, 13.

CHAPTER 9. THE FIRST MISSIONARY JOURNEY

Asia Minor

1. Some scholars would put the council of the apostles before the journey. See ch. 7, note 13.
2. On the route taken see Ramsay, W. M. *The Church in the Roman Empire*, 1893, 18 ff. It seems to us more likely, however, that Paul being unfamiliar with the country followed Alexander's route (which presumably was the shortest and best) to get to the main highway crossing Asia Minor and then turned eastward. See map of this route in Freya Stark, *Alexander's Path*, 1958, 249. There would be no need of stopping at places west of Antioch if no directive of the Holy Spirit was given to do so. The roads did not pass through cities, like our roads.
3. On the situation and history of Pisidian Antioch see *Bible Atlas*, ref. Ramsay, *Cities of St. Paul*, 247 ff.
4. On Paul's speech see Haenchen, 359 f. The account is intended to be typical, not historical.
5. It is surprising to find the Servant Song applied to the missionary rather than to the Messiah; contrast Luke 2:32.

6. On Iconium, see *Bible Atlas*, ref. Ramsay, *Cities*, 317 ff.
7. In the first century the province cannot have been called "Galatia" officially, for its governor is called in an inscription, "governor of the province (provinces?—the word is abbreviated) of Galatia, Pisidia, Phrygia, Lycaonia, Isauria, Paphlagonia, Galatian Pontus, Polemon's Pontus, Armenia." But abridgement to "Galatia" as part for the whole occurs in Tacitus, Pliny, and Ptolemy. See Lietzmann *Handbuch zum Neuen Testament, An die Galater,* 1.
8. On Lystra see *Bible Atlas*, ref. Ramsay, *Cities*, 407 ff. A new road, the *Via Sebaste*, connected Antioch and Lystra. Iconium lay off to one side of it. At the branch road leading to Iconium, Onesiphorus was waiting for Paul, according to the apocryphal story of Paul and Thecla. See Ramsay, *Cities*, 399. For the acts see James, *Apocryphal New Testament* 272 f. Hennecke, E. *Neutestamentliche Apokryphen*, 3 ed. vol. 2. 1964, 243 ff.
9. The story is not quite realistic in having the priest on hand so quickly with his oxen. For a garlanded bull being led see the relief in Avi Yonah and Kraeling, *Our Living Bible.* 313. An appearance of Zeus and Hermes was related in these regions and used by Ovid in his story of Philemon and Baucis, *Metamorphoses, 8,* 611 ff.
10. For material on Derbe, see *Bible Atlas*, 434; Ramsay, *Cities*, 385 ff. However, the true location of Derbe is to be sought at *Devri-Shehri*, "city of Devri" (=Derbe) four kilometers north-northeast of *Sidrova* and four south-southeast of *Kerte-Hüyük*. See M. H. Ballance, "Derbe and Faustinopolis," *Anatolian Studies, 14,* 1964, 139-146. The same author published the Kerte-Hüyük inscription in *Anatolian Studies, 7,* 1957, 147-51. This was taken to be the site of Derbe at the time, but proved to be wrong.
11. There is no clear indication by Luke that a winter was spent in Asia Minor, but chronological considerations seem to demand it. Ramsay in his chapter on "The Pauline Chronology" in *Pauline and other Studies,* 1906, 365 also allows two years for the first missionary journey (which he dates 46-48).

CHAPTER 10.   THE CRISIS AT JERUSALEM

1. The role ascribed to Mark seems humanly plausible but is purely imaginary.
2. Haenchen, 322 thinks the collection taken to Jerusalem is only an echo of the one Paul brought later on. Perhaps Luke wanted Antioch to have the sole glory of having aided the mother church, and for that reason is silent about the offerings Paul brought from Greece. That assumption fits with the one that the author of Acts was an Antiochene.
3. That the journey of Galatians 2:1 ff. is identical with the journey to the council of the Apostles in Acts 15:1 ff. is generally accepted by critical scholars. The journey of Acts 11:30 then is to be identified with that of 15:1 ff. See the discussion by Lake in *Beginnings* 5, 195 ff.; Funk, R. W. "The Enigma of the Famine Visit," *Journ. of Bibl. Lit.*, 75, 1956, 130-136. Since in the arrangement of Luke, Paul and Barnabas would have been present at the time of the persecution of the church by Herod Agrippa I (late in 43 or early 44) there would have been no famine to assuage, for the famine only developed in Palestine in 47–49. See Gapp, S. "The Universal Famine Under Claudius," *Harvard Theol. Rev.*, 28, 1935, 258-65. Meyer, 3, 165 ff.
4. The narration here is imaginary.
5. James the son of Zebedee and his brother John had aspired to being the head men of the church (Mark 10:35 ff.) and must have been disappointed when James, the brother of the Lord, succeeded Peter.
6. The conversation that follows is imaginary.
7. The Acts 15 account has brought out the importance of the occasion by larger staging. We have retained that for the same reason, though Paul's account that he and Barnabas met with only three leaders is probably the whole story.
8. Peter's speech Acts 15:7-11 and 10:1-11:8 to which it refers back were formulated by the author of Acts. Both have the purpose of taking away the laurels of Paul and others who

originated the conversion of Gentiles and placing them on Peter's head. It is, however, put piously: God first persuaded Peter of the right attitude toward the Gentiles. Luke's account of much debate (15:6 f.) gives the participants a short memory (cf. Acts 11:1 ff.). But the incident is a dramatization to bring Peter forward again.

9. By "the poor" he meant not so much the actual poverty of some, but rather "us poor"—that word having already in the Hebrew psalms the nuance of the pious sufferers. Actually, it is an honorary name of the Messianic congregation. It was continued later when the Jewish Christians had left Jerusalem, for they called themselves, or were called, "the poor" (Heb. ebyōnīm, which was turned into a name, Ebionites). On the Ebionites see Brandon, S. G. F., *The Fall of Jerusalem and the Christian Church*, 1951.

10. If Luke here introduces a letter containing a decree of the Apostles (Acts 15:22 ff.) this was a case of bringing related things together. It is excluded for this occasion by Galatians 2:6. See in Ch. 14.

11. We omit here the mission of the two representatives from Jerusalem, which hangs together with the decree.

CHAPTER 11.   THE BATTLE OVER SEGREGATION AT ANTIOCH

1. The RSV tones down "hypocrisy" in Galatians 2:13 to "insincerity."

2. The further attitude of Peter, Barnabas, and Paul is only a reconstruction.

3. The possibility exists that the alleged quarrel over Mark is not historical but has replaced the dispute of Galatians 2:13 (Haenchen, 418).

4. Since for Luke only a personal difference stood between Paul and Barnabas he thinks of Paul as sent out by the congregation (Acts 15:40). On Paul's independent role see Haenchen, 418. The congregations Paul founded from now on are not daughter churches of Antioch. Paul is their father in Christ.

5. See also Haenchen, 418. In Luke's order of the events in 15: 19-33 Silas returns to Jerusalem; yet a few verses later Paul chooses a Silas to accompany him. They thus can hardly be identical. Under the rearrangement adopted for this book it also remains necessary to assume the existence of two men of that name for we hold that the letter of the Apostles was only brought to Antioch while Paul was on his second journey. See ch. 14 at note 20.

CHAPTER 12. THE SECOND MISSIONARY JOURNEY

From Antioch to Troas

1. This is derived from Philostratus, *Apollonius of Tyana.*
2. The Bordeaux pilgrim, bound in the opposite direction, took a route through Hieropolis-Castabala. See *Palestine Pilgrim Texts Society,* 1888, 107, and Ramsay's note on p. 41.
3. See Ramsay, W. M. "St. Paul's Road from Cilicia to Iconium," in *Pauline and Other Studies,* 1906, 273 ff.
4. The remarks about Timothy's mother and grandmother in 2 Timothy 1:5 may rest on apocryphal stories (W. L. Knox). The marriage of a Jewess to a heathen was contrary to Jewish law. Str. Bill. 2, 741. However the woman may have been a slave.
5. If Acts 16:3 declares that Paul circumcised Timothy this is regarded by many as an erroneous tradition. In Galatians 5:11 Paul alludes to the misrepresentation that he preached circumcision. See Haenchen, 421 f. It was part of a rabbinic education to learn to circumcise, and Luke may have thought of Paul as so educated. But see ch. 3, note 4.
6. If Acts 16:4 here has Paul and Silas deliver to the congregations the decision which had been reached by the apostles and elders who were at Jerusalem, the author is trying to represent Paul as their obedient servant, and is not to be believed. In our opinion the decree was not yet given. See ch. 10, n. 10.
7. Connecting the illness of Galatians 4:13 with the hindrance of the spirit of Acts 16:6 is hypothetical but seems plausible.

8. See again 18:23 where the reverse order occurs. Cf. Lake in *Beginnings*, 5, 233. The North Galatian hypothesis thinks of Paul as having proceeded north from Iconium into Galatia proper. Over against this Sir William Ramsay set up the South Galatian hypothesis, according to which Paul used a (supposed) Roman provincial designation "Province of Galatia," in which lay the cities visited on his first journey with Barnabas. Ramsay, accordingly, considered the Epistle to the Galatians as addressed to those same congregations. See *St. Paul*, 102; Meyer, 3, 199; *Bible Atlas*, 435. However, it is unlikely that Paul would have addressed the inhabitants of this part of the province as "Galatians" (Celts) as he does in Galatians 3:1. But Ramsay is right in saying that Paul can hardly have gone into Galatia proper. See also Lake, *Beginnings*, 5, 236, who assumes Paul took the road to Dorylaeum —going north first from Iconium to Laodicea and thence to Nakoleia. We think of him as turning off after passing Antioch, at Metropolis.

9. *St. Paul the Traveler*, 94 f. or *The Teaching of Paul*, 306 ff. For report of the various views and literature see Lietzmann's excursus in *Handbuch zum Neuen Testament, Die Korintherbriefe*, 4th ed., 1949, at 2 Corinthians 12:10.

10. In *Bible Atlas*, 438 and on color map XX we took Paul via Prymnessus, Synnada to Cotiaeum to Adramyttium. Cf. Findlay's map in Hastings, *Dictionary of the Bible*, vol. 3, opp. p. 697. Ramsay in Hastings' *extra volume*, 391 (see also map between pp. 400 and 401) has him take a more northerly course from Dorylaeum down the Rhyndakos River valley, keeping near the Mysian border (in hope that the Spirit would permit him to enter at some other point) and to Artemeia, and thence veer southwestward to Troas. Obviously any route remains the product of guesswork.

11. On the interpretation see Haenchen, 424 n. 4.

12. On the later spread of Christianity into Bithynia see Ramsay, *Church*, 225.

13. The dream of Paul may be only an offshoot of legend—perhaps of one in the sagas about Alexander the Great, who al-

legedly saw a vision of a man in a peculiar garb, exhorting him to cross boldly over the sea to Asia and promised that he would give him victory. See Josephus, *Antiquities, 11,* 8, 5. Lucullus, too, had a vision at Troas; see Plutarch, *Lucullus,* 12.

14. In the so-called Western text a "We" appears already in 11: 28. But this is hardly original; see Haenchen, 317 n. Other "We-sections" are found (apart from chs. 27-28, on which see later) in 20:5-15, 21:1-18. See Dibelius, *Studies,* 199 ff., where the problem is broadened by analogies in other ancient writings.

CHAPTER 13. THE SECOND MISSIONARY JOURNEY

Through Macedonia

1. At Halicarnassus Jews held prayers at the seashore; Josephus, *Antiquities, 14,* 10, 23.
2. On this city see Ramsay, W. M. *Letters,* 327 ff.
3. On the tribunal at Philippi, though of a later date, see Davies, P. E. "The Macedonian Scene of Paul's Journeys," *Biblical Archaeologist, 26,* 1963, 96. Two photos in *Life, 57,* no 26, 1964, 116 f. with Knox's *Paul* article are pertinent for this chapter.
4. See Ramsay, *Church,* 70 ff.
5. On the criticism of the story see Haenchen, 439 f.
6. Without this story the beginning of missions in Europe would have seemed too depressing to the ordinary reader of Acts who did not have Paul's power of faith and endurance.
7. See Davies, l.c. 102 f. It was reconstructed after 1916.
8. The pilgrim of Bordeaux, who passed this way, noted concerning Arethusa in his log "Here is buried the poet Euripides." See the itinerary already mentioned (Ch. 12, note 2), p. 29.
9. The northern part of Illyricum was called Dalmatia (2 Tim. 4:10), the southern part Pannonia.
10. Contrary to Acts 17:15 Timothy went along (1 Thessalonians 3:1-2).

CHAPTER 14.   THE SECOND MISSIONARY JOURNEY

Athens and Corinth

1. On Athens see *Bible Atlas*, 441 f.; Broneer, O. "Athens City
   of Idol Worship"; *Biblical Archaeologist*, 21, 1958, 2 ff.
2. This makes improbable the theory of Curtius and Ramsay
   (see the latter's *St. Paul*, 199 f. and *The Bearing of Recent
   Discoveries*, 101 f.) that Paul was taken before the council of
   the Areopagus which met in the Agora area (so also Cadbury,
   The Book of Acts in History, 51 ff.). There is no indication
   that Paul had to face a court and if that had been the case
   there would have been no other audience as A. D. Nock,
   Gnomon, 25, 1953, 506 n. 5 points out. The alleged super-
   visory activity of the council over education (which has provided some with an excuse to bring Paul before this body)
   has been shown by Haenchen, 456 f. to be baseless.
3. See Dibelius, *Studies*, 80, whose view we here follow as in
   Historical Atlas 77 (with photo of the area D. thought of).
   It may be, however, that Luke is thinking of the hilltop,
   without having realistic knowledge of its nature. So Haenchen, 465. Nock (see note 2) believed that Luke's picture of
   Athens was based purely on literary sources.
4. On the address of Paul see Dibelius, *Studies*, 29 ff.
5. For the Pergamum inscription, see Deissmann, *Paul* 261 ff.
   Apollonius of Tyana (Philostratus, 6, 3) observed that it was
   wiser to speak well of all gods at Athens where one even con-
   secrated altars to unknown gods. E. Norden *Agnostos Theos*,
   1913, 3 ff. has written in detail of this matter.
6. See Broneer, O., "The Apostle Paul and the Isthmian
   Games," *Biblical Archaeologist*, 25, 1962, 2 ff.
7. *Bible Atlas*, 443 ff.; Broneer, O. "Corinth, Center of St.
   Paul's Missionary Work in Greece," *Biblical Archaeologist*,
   14, 1951, 78 ff.
8. Suetonius, *Claudius*, 25. See Meyer, 3, 463.
9. The famous Maecenas, right hand man of Augustus, had a
   freedman of this same name.

10. An inscription "Synagogue of the Hebrews" testifies to the existence of a synagogue at Corinth, perhaps a successor of the one of Paul's day. See Deissmann's work (cited in ch. 15, n. 5) p. 13.

11. On shaking out of garments see Cadbury in *Beginnings*, 5, 246 ff.

12. On the Gallio inscription see Barrett, C. K. *New Testament Background*, 48 f.; Deissmann, *Paul*, 261 f.

13. For a plan showing the location of the tribunal, and a photo of a part of it see Broneer's Article cited in note 7.

14. For the letter of Claudius see Bell, H. I. *Jews and Christians in Egypt*, 1924, 25.

15. On the vow in Jewish custom see Str. Bill. 2, 747-51.

16. See *Bible Atlas*, 446 ff.; Parvis, M. M. *Biblical Archaeologist*, 8, 1945, 62 ff.; Ramsay, *Letters*, 210 ff.

17. Haenchen, 483 holds that Paul's going to the synagogue is an unhistorical tradition, to give the impression that he was the first to preach Christ at Ephesus, while in reality this was done by Apollos (Acts 19:24). "He left them there" (vs. 19) would be excellently continued by vs. 21, as Wendt suggested and thus apply to his friends. As the text stands it is strange that Aquila and Priscilla do not go with Paul to the synagogue.

18. That Luke means to say Paul went to Jerusalem can hardly be doubted. It could, however, be a construction of Luke (so Haenchen, 484). Knox, "The Pauline Chronology," *Journ. of Bibl. Lit.*, 48, 15 ff., accepting this visit as historical, makes it the one of Galatians 2:1 (cf. Haenchen, 480, who points out the difficulties of this view).

19. The rendering of the RSV "I was eager to do" seems too weak, and is based on the assumption that the only money ever brought by Paul to Jerusalem was that of the last journey. One cannot believe that Paul did not make efforts to carry out his agreement earlier. This is the appropriate occasion for him to have made his first payment, and I have construed accordingly; so also Meyer, 3, 38.

20. As noted in ch. 10. Luke, in formulating this letter and plac-

ing it where he did, may have injected into it the earlier action on circumcision. The ecclesiastical-political aspirations reflected otherwise in the letter forbid attributing it to the time of the agreement of Galatians 2.

21. On the interpretation of Acts 15:29 see Str. Bill. 2, 729 ff.
22. Malalas 10, 242. See Spinka and Downey, 52.

CHAPTER 15. THE THIRD MISSIONARY JOURNEY

Through Asia Minor to Ephesus

1. Galatia and Phrygia. See Beginnings, 5, 239. The variation from Acts 16:6 in the order of these terms should not be stressed. Meyer 3, 198 may be right in holding that Luke knew of the letter to the Galatians and introduced mention of Galatia on this account, without being clear about the course of Paul's travel.
2. If the Gospels stress the role of John as fore-runner of Jesus this is partly due to the desire of absorbing his sect. The goal, however, was not fully attained. The sect continued and apparently the Mandeans of Iraq are an offshoot of it. On them, see E. S. Drower, The Mandeans of Iraq and Iran, 1937.
3. The piece Acts 18:24-28 seems to have been fitted in secondarily by the author, and the clause "While Apollos was in Corinth" added in 19:1 to resume the connection.
4. See Dibelius, Studies, 23 f.
5. For such a magical text see Deissmann, A. Light from the Ancient East, 2 ed. 1909, 249 ff. On book costs see Clemen, C. Paulus, 1, 1904, 285.
6. Some think the Christ party had no real existence. See J. Weiss in his commentary on 1 Corinthians.
7. On the rabbinical position see Str. Bill. 3, 343 ff., especially p. 358.
8. In the resurrection narratives of the gospels a later, more naturalistic conception of the event has been developed over against docetism—the teaching that Christ only seemed to have risen. See my Clarified New Testament, 1, The Four-Gospels, 112.

9. James, *Apocryphal New Testament*, 270 ff.; Hennecke, 2, 222 ff.
10. To the Romans, 5:1. In *Bible Atlas*, 449 I gave some credence to the apocryphal tradition.
11. See Ramsay, *Letters*, 210 ff.
12. See Ramsay, *Church*, 470 f. and map of the area; *Letters*, 413 ff.; Johnson, S. "Laodicea and its Neighbors," *Biblical Archaeologist*, 13, 1950, 1 ff.
13. See Knox, J. *Philemon among the Letters of Paul*, 1950.
14. Marcion's text had "in Laodicea" in 1:1. Harnack took Ephesians to be the letter to the Laodiceans. Meyer, 3, 482 thinks Tychicus, authorized by Paul, wrote a circular letter into which any name could be inserted. An apocryphal letter to the Laodiceans was produced in the 2–4 centuries in Latin. See tr. in James, *Apocryphal New Testament*, 478 f.
15. Others would assign it to the Caesarean captivity. The praetorium at Caesarea is mentioned Acts 23:35. On the word see *Beginnings*, 5, 322. On the problem see Dibelius, in Lietzmann's *Handbuch*, on Phil. 1:12 f.

CHAPTER 16.   THE THIRD MISSIONARY JOURNEY

The Crisis in Paul's Career

1. Luke's avoidance of the title of "Apostle" for Paul is an indication that it was denied him at Jerusalem.
2. The Latin Bible's *Anathema sit* became a much used expression in condemning heretics.
3. From 1 Corinthians 11:25 it may have gotten into the gospel tradition. See my *Clarified New Testament*, 1, 100.
4. Bornkamm, G. *Die Vorgeschichte des Zweiten Korintherbriefes*, 1961, thinks there was an invasion of yet another and very different group at Corinth, after Paul had thought everything was settled and that this led him to append the four chapters. (See now Georgi, D. *Die Gegner des Paulus im 2. Korintherbrief*, 1964.) This makes the Corinthian congregation a rather vacillating one. We need not enter into the dismemberment of 2 Corinthians into a compilation of a whole

correspondence as suggested by these writers. The possibility that Paul threw together various drafts of material he had composed but not sent may deserve consideration.

5. On the Artemis of Ephesus and her shrines see Ramsay, *Church*, 125 f.; L. R. Taylor in *Beginnings*, 5, 251 f.

6. This may not be as exaggerated as it seems, for some decades later under Hadrian official Roman coins were struck bearing the name and image of *Diana Ephesia*, proving that the government was bolstering the cause of this deity.

7. On the Asiarchs see L. R. Taylor in *Beginnings*, 5, 256 f. This same type of official existed in other provinces too. In Lycia they were called Lyciarchs; in Syria, Syriarchs, etc. We have suggested at the end of ch. 15 that the Asiarachs helped Paul in an earlier situation.

8. It has been held by some that Paul is referring to the pillars of Jerusalem (Galatians 2:9). So already have some ancient church fathers, and not only modern radicals, like F. C. Baur and the Tübingen school. So great a conservative as A. Schlatter took that standpoint; see his *Paulus der Bote Jesu*, 1934, on 2 Corinthians. However, most scholars believe that these opponents of Paul were men of lesser consequence. They may have been persons sent out by the Pharisaic wing of the Jerusalem church (cf. Acts 15:1, 24). According to Bornkamm and Georgi the invaders who occasioned the writing of chs. 12-15 were Gnostics.

CHAPTER 17. THE THIRD MISSIONARY JOURNEY

Corinth and the Letter to the Romans

1. This we must infer from the fact that Paul later travels to Palestine with congregational representatives. The Book of Acts does not mention his going to Corinth, but that is implied in 20:2 in his going to Greece (Hellas, for Achaia, Acts 19:21).

2. One cannot help feeling that Paul was seeking to get a foothold in Rome, and that the Spanish objective could be postponed; cf. Meyer, 3, 467.

3. In the oldest known text of Romans—a papyrus of about A.D. 200—the doxology of 16:25-27 is found after 15:33. This is a further indication that the letter had ended at that point. The doxology is of Marcionite origin (Harnack).
4. T. W. Manson, "Paul's Letter to the Romans and Others" *Bulletin of the John Rylands Library*, 31, 1948, 224-40. See G. Bornkamm, *Das Ende des Gesetzes*, 1952, 9-92.
5. This carried more persuasion to people conscious living at the turning point of the ages than to a modern reader.
6. Meyer 3, 465 f.
7. Wilamowitz-Moellendorf, Ulrich von in *Kultur der Gegenwart*, 1, 8, 1905, 157 f.

CHAPTER 18.   THE THIRD MISSIONARY JOURNEY

The Return to Palestine

1. Acts 20:4-6 is not entirely clear. Did some of the party go by ship from Corinth to Troas? If all went by land through Macedonia did only Paul and a companion linger at Philippi? Cf. Haenchen, 515 and 517.
2. The secular nature of the Eutychus story was observed by Dibelius, *Studies*, 17 f.
3. Deissmann, *Light from the Ancient East*, 446.
4. Ramsay, *St. Paul*.
5. Dibelius, *Studies*, 155 f. made clear that Luke composed this speech.
6. Meyer, 3, 57 n.

CHAPTER 19.   IN THE HOLY CITY

1. See Str. Bill. 2, 755 ff. on the rabbinic material.
2. On Pentecost, *Ibid.* 597 ff. Josephus uses the Aramaic name form. In the O.T. it is called Festival of the (seven) Weeks (Ex. 34:22; Deut. 16:10), Heb. *Shabu'oth*.
3. The Egyptian. The incident is reported by Josephus, *Ant.*, 20, 8, 6; *Jewish War*, 2, 13, 5. He differentiates the Egyptian and

his attempt to seize power from the "assassins" (*sicarii*), so
Luke is mistaken in mentioning them here.

4. Luke's idea to have Paul address the crowd was an excellent
dramatization. How fitting that he should speak to "Israel" in
the Temple in this period when the doom of that structure
was drawing near! Actually, however, it is unlikely that Paul
was able physically to do so. That he was carried up the stairs
by soldiers (vs. 35) indicates that he was badly beaten and
unable to walk, not as Luke is forced to interpret—to protect
him. Carrying a man would be a poor way to protect him,
since the bearers would be defenseless.

5. See Cadbury in *Beginnings*, 5, 275 f.

6. The high priest Ananias, son of Nedebaeus, held office ca. 47–
59 (see Schürer, 2, 219, 221). He was murdered by the Zealots in September A.D. 66.

7. The story is full of improbabilities, according to Haenchen,
567 ff. The tribune's convocation of and attendance at a
meeting of the Sanhedrin is unlikely. The tribune himself
and the temple authorities could do what was necessary in the
situation. Nobody had any competence to consider Paul's activities in faraway lands. But Luke is trying to achieve certain
effects. Paul's arrest is given greater dignity by having him
brought before the Sanhedrin. His clash with the high priest
provides an opportunity to have Paul prophesy the latter's
death, which had taken place when Luke wrote (see note 6).
Having Sadducees and Pharisees quarrel illustrates the difference between these factions, and makes possible the claim
that Christianity is really a form of Pharisaic Judaism, which
Pharisees should not object to. The real Paul would have
spoken very differently, and the real Sanhedrin would have
acted differently. From our point of view (though perhaps
not from Luke's) Paul appears to be craftily throwing a bone
of contention into the meeting (see the quotations from Far-
rar, in Ramsay, *Pauline and Other Studies*, p. 84 f.). The
general hope of Israel and the Pharisaic resurrection doctrine
were not at issue at all, but rather the question whether Jesus
was the Messiah and whether he had been raised from the

dead prior to any general resurrection. (Luke still has Paul's perspective of 1 Corinthians 15:20.) Greek readers must have thought of the Sanhedrin with contempt in the light of the superior order and propriety that would prevail in the Senate of a Greek and Roman city, Ramsay, Ibid. 97.

8. Luke here uses the *sicarii*, of whose murderous activities at this time Josephus gives information in Ant., 20, 8, 5 and Jewish War, 2, 13, 3.

CHAPTER 20. THE CAPTIVITY AT CAESAREA

1. After a night march of twenty-five miles for the foot soldiers a return on the next day is not very plausible.
2. The reaction we have attributed to James is imaginary.
3. In Acts 23:1-10 no such findings were made by the Sanhedrin. Luke is wording this to set forth Paul's prominence by an outside view.
4. Herod Agrippa II experienced this kind of custody, though on a higher social level (see Josephus, Ant., 18, 6, 6 f.).
5. There is much dispute as to whether the two year period of Acts 24:7 refers to Paul's captivity or to the term of the governorship of Felix which then might be near its end. The position taken affects the chronology. See the special note on that. In our opinion Luke would hardly have known anything definite about a governor's term of office, but he could know about the duration of Paul's imprisonment (cf. 28:30). Josephus' account of Felix's administration requires more time than two years (cf. 24:10 and Schürer, 1, 577 f.). Meyer, 3, 54 dates his recall in 61.
6. Luke's statement arouses objections; see chs. 5-6.

CHAPTER 21. FROM CAESAREA TO MALTA

1. According to Ramsay, St. Paul, 316 they had to go in the role of Paul's slaves. This seems uncertain; Haenchen, 623 n. 1.
2. The Augustan cohort is known to have been in Syria earlier under Quirinius, but at this time, under Agrippa II, was sta-

tioned in Batanaea (Bashan). See Broughton in *Beginnings*, 5, 443 f.; Meyer, 3, 480 n.

3. The westerly wind was advantageous for the direct northerly run from Alexandria to Myra, but if it shifted to the northwest a vessel might be blown to the Syrian coast. This happened to the ship *Isis* of Lucian; see Casson, *The Ancient Mariners*, 1959, p. 235 f.

4. The ship on which Josephus went to Rome is said to have carried six hundred persons, *Life*, 3.

5. The northwest winds began to blow in August, according to Pliny, and lasted forty days.

6. On Fair Havens see *Bible Atlas*, 455. For details see Smith, J. *Voyage and Shipwreck of St. Paul*, 4th ed. 1888, 82, 262 ff. Note the opinion on p. 271 that a ship could winter there without much danger.

7. Phoenix (Phoenikias). This is taken by navigational experts to have been near the present Lutro, the best harbor on the south coast of Crete. See *Bible Atlas*, 455; Smith, *The Voyage and Shipwreck of St. Paul*, 88 ff. Thus Captain Spratt is quoted as saying, "It is the only bay in which a vessel would be quite secure in winter" (see Smith, 91 f.). The matter is rendered somewhat problematic by the words of Acts 27:12, a harbor "looking southwest and northwest." Smith defends the interpretation that this refers to its opening to the northeast and southeast from the standpoint of a ship at sea (the RSV translates according to this view). Wordsworth observed that there is a bay on the west side of the promontory containing Lutro which is named Phineka and which is open to the west. He would localize the intended harbor there (see also Lake in *Beginnings*, 5, 342 and Haenchen, 626 f.). But the visits of the yachtsman Tennant at Lutro in Smith's Appendices I and II should not be overlooked (pp. 261 f.; 269 f.). I would trust the realistic judgment of seafaring men that Lutro was the intended stopping place, even if the narrative description did not fit it, for an error could easily creep in in such a matter as remembering or copying out the directions in which a harbor faced. No one in his right senses

would go past the best harbor to winter in one that was not secure. From Lutro harbor the grand pyramid of Mt. Ida is visible forty miles away.

8. The item in 27:9-11 brings Paul to the fore, but stands outside of the "We-account," which resumes in vs. 15 (but perhaps already in vs. 12).

9. The Northeaster. On the Greek terms of direction see Lake and Cadbury in *Beginnings*, 5, 338 ff. Cf. *Bible Atlas*, p. 456.

10. The name-form "Clauda" was used by an old Cretan Greek whom Tennant consulted, Smith, 259. "Cauda" is probably the Latin name-form.

11. Undergirding the ship. What is meant has produced much discussion. See Cadbury in *Beginnings*, 5, 345-53. Smith's reference to nineteenth century procedures (108 ff.) and the Smartley painting of St. Paul's vessel (opp. p. 141) are of interest. Breusing, H. *Die Nautik der Alten*, 1886, 170 ff. thinks the girding was longitudinal.

12. The lowering of the gear is taken by Smith, p. 111 f. to refer to the yard with the sail attached to it. But for the view adopted here see Haenchen, 628 n. 2 and the references there given to Renier.

13. The incident of vss. 21-26 is no "We"-material, but (like vss 9-12) was injected into what is primarily the narrative of a journey. See Dibelius, *Studies*, 213 f.

14. Josephus, too, was shipwrecked in the Adria a few years after Paul; see his *Life*, 3. Ptolemy includes the sea between Crete and Sicily in the Adria.

15. On Koura Head see Smith's report of a court martial at which the lookout of a British ship testified that at the distance of a quarter of a mile the land could not be seen but that he saw the surf. Thus those on Paul's ship likewise could not be aware of the nearness of land until they reached the entrance of the bay. The distance from Clauda to Koura Head is 476.6 miles, which at the rate of drift that Smith ascertained from experienced navigators of sailing ships, would take thirteen days, one hour and twenty-one minutes (Smith, 126 f.). The fourteenth day of Acts is thus reliable.

16. On soundings here see Admiralty chart in Smith opposite p. 129.
17. It should be noted that this is not "We-material."
18. The story is puzzling in some respects. Where were the captain and the ship-owner? If the boat had not been set adrift could not all have made shore and the ship perhaps have been saved? Smith, 137 n. notes that there was no possible advantage in putting out the bow anchors. One can see that the important thing for the sailors was to get the boat into the water. Those who think the ship could have been saved are mistaken. A sailing vessel under such circumstances was ruined from the strains suffered. See Smith, 144 f.
19. The incident of vss. 33-37 brings in Paul again in a vivid manner, as was the case in vss. 9-12; 21-26; 30-32. It is not "We-material."
20. In vss. 39-44 we again have third person material primarily focused on the happenings. Indeed the words "wishing to save Paul" can be suspected of being an addition by Luke in adapting an existing shipwreck narrative to his purpose. (This is Dibelius' opinion of the shipwreck narrative, following a cue of Norden, op. cit. 313.) As he observes it is strange that nothing is said of how Paul fared, for whose sake the centurion allegedly had interfered; Dibelius, Studies, 214.
21. Acts 28:1-2 are a snatch of "We-material." The "natives" are "barbarians" in the Greek. From the Hellenistic point of view only those who shared in the Hellenistic culture and could speak the Greek language were not barbarians.
22. Acts 28:3-6 is an enclave of material of different origin, secular in spirit. See Dibelius, Studies, 17 f. It lacks a Christian conclusion (cf. Acts 14:15 f.). Its historicity is rendered uncertain on several grounds: there are no poisonous snakes on Malta; Spratt, Travels and Researches in Crete, 2, 1867, 7, and the story has a parallel in the funerary inscription of a shipwrecked mariner who escaped death in the waves, only to be bitten by a serpent and die when ashore in Libya; quoted from Wettstein by Haenchen, 638 n.

23. The title of Publius is vindicated by inscriptions found at Malta (*Beginnings*, 4, 342). His name is a *praenomen* or first name, which as noted in ch. 1 was not ordinarily used. For this reason Ramsay, (*St. Paul*, 343), thought the man's name was really Popilius, which is a *nomen*, or clan name. Meyer, 3, 30 n. asserts that first names were used in households, but not outside. Zahn, 846 thinks use of the first name shows intimacy between Paul and Publius.
24. 28:7-10 are "We-material."

CHAPTER 22. ARRIVAL AND CAPTIVITY AT ROME

1. Acts 28:11-16 are "We-material."
2. On the names and emblems of ships see Casson, *The Ancient Mariners*, p. 214.
3. On the celebration for the arrival of the grain fleet see Casson, 236 f.
4. Horace, *Sat. 1*, 5, 3.
5. In Acts 28:15 Paul is met by Christians from Rome—first at Forum Appius and then at Three Taverns. He thanks God and takes courage. But one must be suspicious of this verse, as an interpolation made at the time when Acts was received into the canon. For the preceding verse ends with "so we came to Rome," and this cannot be taken with Ramsay, *St. Paul*, 346 f. as referring to the district of the capital, as *Beginnings*, 4, 345 points out. Owing to the interpolation, the beginning of vs. 16 was altered. Luke's purpose was to show that Paul crowned his career by carrying the gospel to Rome. He has prepared the way for it with his whole narrative since Paul's last trip to Palestine. Had he wanted to tell of Christians at Rome before Paul, he would also have brought them in to associate with the imprisoned man and to serve him. But Paul alone is propagandizing Christianity in the concluding verses of Acts. Seen in this manner Acts 28 becomes the great climax: Paul brought Christianity to Rome. But in receiving Acts into the canon in the latter part of the second century

churchmen could not let this impression stand. The Epistle
to the Romans showed that there was a Christian congregation at Rome before Paul, and if so it could be assumed that
the arriving apostle was properly received. Not only one but
two delegations went forth to meet him.

6. For the correspondence of Paul and Seneca see James,
   Apocryphal New Testament, 480 ff.; Hennecke, 2, 84 ff.
7. If Paul was a prisoner for two years at Caesarea it is incredible that the Jews at Rome would have known nothing of the
   charges. Luke wants to give Paul an ideal, unprejudiced Jewish assembly before which to present the Christian gospel
   for the last time. Thus the break with Judaism is made fully
   dramatic and decisive after the anticipatory incidents of Acts
   13 and 18. See Haenchen, 650 ff. on the historical improbabilities of Luke's construction.
8. What Paul had to offer the Roman empire is set forth briefly
   in Ramsay, *Pauline and Other Studies*, 1894, 99 f.; more fully
   in his *The Church in the Roman Empire*.
9. Ramsay, *Teaching of St. Paul*, 352 held that the case against
   Paul was dismissed, because no accuser appeared within the
   eighteen months limit set by Claudius. This is placing too
   much reliance on Acts 28:21. But the question whether Paul
   was set free and was able to resume his travels is bound up
   with the problem of the authenticity of the Epistles to Timothy and Titus, as well as that of a second captivity after a
   journey to Spain. In *Bible Atlas*, 461-64 I took a more posi-
   tive view, partly because of holding Philippians to have been
   written from Rome, and partly because of the statement of
   1 Clement, written about 95 A.D. at Rome, that Paul had
   reached "the limits of the west," which can only mean the
   straits of Gibraltar. But if Philippians mirrors an Ephesian
   captivity the case is gravely weakened. The Spanish journey
   may just be an inference from Rom. 15:24. The destruction
   of the Christian community in the persecution of Nero prevented any continuity of tradition. The material offered in 2
   Tim. 4:10 ff. could be understood from the situation of the
   captivity in Caesarea; see Dibelius, in Lietzmann's *Handbuch*,

Timotheus I-II, Titus, 3 ed. 1955, on that section. However, for the purposes of biography these items, controversial as they are, add little light.

CHAPTER 23. BEFORE CAESAR

1. For our imaginary reconstruction of the trial of Paul we have used Philostratus' account of the trial of Apollonius of Tyana before the emperor Domitian. This enabled us to do without the fictional persons of the apocryphal Acts (see James, *Apocryphal New Testament*, 270 ff., or Hennecke, 2, 221 ff.). Philostratus was close to the wife of the Emperor Septimius Severus, and thus to life at the imperial court. He is apt to have had realistic knowledge of how trials were conducted. Unlike Paul, Apollonius escaped death and was able to go to Godes in Spain. On the numerous questions of Roman law involved in Paul's appeal and trial and all the uncertain answers see Cadbury in *Beginnings*, 5, 321 ff.
2. See Josephus, *Life*, 3.
3. Malalas, 10, 257. This author gives physical descriptions also of the emperors.
4. A Roman custom in executions, Tacitus, *Hist.* 4, 11.
5. On the traditional place of execution see Barnes, A. A. *The Martyrdom of St. Peter and St. Paul*, 1933, 74; Lietzmann, H. *Petrus und Paulus in Rom*, 1927, 170.
6. The Lucina story enjoys no very early attestation; see Lietzmann, 188.

Index

Abraham, 97, 183, 200
Acco, 212
Achaia, 152, 168
Achaicus, 167
Achilleum, 131
Acre, 212
Acro-Corinth, 150
Acts of the Apostles, 269 f.
Acts of Paul, 175
Adam-Christ, 200
Adana, 71, 126
Adra'a, 58, 284
Adramyttium, 130, 206, 240, 292
Adria, 244, 251
Adriatic, 249, 250
Aegae, 71
Aegean Sea, 157, 241
Aeneas, 249
Aeschines, 207
Aesculapius, 71
Aetna, Mt., 249
Agabus, 80, 107, 212, 222
Agora, 155, 294; see also marketplace
Agreement, 116, 160, 181, 213, 216

Agrippa, 236 ff.
Agrippina, 258
Aleian Field, 71
Alexander the Great, 21, 26, 41, 83, 125, 130, 208, 211, 212, 287, 292
Alexander, Jewish leader, 188
Alexandria (Egypt), 30, 42, 249, 250
Alexandria Troas, 130 f.; see Troas
Alexandrian, 30, 165; ship 241, 248, 250
Aliturus, 259
Altar, 29, 147, 222, 294
Amana R., 54
Amanus Mts., 25, 125
Am-ha'arets, 40
Amphipolis, 139 f.
Amyntas, 99, 102
Ananias, of Damascus, 55 f., 59 ff., 61
Ananias, high priest, 225, 230, 300
Anastasis, 146
Anazarbus, 71

Anchors, 245, 304
Ancyra, 128
Andronicus, 189
Angel, 43, 130, 172
Antioch (Syria), 25, 41, 74, 75, 76, 77 ff., 83, 88, 97, 116, 117, 124, 125, 158, 159, 160, 161, 162, 198, 219; Church or congregation, 80, 105, 117, 161; Jewish community, 79
Antioch (Pisidian), 96, 127, 287
Antiochus of Commagene, 102
Antiochus III the Great, 211
Antiochus IV Epiphanes, 79, 84, 286
Antipater, 102
Antipatris, 229
Anti-Semitism, 81, 188
Antonia, 222, 227
Antony, Mark, 20, 134
Aphrodite, 20, 91, 151, 170
Apocalypses, 34
Apollo, 84, 126, 157
Apollonia, 140
Apollonius, 71, 294, 307
Apollos, 153, 165, 168 f.
Apology, 192, 194
Apostle, 54, 57, 63, 81, 181, 194, 213, 297
Apostleship, 192 f.
Appeal to Caesar, 234 f., 236, 238
Appian Way, 250, 252, 264
Apuleius, 150
Aquila, 151, 156, 157, 164, 189, 198, 295
Arabia, 57 f., 59, 61, 283
Aramaic, 17, 32, 58, 110, 216, 223, 276
Aratus, 71, 148
Arcana, 74
Archippus, 177
Areopagus, council of the, 149, 294

Aeropagus, 147, 294; see Hill of Ares
Aretas, king, 59, 61, 284
Arethusa glen, 140
Aristarchus, 176, 187, 232, 240
Aristotle, 140
Art, 146
Artemeia, 292
Artemis, 93, 158, 187 f., 189
Ascetic, 170
'Asereth, 220
Asia Minor, 13, 27, 72, 95, 96, 104, 127, 131, 160, 196
Asia, province, 127, 163, 165, 187, 204
Asiarchs, 179, 187 f., 298
Assassins, 223, 233
Assos, 130, 206 f., 240
Athenodorus, 18
Athens, 20, 100, 144, 145 ff., 153, 294
Athletics, 19, 86 f.
Athos, Mt., 140
Atomos, 232
Atonement Day, 242
Atoning death, 120
Attalia, 104, 105
Attica, 144
Augustan Cohort, 240, 301
Augustus, 13, 99, 134, 251
Author of Acts, 58, 88, 98, 101, 132, 207, 209, 218, 225, 255; see also Luke
Aziz, 232
Azotus, 46

Bannus, 38, 40
Baptism, 55, 68, 136, 164, 200; of John, 37, 164
Barbarian, 128, 129, 176
Bariesus, 92; see also Elymas

Barnabas, 62, 75, 77 ff., 87, 89
  ff., 93, 94 ff., 100 f., 105 f.,
  107, 109, 114, 119, 121, 122,
  159
Basket, 61
Bathing, 38
Beasts, wild, 175
Beating, 185
Benjamin, 14
Berenice, 236
Beroea, 143, 144, 145, 204
Berytus, 25
Beth-horon, 26
Bithynia, 129, 131
Blindness, 51, 55, 93
Boasting, 194
Book-burning, 167
Bostra, 58, 284
Brundisium, 133, 250
Brutus, 61, 145
Buffeting, 72, 129
Burrus, 252, 258

Cadmus, Mt., 176
Caesar (Roman emperor), 15,
  234 f., 239, 244, 259
Caesar, Augustus, 13
Caesar, Julius, 15, 26, 61, 151
Caesarea, 24, 25, 46, 63, 75,
  158, 204, 212, 227, 229, 230,
  233, 239, 250
Caesarea Philippi, 236
Caiaphas, 31, 41, 60, 278
Caligula, 74 (edict), 258; see al-
  so Gaius
Caliph, 217
Campanian Way, 250
Canal, Corinth, 150
Capri, 249
Captivity, second, 256
Capua, 250

Carmel, Mt., 25, 212
Casius, Mt., 89
Catacumbas, ad, 252
Cauda, 242; see also Clauda
Caystrus River, 158
Celibacy, 170
Celts, 128, 163, 182; see also
  Galatians
Cemetary, 251
Cenchreae, 150, 157, 198
Centurion, 224, 227, 240, 241,
  245, 246
Cephas, 109, 181
Cephas party, 168
Cestius, tomb of, 264
Cestrus River, 94
Chalcis, 236
Charge, 137, 142, 153, 155, 230,
  235
Charon, 79
Charonion, 79
Chelidonian islands, 211
Cherubim Gate, 78
Chief man of the island, 247
Children, 212
Chios, 207
Chloe, 168
Chrestus, 152
Christ, Jesus, 130, 152, 170,
  174, 183, 199
Christ party at Corinth, 168
Christian (name), 81 f.
Christianity, 96, 104, 149, 152,
  171, 197, 247, 254
Christians, 170, 197 f., 212,
  226, 241, 250, 252
Chronology, 272, 273, 274, 275
Church discipline, 170
Cicero, 137, 203, 251
Cilicia, 13, 20, 61, 71, 137, 162,
  230
Cilician Gates, 126, 164
Cilicium, 16

Circumcision, 14 (of Paul), 19, 107, 115, 171, 181, 183, 184, 217, 276
Circus Maximus, 252
Citizen, Tarsian, 14, 277; Roman, 138, 224
Citizenship, Roman, 139, 201, 224
Clauda, 242; see also Cauda
Claudius, 74, 152, 156, 197, 227, 232, 236, 249, 258; letter, 156
Claudius Lysias and his letter, 227
Clean and unclean, 33, 119
Clement, 179; of Alexandria, 161; of Rome, 267
Cleopatra, 20
Cnidus, 241
Collection for famine, 107
Collection raised by Paul, 186, 191, 217, 231
Colophon, 18
Colossae, 164, 176 f.
Colossians, Ep. to the, 175 ff.
Colossus, 211
Confession of faith, 68
Conscience, 34
Consecration of missionaries, 88
Coressus, 158, 175
Corinth, 149, 150 ff., 165, 174, 186 (intermediate trip), 190, 191, 196, 197, 204
Corinthian letters; 1 Epistle, 149; 2 Epistle, 191 f.
Cos, 211
Cotiaeum, 130
Covenant, 68 (new), 183 (two), 193
Craft, 18, 82; see also trade
Creator, 101
Crete, 241
Crispus, 152, 154
Cross, 185, 215

Crucified, 49, 153
Cumae, 249
Curses, 182
Custody, 231
Cybele, 100
Cydnus, R., 19, 24, 65
Cynics, 19
Cypriote, 215
Cyprus, 24, 62, 75, 89 f., 95, 105, 121 f., 232, 241
Cyrenaica, 243
Cyrene, 75
Cyzicus, 131

Damaris, 145 f.
Damascus, 46, 48, 51, 57, 59, 194; Vision, 50 f., 226
Daniel, 41, 44, 135
Daphne, 78
David, 97
Days, observance of, 202
Deaconess, 198
Deacons, 212
Dead Sea, 35 f.
Decapolis, 46
Declarations of going to Gentiles, 98, 154, 254
Decree of Apostles, 159, 171, 218
Delegations at Rome, 251
Delos, 157
Demetrius, 187
Democritus, 170
Demon possession, 136 f., 166
Depression of Paul, 151
Derbe, 102, 103, 126
Diana Ephesia, 189
Dionysius, 149
Dionysus, 20
Dioscuri, 248
Disciples of Apollos, 165
Dora, 25

Dorylaeum, 129, 130
Drag, 243
Drusilla, 232
Drusium, 25
Dusares, 59
Dust, 99, 224
Dyrrachium, 133

Earthquake, 74
Education of Paul, 17
Egnation Way, 133, 139, 143
Egypt, 80, 106
Egyptian prophet, 223
Elders, of Ephesus, 208 f.; at
    Jerusalem, 114, 159, 217
Eleusinian mysteries, 150
Eleusis, 150
Elymas, 92 f.
Emesa, 52, 232
Epaenetus, 198
Epaphras, 177
Epaphroditus, 179
Ephesian writings, 166, 179
Ephesians, Ep. to the, 177, 178
Ephesus, 127, 156, 158 f., 163,
    164 ff., 168, 175, 176, 180,
    186, 187, 190, 198, 207, 208,
    222
Epicureans, 145, 146
Epileptic attacks?, 129
Epiphania, 79
Essenes, 31, 35
Essenism, 279
Estates, 250
Ethnarch, 61
Eunice, 127
Euodia, 179
Euphrates, 163
Euraquilo, 242; see Northeaster
Euripides, 140, 209
Europe, 130, 131

Eutychus, 205
Exorcism, 136, 166

Fair Havens, 241 f., 244
Faith, 68, 183, 198 f.; in Christ,
    113, 116
Famagusta, 90
Famine, 80, 106
Farewell address, 209
Fast, 242
Father, break with, 69 f.
Fear, 152
Felix, 223, 227, 229, 232 f., 259
Festus, 233 ff., 240
Fighting, 190
Foolishness, 194
Forgiveness, 131
Formia, 250
Fortunatus, 167
Forum of Appius, 251
Four Chapters of 2 Cor., 187

Gaeta, gulf of, 251
Gaius, 74, 78; see also Caligula
Gaius, 152
Gaius of Derbe, 103, 127, 187,
    204
Galaaditis, 49
Galatia, 99, 100, 128, 182; Ga-
    latia and Phrygia, 163
Galatians, 128, 130, 181; see al-
    so Celts
Galatians, Ep. to the, 181 f.
Galilee, 37, 40, 46, 78; lake of,
    48, 49
Gallio, 155 f., 272
Gamaliel, 32, 34, 42, 278
Gangites, 134
Garment, 154, 224

Gear, 243
Gentile-Christians, 119
Gentiles, 14, 20, 40, 42, 56, 57, 63, 67, 76, 81, 97, 98 f., 106, 111, 115, 154, 167, 183, 198, 201, 216, 217, 236, 254
Ginnaea, 48
Girdle, 212 f.
Glossalaly, 172 f.
God-fearers, 99, 101, 111, 154
Golgotha, 215
Gospel, 120, 182, 196, 197, 198, 199
Grain, prices, 80; ship, 241, 248, 250
Greece, 20, 144, 160, 196
Greek Bible translation, 32
Greek language, 58, 110, 223
Greeks, 75, 81, 200
Grief, godly, 191
Gymnasium, 19

Herod Antipas, 37, 59, 81
Herod Agrippa I, 75, 80, 81, 106
Herod Agrippa II, 236 ff.; see Agrippa
Herodias, 59
Herodotus, 158, 211
Hierapolis, 176 f.
High priest, 31, 32, 42, 225
Hillel, 34
Hippocrates, 211
Hippodamus, 78, 211
Hippodrome, 78, 85
Hispania, 163; see also Spain
Holy Places, 215
Homer, 19, 68, 131, 158
Hope of Israel, 226, 237, 253, 254
Horace, 251
Hypocrisy, 119

Hagar, 59
Haggadah, 33
Hagra, 59
Haifa, 25; see Sycaminos
Hair cutting, 157, 222
Halakah, 33
Halicarnassus, 72, 211
Handkerchiefs, 166
Hannibal, 211
Healer, 100, 166, 247
Hebrew, 20, 32, 274
Hellenists, 32, 41, 42, 45, 63
Hellenization, 125
Heracles, 67, 102
Heraeum, 207
Hermes, 84, 101
Hermon, Mt., 49 f.
Hermus River, 135
Herod the Great, 25, 27, 78, 233

Iberian peninsula, 163
Iconium, 99 f., 127
Idol, 146
Idol sacrifice, 171
Ignatius, 175
Ignorance, time of, 148
Illness of Paul, cf. 127, 129; hindrance, 127
Illyricum, 143, 182
Imbros, 131
Immorality, 169
Imperial province, 229
Imprisonment, 175
Inscription, 30, 223
Ionia, 157
Irony, 194
Isaiah, 135, 254
Isauria, 102
Isis mysteries, 150
Israel's salvation, 116, 201

Issus, 24, 125, 126
Isthmian games, 150
Isthmus of Corinth, 150
Italy, 133, 143, 197, 241

Julius, centurion, 240
Junias, 19
Justification, 33, 120, 183, 200, 201

James, son of Zebedee, 75, 80
James, the Lord's brother, 63, 109, 116, 118, 158, 160, 181, 213, 216, 217 f., 220, 221, 230
Jason, 142
Jericho, 39
Jerome, 148
Jerusalem, 21, 26, 40, 46, 74, 78, 80, 158, 198, 226, 228; First Visit, 61 ff.; Second Visit, 108 ff.; Third Visit?, 158
Jesus, 37, 39, 42, 44, 49, 50, 55, 63, 73, 75, 81, 97, 110, 115, 135, 136, 142, 146, 195, 253
Jesus Justus, 176
Jews, 42, 78, 81, 90, 134, 156, 158, 171, 198, 211, 233, 252, 258
John the Apostle, 109, 160, 181, 213
John the Baptist, 37, 39, 97, 164
John Mark, 90, 95, 105, 114, 122; see also Mark
Jordan, 38, 39 f., 46, 49
Josephus, 258
Journeys of Cilician period, 71
Judaism, 69, 97, 98, 183
Judas, 52, 54
Judas Barsabbas, 159
Judea, 62, 63, 64, 80, 117, 174, 253
Judgment, 149
Julian emperors, 145
Julias, 236
Juliopolis, 15

Kerte-Hüyük, 102
Khan, 50
King, Jesus, 142
Kingdom of God, 49, 135, 253
Kings, Paul before, 236
Koran, 253
Koura head, 244 f.

Lamus River, 71
Laodicea, 164, 176 f.
Laodiceans, letter to, 177
Larnaka, 90
Lasea, 242
Lashes, 71
Law (of Moses), 21, 32, 34, 37, 112, 155; Roman, 155
Leather-worker, 18
Lechaeum, 150
Legalism, 180, 183
Legends, 33
Lesbianism, 207
Lesbos, 207
Letter, 46, 159, 165; Letters of Paul as literature, 203; Indispensability, 203; Sources for his life, 269
Libertines, 30
Liberty, 160, 183, 220
Licinius, 255
Life eternal, 33, 57
Lifeboat, 245
Limnai, 96
Lincoln's address, 198
Lion, 139 f., 175, 207
Lois, 127

Lord's Supper, 55 f., 118, 119, 123, 172, 183
Lucina, 267
Lucius of Cyrene, 81
Lucullus, 292
Luke, 80, 92, 93, 132, 138 f., 147, 148, 149, 152, 157, 159, 163, 165, 167, 189, 205 f., 210, 214, 223, 224, 226, 231, 238, 254, 256; see also Author of Acts
Luther, 198
Lycaonia, 99, 107
Lycia, 211, 241
Lycurgus, 140
Lycus, 25, 176
Lydia, 135 f., 139, 179
Lystra, 99, 100 f., 127, 162

Macedonia, 20, 131 f., 141, 143, 160, 174, 186, 190, 191, 196, 205
Maeander River, 176, 208
Magic, 167
Magical books, 166
Magician, 92, 232
Magistrates, 137 ff.
Magus, 91, 92
Malaria, 16, 129
Malea, Cape, 150, 241
Mallus, 71
Malta, 246, 247, 249; see also Melita
Manaen, 81
Maranatha, 118, 266
Marathon, 144
Mark, 176 f.; see also John Mark
Marks of Jesus, 185
Marketplace, 146, 147; see also Agora
Marmara, Sea of, 131
Marriage, 170 f.

Martyrology, 256
Mary, 108
Matala, Cape, 241
Meals, congregational, 172
Mecca, 58
Meeting day, 253
Megara, 150
Melita, 246; see also Malta
Merits, 33
Mesara, 242
Message, 244
Messiah, 42, 44, 142, 237
Messianic Hope, 253
Messina, straits of, 249
Metropolis, 128
Miletus, 180, 207, 208
Milton, John, 34
Mnason, 215
Money, 174
Mopsuestia, 71, 126
Mopsus, 126
Moses, 53, 217
Mother Church, 254
Mount of Olives, 223
Mummius, L., 150
Mygdonia, 140
Myra, 212, 241
Mysia, 130, 240
Mystical ideas, 172
Mytilene, 207

Nabataeans, 58
Names, Roman, 14 f., 224
Nazarenes, 39, 40, 43, 45, 46, 47, 48, 53, 55, 62, 79, 87, 109, 230
Nazareth, 37
Nazirite, 221
Navigation, 204, 242, 248
Neapolis, 133, 205
Nebo, Mt., 37
Nero, 150, 234, 257 f.

Nestor, 18
Nicaea, 131
Nicodemus, 110
Nicomedia, 131
Nile, 80
Northeaster, 242
Nympha, 177

Obelisk, 250
Octavia, 258
Old Testament, 202
Olympia, 83, 84
Olympic Games, 76, 83 f., 97
Olympus, 141, 144
Onesimus, 177
Orontes River, 25, 77, 78, 89
Ossa, Mt., 144
Ostia, 249
Ovid, 203

Palestine, 80, 95, 106, 158
Pallas, 232, 258
Pamphylia, 94
Pangaeum, Mt., 133, 139
Panormus, 158
Paphos, 90, 91, 93
Paradise, 194
Parmenius, 78
Parthenon, 146
Parting at Miletus, 210
Passion story, 69
Passover, 204
Pastoral Epistles, 202
Patara, 211
Paul-name, 14, 93
Paul party, 168
Paulus, L. Ae., 15, 143
Pausanias, 148
Paximades, 242
Pedagogue, 183

Pelion, Mt., 144
Pella, 143
Peloponnesus, 150
Peneious River, 144
Pentecost, 173, 175, 205, 207,
   219, 220, 221
Peraea, 37, 46
Perga, 94, 95, 103
Pergamum, 135, 148
Pericles, 145
Persecution of Paul, 45 ff., 63
Perseus, 143
Pessinus, 128
Peter, 48, 61 ff., 75, 80, 109,
   115 f., 117 ff., 158, 159, 160,
   166, 169, 181, 183, 213
Petra, 58
Petronius, 77
Pharisaic element in Church, 108,
   109, 118, 119
Pharisaism, 32, 35, 56, 223, 237
Pharisee, 17, 31, 37, 75, 225,
   226, 231
Phidias, 146
Philemon, Ep. to, 175, 177
Philip, evangelist (and daugh-
   ters), 46, 212
Philip of Macedon, 133, 143
Philip, tetrarch, 236
Philippi, 133 ff., 138, 141, 145,
   152, 179, 205
Philippians, Ep. to the, 175,
   178 f.
Philo, 19, 30, 106, 165, 279
Philosophers, 18, 147, 149
Philosophy, 21, 32, 149, 165,
   195, 278
Phineas of Tiberias, 78
Phoebe, 198
Phoenicia, 211
Phoenician, 20
Phoenix, 242
Phrygia, 96, 163
Phrygia and Galatia, 128

Pieria, 89
Pilate, Pontius, 27
Pillars, 213; of Hercules, 20, 197
Pinarus River, 125
Pion, 158
Pioneer, 197
Piraeus, 144
Pisidia, 96
Planted gospel, 196
Plato, 173
Pliny, 248
Plot, 205, 227
Plutarch, 83, 137
Polemic, 192
Politarchs, 141 f.
Polybius, 150
Polycrates, 207
Pompeiopolis, 71
Pompey, 73, 95
Pontine Marshes, 251
Pontus, 203
Poor, 159, 213
Poppaea, 258, 259
Porta Capena, 252
Portrait, 154
Portus, 250
Poseidon, 131, 150, 157
Postscript, 185
Power, 131, 195
Praetorian camp, 252; guard, 258
Prayer, 214; Paul's, 131
Priene, 208
Priests, 101, 259
Priscilla (Prisca), 152, 156, 157, 164
Prison, Paul's, 175
Prisoners, 239, 246
Proconsul, 91, 96, 151, 155, 229
Promontory, Holy, 211
Prophecy, 137, 173, 209
Prophet, 80, 81, 140, 195, 237
Propontis, 131

Proselytes, 67, 186
Prostitution, 170
Ptolemais, 212
Publius, 247
Publius Servilius, 102
Punic, 20
Purification, 221
Purple, 135
Puteoli, 249, 250 (distance from Rome), 259
Pydna, 143; new, 144
Pyramus, 71
Pythagoras, 158, 207

Rabbi, Paul no, 32, 169, 278
Ramsay, W. M., 128, 129, 208, 255
Rebellion against Paul, 186
Renan, E., 88, 176
Repentance, 148
Resurrection of Christ, 174, 205, 237, 255; of the dead, 173 f., 226, 231, 237, 238, 255
Revelation, 57, 73 f., 107, 108
Rhegium, 249
Rhegma, 19
Rhetor, 165, 230
Rhodes, 72, 211
Rhodian fleet, 211
Rhosus, Mt., 25
Righteousness, 57, 199
Riot, 78
Ritual law, 68, 165, 183
Ritualism, 180
Rivers, 72
Roma, 188
Roman citizen, 138, 139, 227; colony, 96, 130, 134, 151, 153; congregation, 197; law, 96, 227
Romans, Epistle to the, 149, 197 ff., 202 (impact)

318   INDEX

Rome, 77, 80, 133, 151, 176, 197, 226, 233, 238
Rufus, 76

Sabbath, 20, 58, 67, 81, 97, 100, 134, 141, 144, 158
Sacrifice, 68
Sadducees, 31 f., 33, 41, 225, 231, 278
Sailing ships, 240
Sailors, 245
St. Paul's Bay, 246
St. Peter's Square, 250
Saints, 173, 174, 191
Salamis, 90
Sammonium, Cape, 241
Samos, 131, 157, 207
Samothrace, 131, 133
Sanhedrin, 224 f., 227, 230
Sappho, 207
Sardis, 135, 157, 164
Sarus, 71
Satan, 112, 129, 169
Satyrs, 172
Saul, 14, 15, 50, 87, 93
Scaeva, sons of, 166
Scopus, Mt., 27, 48
Scourging, 224
Scripture, 32
Scripture-proof, 33, 254
Scythians, 176
Scythopolis, 46
Sebaste, 233
Sect, 96, 253
Seleucia, 25, 77, 89
Seleucids, 77, 81
Seleucus I, 79, 81, 89, 96
Senatorial province, 229
Seneca, 155, 251, 258
Sergius Paulus, 91 f., 96
Serpent, 246 f.

Shammai, 34
Shipwreck, 72, 242
Sicarii, 233
Sicily, 244, 247, 249
Sicyon, 79, 150
Sidon, 240
Silas, 123, 144, 146, 153, 157, 159
Silence of women, 173
Silpius, 78
Silversmith, 187
Simon Magus, 92
Singon Street, 79
Sister, 23, 47, 108, 216
Sister's son, 216, 227
Slave, 69, 136 f., 171, 250
Slavery, 151, 177
Smyrna, 180
Socrates, 140, 150
Sojourners, 160
Soldiers, 222, 245, 246
Soli, 71, 148
Solyma, Mt., 211 f.
Son of man, 41, 44, 45, 135
Sosthenes, 156
Spain, 20, 197; see also Hispania
Spanish journey, 197
Speech, 97 f., 101, 147 ff., 223 f., 230 f., 236 f.
Spirit, Holy, 43, 44, 55, 87, 91, 94, 99, 127, 128, 133, 143, 144, 163, 164, 184, 186, 209, 213, 254
Spiritual gifts, 173 f.
Spiritual man, 185
State, 201
Status quo, 171
Stephanas, 152, 167, 168
Stephen, 42, 43 f., 256
Stocks, 138
Stoics, 19, 32, 145, 146, 155
Stoning, 45, 101 f., 185
Strabo, 207

Straton's tower, 233
Street called Straight, 51
Strymon River, 139
Subject to authority, 201
Sultan Dagh, 96
Sunday, 205
Sybil, 249
Sycaminos, 25
Symeon Niger, 81, 87
Synagogue, 17, 30, 39, 58, 71,
  90, 96, 100, 141, 146, 152,
  153, 158, 226
Syntyche, 179
Syracuse, 249
Syria, 77, 87
Syrian Gates, 125
Syrtis, 243

Tablet of warning, 30
Tackle of ship, 243
Tarsus, 13, 15, 33, 63, 74, 75,
  126, 162
Tatian, 161
Taurus Mts., 15, 16, 24, 95, 126;
  pass, 15, 162
Tavium, 128
Teachers, 80, 81; strange, 186
Temple, 29 f., 42, 43, 47, 74 f.,
  221 ff., 230; state, 41; viola-
  tor, 222, 231
Tenedos, 131
Tent, 18; tent-maker, 18, 276;
  see also leather-worker
Tertullian, 148, 154
Tertullus, 230
Testimonies, 69
Tetrarchy, 236
Thales, 158, 207
Thasos, 131
Theater, 19, 187
Theology, 149
Therapeutae, 30

Therme, Gulf of, 140
Thessalonians, 1 Epistle to the,
  154
Thessalonica, 141, 143, 144,
  153, 154, 232
Thorn, 103, 129
Thracian Sea, 140
Three Taverns, 251
Thucydides, 214
Thyatira, 135
Tiber River, 91, 227, 228, 249
Tiberius, emperor, 20, 74
Tiberius Alexander, procurator,
  106
Tigellinus, 258
Timothy, 101, 127, 136, 146,
  153, 157, 162, 175, 182, 184,
  186, 204, 213; Epistles to
  Timothy, 127, 202
Tithing, 33
Titius Justus, 154
Titus, general, 78
Titus, 82 f., 86 f., 107, 115 (cir-
  cumcision of Titus rejected),
  162, 186, 190, 191, 192, 193;
  Epistle to, 203
Tmolus, Mt., 157
Tongues, 164, 172 f.
Trade, 18, 82; see also craft
Trade route, 163
Tradition, 34
Trance, 63
Transgression, Gentile, 148
Travel plans, 174
Trial, 234, 257 ff.
Tribal associations, 17
Tribunal, 137
Tribune, 222 f., 225 f., 227, 231
Troas, 130 ff., 132, 190, 205,
  206; see also Alexandria
Trophimus, 205, 222
Troy, 131
Twelve men, 164
Twin brothers, 248

Tyche, 79
Tychicus, 177, 205
Tyrannus, 165
Tyre, 25, 212
Tyrian ladder, 25

Unchastity, 160
Unclean or uncleanness, 120
Ungirding, 243
Unhindered, 255
Unity, 110
Unknown god, 147 f.
Unleavened Bread, feast of, 205

Wall, 61
Washing of hands, 134
Way, 165, 223, 231
Weakness, 131
We-sections, 132, 205, 210 f.,
    240, 247, 252, 293
White River, 94; see Cestrus
Widows, 171
Wilderness, 35
Window, 61
Wisdom, 153
Women, 171, 173
Wonderworker, 166
Works, good, 120
World's Fair, 83

Valetta, 248
Vegetarianism, 202
Veil 171
Vesuvius, Mt., 249
Via Sebaste, 99
Virgil, 249
Vision, 44, 50, 63, 73 f., 155,
    199, 223, 226, 244
Visitors, 118
Voluntary giving, 192
Vote, 242
Vow, 157, 218, 221

Xanthus, 211
Xenophanes, 13

Yoke-fellow, 179

Zadok, 31
Zealot, 233
Zeus, 25, 83, 84, 89, 101